The Thames Valley:
Past, Present, and Future

A Snapshot of English Life

Published in 2024

Copyright © 2024 Jim Donahue Images

All rights reserved. Apart from any fair dealing for the purpose of private study, research, criticism or review, as permitted under the Copyright, Designs and Patents Act, 1988, no part of this publication may be reproduced, stored in a retrieval system, or transmitted in any form or by any means, electronic, electrical, chemical, mechanical, optical, photocopying, recording or otherwise, without the prior written permission of the copyright owner. Enquiries should be addressed to the Publishers.

Every attempt has been made by the author and publisher to secure the appropriate permissions for materials reproduced in this book. If there has been any oversight we will be happy to rectify the situation in future editions.

A CIP catalogue record for this book is available from the British Library.

ISBN: 978 0 85704 378 8

Halsgrove
Halsgrove House,
Ryelands Business Park,
Bagley Road, Wellington,
Somerset TA21 9PZ
Tel: 01823 653777
Fax: 01823 216796
email: sales@halsgrove.com

Part of the Halsgrove group of companies
Information on all Halsgrove titles is available at: www.halsgrove.com
Printed and bound in India by Nutech Print Services

The Thames Valley: Past, Present, and Future

A Snapshot of English Life

Jim Donahue

Halsgrove

Contents

Introduction 1

Part 1: The Past: A Time-line of Thames Valley History 9

   1. Pre-historic through Roman Britain
 — Hand Axes, Crop Circles and Earthworks 11
   2. 410 AD - 1066: Anglo-Saxon Britain
 — Christianity, King Alfred and the Vikings 25
   3. 1066 - 17th Century: The Norman Conquest through the Civil War
 — Kings, Castles and Manors 41
   4. 18th and 19th Centuries: Development of today's towns and villages
 — Horses, Boats and Trains 71
   5. 20th Century to the present
 — Cars, Planes and Rock Stars 99

Part 2: The Present and Future: Thames Valley Community Life and Future Challenges 127

   1. Windsor and Eton 129
   2. Slough 135
   3. Maidenhead, Marlow and Cookham 138
   4. Henley-on-Thames 144
   5. Reading 150
   6. Pangbourne and Whitchurch-on-Thames 154
   7. Hardwick Estate community 160
   8. Goring-on-Thames and Streatley 165
   9. Wallingford to Abingdon 176
   10. Oxford 180

Parting Thoughts 193

Acknowledgements and References 195

Index 199

Introduction: A snapshot of English life

As an American who moved to the UK as an adult, I can appreciate with fresh eyes some of the many wonderful things about living in England, and the Thames Valley in particular, that many people who have grown up here often take for granted. In the 25 years that I have lived here, one of the things that I still regularly hear from people I meet is — "you're an American, what are you doing here?", in a surprised tone implying that I must be either lost or daft as the only possible explanations for my having abandoned the American dream everyone sees on television and films for "dreary old England". Well the short answer is that I live here because I like it here. England may be old, but it is anything but dreary.

As I have been asked why I choose to live here so many times, I have put a bit of thought into my answer. If I had to choose the three best things about living in the Thames Valley compared to living in other parts of the world, I would point to:
- its rich and fascinating history
- the vibrant quality of community life
- the exceptional beauty of the countryside

Not that everything is perfect. I have come to learn about some of the challenges facing communities in the Thames Valley in recent years through my work as a Parish Councillor in my village in Oxfordshire.

These qualities and issues are shared by many other regions of England, but by focussing on the Thames Valley, I was able to explore these themes in depth. My preparation for writing this book has included extensive research into British history, photography of Thames Valley people and landscapes over a 10 year period and participation in some of the many community groups that I have been privileged to be involved with. I have also taken an interest in investigating local issues that communities across the Thames Valley have been struggling with and working to understand what can be done to address them.

I've included photos throughout to paint a picture — or more accurately, 'take a snapshot', of life in England as seen in the Thames Valley. The photographs in this book are generally my own unless otherwise indicated. I have used some historic images and those of other local artists and photographers where they have captured things better than I could. My goal as been to use photographs to:

- Portray the timeless nature of the area — so well preserved as a result of the actions of passionate residents over the years.
- Bring to life some of the historic buildings and monuments in the region that many will be aware of but may not fully appreciate. I particularly like photos that show how historic sites are still significant in modern life, but in very different ways.
- Capture people engaged in community activities with a vibrancy that is unique to England and the Thames Valley.

Putting this book together is my attempt to share what I have learned about England in the past 25 years in a relatively concise, visual and easy to understand manner. I have made an effort to explain any terms or customs that may not be obvious to the general public — basically anything that was not apparent to me when I first moved here!

The book is divided into two parts:

- **Part 1: The Past — A Time-line of Thames Valley History:** I share the fascinating stories of some of the most important men, women, events and places that have made this area such a strategically important part of England for more than 5000 years — from evidence of prehistoric settlements to important findings from Roman, Anglo-Saxon and Medieval periods leading up to the development of the modern villages and towns we know today. The photos in this section focus on the remnants of history that are still visible and continue to have relevance to life in the Thames Valley today.
- **Part 2: The Present and Future — Community Life and Future Challenges**: I take you on the 75 mile journey along the river from Windsor to Oxford to give you a feel for what it is like to live in the Thames Valley today. I include several case studies that both celebrate the area's vibrant community life and explore key challenges communities are facing, providing insight into how these kind of issues can be addressed at the community and local government level in England. By better understanding some of the most important local issues, the reader will learn about the trends shaping the area's future.

Finally, I hope this book comes close to documenting how rich and satisfying life can be along this beautiful stretch of the Thames and gives you an incentive to visit or further explore the area for yourself!

Below: The Chiltern Hills on a summer's evening at Stonor outside of Henley.
Opposite page: Rowers on the Thames near Henley-on-Thames on a misty autumn morning.

What is the Thames Valley, anyway?

As the Thames Valley region is not a county, borough or council, there is no official definition of it. It is generally considered to be the area within easy reach of the River Thames beyond the London metropolitan area, past around Heathrow Airport and Windsor.

- In London, the Thames is a broad and mighty river, historically associated with images of the Houses of Parliament, the Tower of London and international trade with the British empire.
- Beyond the tidal waters of London, the Thames becomes a narrower and gentler river, meandering its way through the English countryside to Oxford and narrowing further as it approaches its source in the Cotswolds.
- The physical Thames River Basin covers a geographic area extending to the source of the Thames and to the sources all its tributaries, such as the Cherwell, Evenlode and Windrush Rivers. This is a much larger region than is commonly understood to be the Thames Valley as it stretches into the Cotswolds and includes all of Greater London out to the Thames Estuary and the North Sea.

The Thames Valley most people know today is based on a number of informal understandings such as:

- A collection of picturesque towns and villages dotted along the more scenic parts of the River Thames such as Cookham, Marlow, Goring and Henley-on-Thames.
- Home to the leading concentration of high-tech firms in the UK located along the M4 corridor at business parks in Reading, Slough, Bracknell, Newbury and Oxford.
- An area covered by various organisations using the name in their title, each with their own definition of the region, e.g. Thames Valley Police, Thames Valley Windows and Tyres, and the Thames Valley Football league. The Thames Valley Police has responsibility for all of Berkshire, Oxfordshire, and Buckinghamshire. The Thames Valley Premier Football league has five divisions with over 50 teams representing towns and villages stretching from Windsor to Newbury.

For the purposes of this book, I will use the map below as a reference which focusses on villages and towns within easy reach of the Thames between Windsor in the south and Oxford to the north, or along the M4 Motorway from Junction 6 at Windsor to Junction 13 at Newbury. For me, the heart of the Thames Valley is shown in the map below.

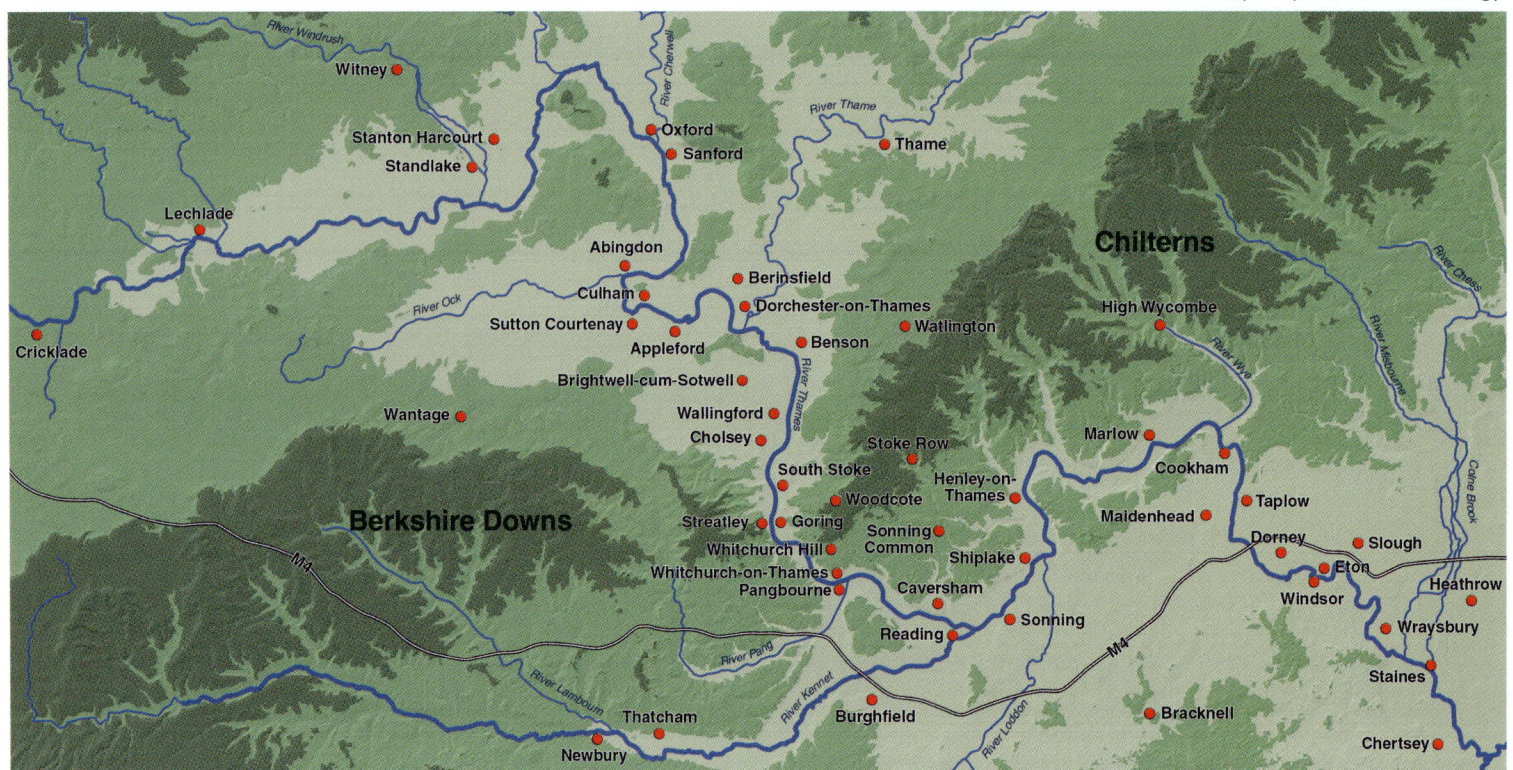

An overview of the Thames Valley. Map: Oxford Archaeology.

Oxford 8s Rowing competition held each May, where the Thames is known as the Isis.

Some background on the River Thames

The river itself is, of course, the reason for the existence of the Thames Valley. Despite the river's strategic and economic importance, it is no longer used for shipping and trade beyond London. Even in London, commercial ports are predominantly located to the east, towards the Thames Estuary. In the Thames Valley, the river itself is now a source of recreational pursuits such as boating, rowing, fishing, walking, swimming and is generally a picturesque and enjoyable place to live and work.

At 215 miles (346 km), the Thames is the longest river within England and the second-longest in the United Kingdom, after the River Severn, which is only about 5 miles longer. The Thames is certainly not one of the longest rivers in the world, but its historic importance for London and England as a whole make it one of the world's most famous rivers.

The earliest documented reference to the river is thought to be when Julius Caesar called it by its Latin name, Tamesis, in his account of his second expedition to Great Britain in 54 BC. The river is still referred to as the Isis locally in Oxford, probably stemming from the Latin name. Many historians and cartographers previously considered the true name of the river to be the Isis from its source in the Cotswolds down through Oxford to Dorchester-on-Thames where the river joins the tributary River Thame (without an 's'). According to this definition, only after the junction of these rivers should the two names be combined to form the River Thames. The Henley-on-Thames bridge includes two sculptures that refer to this naming of the Thames — one of a bearded man's head called Tamesis, or Old Man Thames, on the downstream side, and one of a woman's head called Isis on the upstream side. In the photos shown on this page, the logo of the Henley Royal Regatta headquarters, located next to the bridge can be seen above Old Man Thames. The Leander Club Flag, home to Britain's most elite rowers, can be seen above Isis. Modern maps call the river the Thames for its full length although the Ordnance Survey map labels it as "Thames or Isis" through Oxford.

The source of the Thames —is an underground spring in the Cotswold hills near the village of Kemble, just south of Cirencester. For most of the year, the spring is not visible until about a half a mile downstream when it reaches a place where it becomes a spring known as Lyd Well. In the wetter seasons, water often bubbles up from the well to form the start of something resembling a stream or tributary river. The photo of the well on the opposite page was taken in the wet winter season — even this early section of the Thames is dry for much of the year.

For the first several miles of the Thames, the river appears to be nothing more than a narrow creek. It is not considered to be navigable — even by canoes or small boats — until it reaches Cricklade, about 10 miles downstream where the River Churn joins the Thames. Some people have argued that the true source of the Thames to be the source of the Churn at Seven Springs near Cheltenham, although Kemble is the source used in maps.

Only when the river gets to Lechlade-on-Thames, a further 12 miles downstream from Cricklade, does it reach the point where it is navigable by larger boats, resembling the river seen in much of the Thames Valley today.

The river drops about 70m in altitude from the first lock at Lechlade to the point it reaches the tidal waters in London after the final lock in Teddington.

Top photo: Old Man Thames sculpture on Henley bridge, with logo of Henley Royal Regatta Headquarters above it.

The Tideway —The river in London east of the Teddington lock is subject to the tidal flows of the North Sea and is referred to as the Tideway. The mouth of the Thames, where the river joins the North Sea east of London, is called the Thames Estuary. Above Teddington to the source near Cricklade, the Thames is unaffected by the tide and remains relatively stable, other than from seasonal flooding.

Locks and weirs — There are a total of 45 lock and weir combinations from Lechlade to Teddington that are designed to control the level and flow of water on the river, ensuring it remains navigable and managing the effects of flooding.

There is typically a drop of between 1 and 2m at each lock (known as the fall). Each section of the river between locks is known as a 'reach'. The locks are designed to allow boats to smoothly transition between these different levels of the river. The Sandford Lock, shown on the opposite page, has the deepest fall of any lock on the river of 8 ft 10in (2.69m).

Weirs are a type of dam or wall built across the river to raise the level and depth of the river. Weirs were originally developed by mill owners to ensure there was sufficient force of water to turn the mills by creating a sort of artificial waterfall. Locks are always located near a weir to allow boats to pass through the changes in river heights at weirs. These lock and weir combinations help keep the river relatively level within each reach and sufficiently deep for the full length of the river to make it reliably navigable. Water flows over or through the weirs when river levels are high. Sluice gates in the weir can be opened or closed by lock keepers to manage the flow of water through each weir. During rainy periods, especially in winter, when the river levels are high, sluice gates are normally fully open to reduce flooding upstream.

Bottom Photo: Isis sculpture on the Henley bridge, with the flag of the co-located Leander Rowing Club building above it.

Left: Lyd Well, near Kemble, where the first sighting of the Thames above ground can normally be seen emerging in the wetter months of the year.

Below: Sandford Lock with a boat exiting downstream after the lock gates have opened. There is almost a 9 foot (2.69 m) drop between the reaches of the river on either side of the lock.

Managing the river over the centuries

Prior to the present system of locks being put in place from the 17th to 19th centuries, early settlers would have experienced a much wider and shallower river surrounded by areas of marshland. There would have been many more crossing points at fords where river levels were low, with the river depth varying widely depending upon the weather and time of year. Settling near the river would have been difficult due to flooding and marshland except for areas on higher ground, which may be a reason that iron age hillforts were common along the Thames.

The river's steady current would have allowed for at least small boats and fishermen to use it across its full length, but gradual proliferation of mills with weirs, especially from Henley to Oxford, meant that river travel was difficult in many sections well into the 19th century.

- **Watermills** — were established at many points along the river by the time of the Domesday Book in 1086. Mills were an important technology to enhance agricultural productivity as they were the only source of power other than that generated by oxen or manual labour. One of the main drivers for creating early weirs across the river was the need to divert water into private mills to ensure there was a sufficiently powerful fall to generate the power needed to grind wheat, barley, and other grains. The higher the drop from the weir, the more power there would be to turn the mill.
- **Early weirs** — not only ensured that mills were productive, they also had some benefits in controlling river depth and flooding on the river. The downside was that the privately owned weirs presented obstacles for boats travelling along the river for trade. The fees charged by weir owners and time-consuming processes for getting past them were a significant cause of tension for those wanting to use the river for trade.
- **Flash locks** — were set up at many weirs from the 13th century to enable barges and other vessels to pass through as demand for trade and fishing increased. Flash locks consisted of wooden bars set up next to or in the middle of a weir which could be released to let a vessel through They were not an ideal experience for either boat or mill owners. Vessels going downstream had to prepare for an exhilarating whoosh or 'flash' when the locks were opened. Boats going upstream undertook a complex process involving the removal of boat paddles and a winch and pulley system to get them over the lock or weir. A diagram of the Whitchurch flash lock and winch system from 1786 is shown on the next page. Opening the lock also reduced the upstream water level temporarily, sometimes impacting the productivity of the mill for a day or more until the levels rose again.
- **Fishing weirs** —In addition to weirs from millers, fishermen also built their own weirs to trap fish. They were typically smaller than weirs at mills, and did not normally cross the entire width of the river, but were still problematic for larger barges. The 12th century Magna Carta even included a special clause stating that all fish weirs should be cleared from the Thames and other waterways, although it didn't seem to have had much effect.

By the 14th century, Henley-on-Thames was the furthest point where trade was considered 'ordinarily navigable' to London, contributing to its growth as a market town. Above Henley, the number of weirs made navigation difficult. In the 1600s there were about 20 flash locks between Henley and Oxford where there were only 5 between Henley and London. From Henley it was much easier to travel the 25 miles to Oxford by road as opposed to about 50 miles by river through all those flash locks.

Closer to Oxford, the river became completely unnavigable for larger barges. Improvements were initiated by a commission established in 1605 which aimed to improve navigability between Oxford and Burcot, near Culham. Barges were finally able to pass by 1635 after the introduction of pound locks at Iffley, Sanford and Abingdon.

Pound locks —The gradual introduction of pound locks across the Thames was a major improvement over flash locks. Pound locks, still used today, consist of large water chambers, enclosed by gates at either end, that act as a type of elevator to more effectively manage the changes in water level at each lock. It took nearly 200 years, until about 1800, before all locks in the Thames were converted to pound locks.

Weir at Pangbourne with Whitchurch Lock Keeper's House in background.

Even with the improvements completed by 1635, navigation was still a challenge and further improvements were needed.

- From 1751, the **Thames Navigation Commission** was responsible for making improvements and attempting to wrest control of the river away from private mill and weir owners. This ultimately made the Thames a more useful waterway for commerce, even as nearly all commercial shipping on the river was gradually replaced by pleasure craft and recreational activities after the arrival of the Great Western Railway in the 1840s.
- The Thames Navigation Commission's mission was 'improving and completing the navigation of the Rivers Thames and Isis from the City of London to the Town of Cricklade'. A total of ten new pound locks were built by 1778 between Boulter's Lock in Maidenhead and Mapledurham, just west of Reading. Each lock removed approximately half a day's travel for the crews.
- The **Thames Conservancy** — took over responsibility for managing the river, initially responsible for London from 1857 and then for all of the river to Cricklade from 1866. The Great Stink of 1858 focussed the government and public opinion on cleaning up the Thames, especially in London. As described later, no new flows of sewage into the river or its tributaries were allowed and existing sewage flows were diverted away from the river.
- All weirs still owned by private mills were finally transferred to the Conservancy. Refurbishment and replacement of older pound locks carried on for over 50 years including a new lock at Sunbury in 1927, and replacement locks at Marlow and Iffley.
- In 1885, the **Thames Preservation Act** formally changed the emphasis from commercial navigation to preserving the Thames for public recreational activities in support of the golden age of Thames boating that continued until the start of the First World War.

The 1974 Water Act — created the Thames Water Authority to become the centralised regional body responsible for water supply and treatment and disposal of sewage within the overall Thames river basin. The authority was also responsible for some environmental services such as flood management and land drainage.

The 1989 Water Act — Under Margaret Thatcher's Conservative government, privatised water supply and sewage responsibilities followed the earlier privatisation of telecoms and energy industries. Thames Water was given responsibility for managing the regional water supply across London and the Thames Valley, as well as for sewerage and sewage disposal activities.

The National Rivers Authority (NRA) was created as navigation authority for several key rivers, including the non-tidal Thames. **The Water Services Regulatory Authority,** also known as **Ofwat,** was created to regulate economic aspects of the water companies including limits on pricing, taking into account proposed capital investment schemes such as building new wastewater treatment works.

The Environment Agency — took over ownership of river's locks and weirs and overall river management from the NRA in 1996.

As of 2024, the Environment Agency still owns and operates the Thames river weirs and locks, including responsibility for managing the river levels. They employ the lock keepers and own the lock houses where many lock-keepers still live.

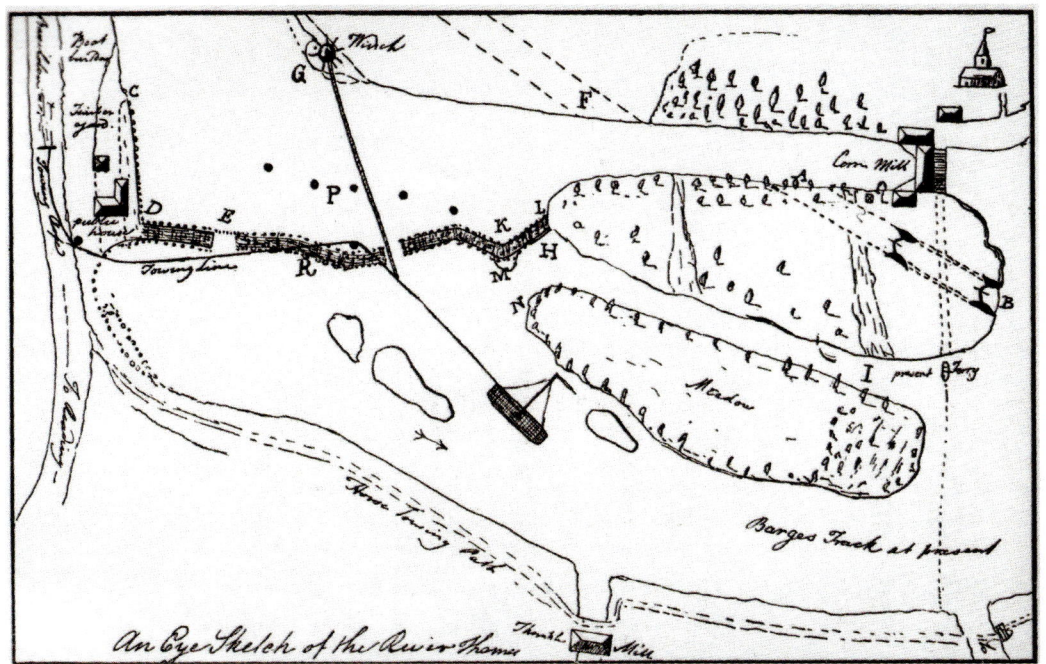

Diagram of Whitchurch Flash Lock from 1786 with boat being pulled upstream by winch located opposite the Swan Pub.

Part 1: The Past — A Time-line of Thames Valley History

Wherever you go in the Thames Valley, you will most likely be within a stone's throw of some site of special historical significance—whether it's an ancient road or settlement, the site of some forgotten struggle, or a former archaeological excavation. Perhaps a pillbox or historic home that you pass on a regular basis without fully appreciating its significance. The area is steeped in such a colourful history that you can't really appreciate what it is like to live in the Thames Valley today without some understanding of the rich context of its past.

You will not find any other books on the general history of the Thames Valley, yet many aspects of its history are well known as part of the broader history of England and the British Isles. The history presented here has been pieced together for the first time from other accounts of local and national history to tell the important story of the Thames Valley region of England.

Some of the key characters in the story are men and women that you may have previously been aware of for other reasons, but I hope you will come to see them as pioneers in shaping the history of the Thames Valley. I have chosen to highlight 30 individuals here as some of the more well-known men and women of the Thames Valley that you will come to know in the following pages. These figures, of course, are only a small sample, of the many, many individuals, communities, businesses and other organisations that have shaped its history.

It is hard to overstate the strategic importance of the Thames Valley in England's history.

- There is widespread evidence that the Thames Valley was home to some of the earliest pre-historic humans to migrate to Britain, forming some of its earliest permanent settlements—some as old as 5000 years.
- The area is criss-crossed with ancient roads and trails and dotted with sites of iron age forts and Roman villas.
- It has played host to decisive battles between Anglo-Saxon Kings with the Vikings and was home to countless Kings and Queens since the Norman Conquest.
- It is not possible to give full justice in this book to the great influence that both Windsor Castle and Oxford University have played for nearly a millennia.
- During the Civil War, the Thames Valley acted as the headquarters for the Royalist government and was also an important base for Parliamentary forces.
- Before the advent of automobiles, it was a major route for river and canal transport and played host to one of the busiest stage coach routes in the country. The opening of Brunel's Great Western Railway in the 1840s was a major catalyst for the region's growth.
- It continued to play an important role in the 20th Century, attracting world-renowned industrialists, authors, artists, and athletes.
- The region played a number of crucial roles in the Second World War, especially as a strategic base for airfields acting as a launch pad for the D-Day invasion.
- Today the Thames Valley is known as a centre for global business in both high tech industries along the M4 and in advanced scientific research and development in the area surrounding Oxford.

Prominent Figures in Thames Valley History

Julius Caesar

St Birinus baptising the local Wessex King

St Frideswide, Patron saint of Oxford

King Alfred the Great

William the Conqueror

Henry I and Reading Abbey

Empress Matilda

King John and the Magna Carta

Henry VI and Eton College

Henry VIII

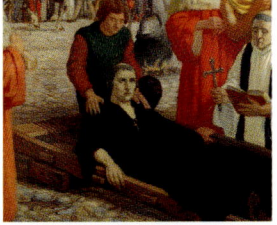
Hugh Cook of Faringdon

Charles I and the Civil War

Isambard Kingdom Brunel

William Henry (WH) Smith

Joseph Bazalgette

Lord Desborough of Maidenhead

Nancy Astor of Cliveden

William Morris, Lord Nuffield

Kenneth Grahame

Sir Charles Day Rose

George Palmer, Huntley & Palmer biscuits

J.R.R. Tolkien

Sir Stanley Spencer

Greenham Common Women's Peace Camp

Jimmy Page and Led Zeppelin

Sir John Madejski

Sir Steve Redgrave

Ricky Gervais and *The Office*

Prime Minister Theresa May

The Prince and Princess of Wales

1. Pre-Historic through Roman Britain
— Hand Axes, Crop Circles, and Earthworks

The changing route of the Thames — When the first humans visited the area about a half a million years ago, the River Thames would have been very different and the actual valley would not have been as deep. There was a river that flowed from its source in the Cotswolds across what is now Oxfordshire, but downstream from Goring, the river had a more north-easterly direction, carrying on somewhat north of Reading, past Marlow and Cookham, then through the vale of St Albans to the North Sea via Essex and Suffolk. During the Anglian Ice Age, about 450,000 years ago, glaciers advanced further south than at any point in history, covering most of East Anglia. The advancing ice sheet over-ran the previous route of the river to the North Sea, forming a lake when the water could not reach the sea. This lake overflowed and forced the river it take its present more southerly route via London. The river is thought to have made a turn at today's bend in the river near Cookham's Winter Hill, continuing towards Maidenhead, eventually forming the rest of today's Thames Valley into the sea via London.

The Goring Gap — Today's route of the river through Goring is via a relatively narrow gap in the chalk hills bordered by the Berkshire Downs to the west and Chiltern Hills to the east. During the 2-3 million years of the Earth's Ice Age, the land has slowly risen and, as a response, the river cut down through the chalk hills to the point where they are now two distinct ranges of hills.

The ancient Ridgeway, which follows the Chiltern and Berkshire Downs escarpments, crosses the river at the Goring Gap, thereby making it one of the oldest Thames crossing points. For at least 5000 years, the Ridgeway Trail connected the area with East Anglia and Wessex and was a possible route of migration between these two regions. A Roman road also crossed the river in this area, connecting the town of Silchester (Roman name Calleva) with other settlements. Much later, the Goring Gap was chosen by Isambard Kingdom Brunel as the only low-gradient route through the hills for his Great Western Railway heading west from London to Bristol.

Opposite page: Alpacas from farm now on the site of the Bozedown Iron Age Hillfort at Whitchurch Hill overlooking the Thames on the edge of the Chilterns. Below: A map showing the Goring Gap between the Berkshire Downs and the Chilterns. Map: Oxford Archaeology.

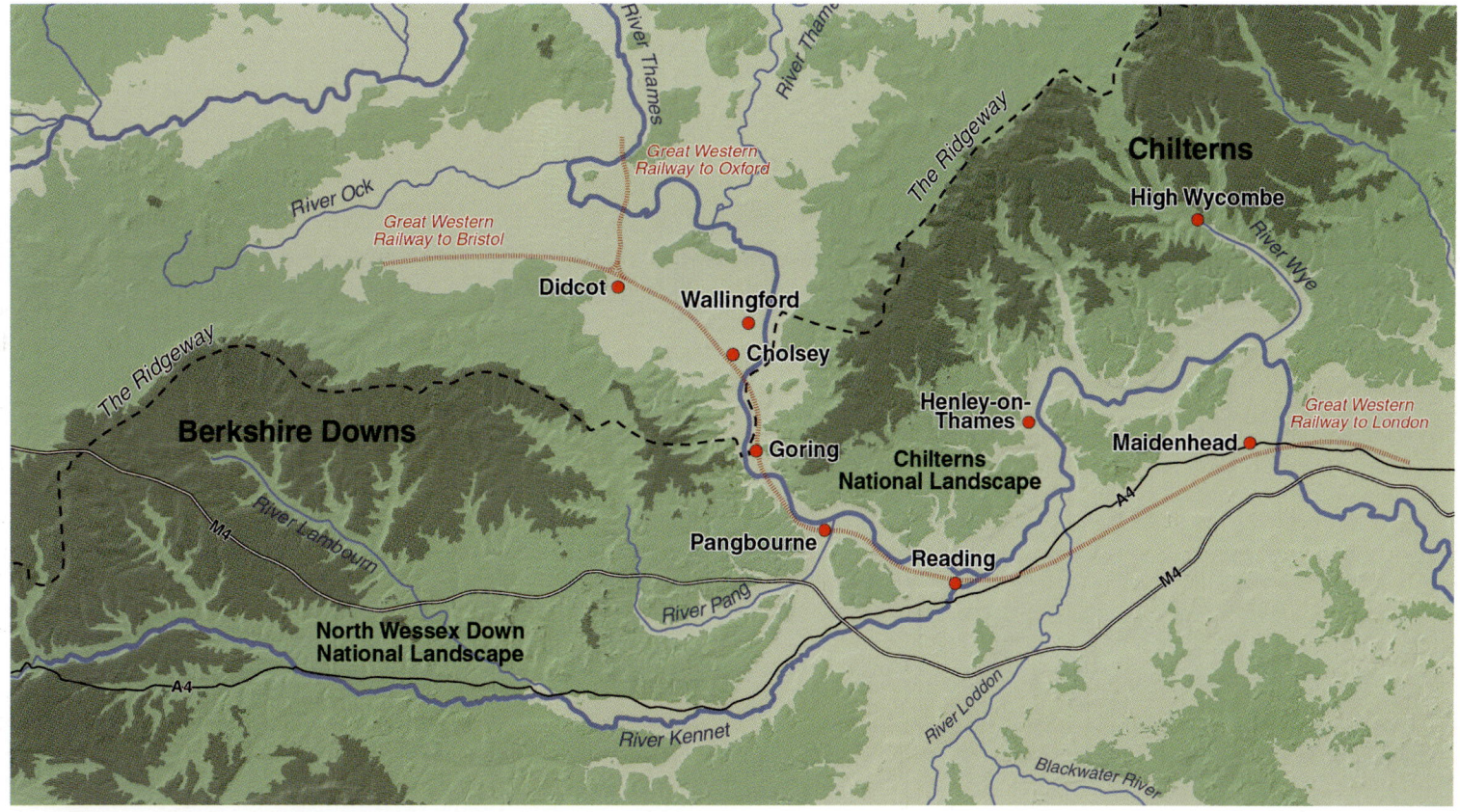

Prehistoric Britain

Prehistory refers to the time before there were written records. Despite a lack of documentation, there is ample evidence of early humans living in the Thames Valley in the form of stone age artefacts, and ancient ritual and burial sites. Examples of these findings can be seen at the Reading Museum and in Oxford at the Pitt-Rivers, Natural History and Ashmolean museums. The Ashmolean organises its collection of British prehistoric artefacts into the following periods:

- **The Palaeolithic Age** — from at least 750,000 years ago, when humans first occupied what is now coastal East Anglia, down to around 12,000 years ago. This is also known as the Old Stone Age, when early humans used stone tools and lived a nomadic lifestyle. One of the earliest signs of human presence in the Thames Valley is from Highlands Farm just west of Henley-on-Thames, possibly about 500,000 years ago. Palaeolithic flint hand axes have been found throughout the Thames Valley, although in Oxfordshire quartzite was used for hand axe manufacture alongside flint.
- **The Mesolithic Age** — following the end of the last Ice Age, about 11,500 years ago, when new kinds of flint tools were introduced. This is also known as the Middle Stone Age. Britain only became an island, fully detached from Europe, from about 6000 years ago, as the English Channel and North Sea were gradually submerged when the climate warmed and the residual ice from the last glacial period finally melted. The land had then became densely forested with hazel, birch, lime elm and oak, and the main larger animals were red and roe deer, elk and pig. Humans were still predominantly nomadic hunter-gatherers and activity seems to have been focused along river valleys such as the Thames.
- **The Neolithic Age** — also known as the New Stone Age, dates from about 6000 to 4300 years ago. This was the time when humans first settled in certain parts of the country conducive to farming, fishing and hunting such as the Thames Valley. The start of the Neolithic Age is traditionally defined by the change from nomadic tribes hunting and gathering to settled communities growing crops, such as barley and wheat, and breeding animals, including sheep, goats, cattle and pigs. Flint hand axes, arrowheads, and other implements have been found from this era throughout the Thames Valley.

View over the Goring Gap from the Chiltern Hills towards the Berkshire Downs at Streatley, where the ancient Ridgeway, known as Britain's oldest road, crossed the Thames. The route is thought to have been used by Neolithic settlers from Europe with knowledge of farming. Brunel's GWR bridge at Gatehampton, seen in the centre, also took advantage of this gap through the chalk hills.

Up to 400,000 years ago — hand axes

Hand axes were typically made of flint which is commonly found in chalk terrain. Hand axes were an all-purpose 'Swiss Army knife tool' but believed to have been primarily used for meat butchery in Britain.

- In 1919, a very large flint hand axe, estimated to be 450,00 years old, was found at Canon Court Farm in the Furze Platt neighbourhood of Maidenhead. At 32.3 cm long, is it thought to be the largest hand axe ever found in Europe, and so large, that it was probably only useful as ceremonial value. Over 2000 other smaller hand axes have been recovered from the same area making the stretch along the river between Cookham and Maidenhead one of the most prolific areas for hand axe finds in Britain.
- The oldest hand axes in the Thames Valley were found at Henley's Highland Farm, estimated to be 500,000 years old. The site is now being developed with new homes, but a thin strip of land is protected as a Site of Special Scientific Interest (SSSI) to enable future archaeological investigations.
- Over 200 Palaeolithic flint artefacts were found at a gravel pit in Berinsfield south of Oxford as well as a number made from quartzite stone. Evidence from fossil bones found in the regional gravel pits suggests that animals from this time included woolly mammoth, woolly rhinoceros, horse, cave bear, cave lion, and arctic fox.
- You can see a some of the oldest hand axes from the Thames Valley in the Oxford Natural History Museum. Their display includes a 400,000 year old hand axe found in a gravel pit in Long Hanborough, about 10 km northwest of Oxford, not far from Blenheim Palace.

Above right: The Furze Platt Hand Axe – the largest Hand axe ever found in Europe. Impressive, but probably too large to be of much practical use! Photo: Natural History Museum, London, Science Photo Library.

Right: A narrow strip of land at Henley's Highland Farm is now used as a footpath and protected as an SSSI to enable future excavations.

Retired bricklayer and hobbyist flint shaper, Peter Woolhouse, pictured right, has found the six prehistoric hand axes (shown below) in the Reading area in recent years whilst either working on construction sites, through the course of gardening or just out for a walk. Peter found some of the hand axes in Earley and Tilehurst in suburban Reading, and others in Ipsden, Yattendon and Whitchurch. When I asked him how old they were, he shrugged and said — "I don't really know — maybe a couple hundred thousand years?"

At least five other stone age flint hand-axes have been found in Whitchurch-on-Thames in recent years by residents in their gardens or other areas of the village. Two of these were found in a garden on Swanston Field road in 1985. These were validated by a researcher from Pitt Rivers Museum in Oxford to be Palaeolithic hand axes, dating some 150,000 to 250,000 years ago.

My discussions with Peter and other local historians were indeed part of my inspiration for writing this book. If they could find evidence of human activity going back that far whilst working in the garden or out for a walk, what other important history might have happened in this area in the meantime?

Right: Former bricklayer and hobbyist flint shaper Peter Woolhouse.
Below: Some of the hand axes Peter found in the Reading area.

Approximately 220,000 years ago — woolly mammoths

A major finding of woolly mammoth bones was unearthed In 2017, by Sally and Dr Neville Hollingsworth, at Cerney Wick Quarry, near the source of the Thames at Cricklade. The site, with well-preserved remains of least four mammoths and many hand axes was featured on a David Attenborough BBC documentary where it was speculated that this gave strong evidence that Neanderthal man may have been hunting the mammoths. The site is thought to be on a previous route of the River Thames three km from its present route.

10,000 years ago — Post Ice Age hunting at Gatehampton

Findings of flint tools at Gatehampton Farm, near Goring, suggest that it was an area for seasonal hunting and butchery, set amidst chalk grassland. Mesolithic hunters using 'Long blade' flint tools are thought to have ambushed migrating animals at a shallow river crossing there, in the narrow the Goring Gap section of the river. A Neolithic settlement on the Berkshire side of the river was found in 2001 by archaeologists on the Time Team television show, supporting the idea that this river crossing was a place of special significance for early nomadic humans.

The river crossing at Gatehampton, shown on the right, is what some historians refer to as a 'persistent place' of historical significance through the ages. It was a strategic crossing for later generations based on the discovery of Roman villas on either side of the river, the mention of a Manor House and mill in the Domesday Book, and the site chosen by Isambard Kingdom Brunel for his Great Western Railway bridge over the Thames. Gatehampton is now a quiet rural spot accessed primarily via the Thames Path, however Brunel's railway bridge from 1840 is still very much in use and Thames Water boreholes at Gatehampton provide fresh spring water to much of Oxfordshire.

6000-4000 years ago — The first settlers

Like Gatehampton, Dorchester-on-Thames was a persistent location that early humans chose to settle in over many centuries. A number of important archaeological findings around Dorchester indicate that Neolithic farmers began to clear away the forests to provide food for some of the first permanent settlers in the Thames Valley 4000 to 5000 years ago. The extensive evidence of human burial and other ceremonial monuments located below the prominent Wittenham Clumps at the strategic intersection of the River Thames and Thame all add to the belief that the area was a settlement of special significance.

- Wheat and barley were thought to be the earliest crops. Domesticated animals during this period would have included cattle, pigs and sheep, although they would have looked very different from today's farm animals.
- Evidence was found of a large circular henge of a similar age and size to the more famous henges at Avebury and Stonehenge. The monument, known as Big Rings, was a circular double ditch henge that measured almost 200 metres in diameter. It may have been topped with timber structures or standing stones. This henge was initially found through aerial photographs of crop marks in 1938 by Major George Allen (see photo next page) using his own private plane with a specially designed camera. Major Allen owned a private airfield at nearby Clifton Hampden and collected images of a number of hillforts and other archaeologically significant sites in the 1930s.
- After the war, the henges and many other sites of special interest were destroyed to make way for gravel quarrying and the sites are now beneath a series of large lakes used for fishing and sailing. Thankfully, before their destruction, a number of important archaeological excavations were completed between 1946 and 1951 validating the prehistoric significance of the area.
- Further excavations were completed in 1981 during construction of the Dorchester bypass road, now the A4074. This road coincides with a narrow rectangular neolithic structure about 1.8 km long called a cursus, also slightly visible in Major Allen's photo. The monument is made of two parallel earthwork walls about 64m apart. Human bones recovered near this monument have been dated to between 4000 to 5000 years ago. The function of this monument is unknown, but it is thought to have been used for

Brunel's rail bridge at Gatehampton in the Goring Gap – the site of seasonal hunting 10,000 years ago and much more over the ages.

rituals that may have included processions. Other neolithic burial sites were found in nearby Benson, Abingdon and North Stoke. The Dorchester Cursus seems particularly significant due to its position by the river with an unusually large number of smaller circular burial sites found nearby.

- The road intersection shown in Major Allen's photo above Big Rings is now the roundabout at the intersection of the A4074 and the A415 road to Abingdon. Berinsfield was later built on the north side of the road, also the site of a number of quarries with many important neolithic findings. Deacon's Garage continues to be located at this roundabout. Today there is a motorcycle shop and the H Cafe at Deacon's that is a popular meeting place for motorcyclists on most sunny weekends. Things may have changed in 5000 years, but the site is still a popular meeting place with its own distinctive rituals.

Above left: Major Allen's aerial photo of Big Rings Henge at Dorchester in 1938.© Ashmolean Museum.
Below left: The site today is covered by fishing and sailing lakes, resulting from gravel quarrying.
Below right: The entrance to the 5000 year old cursus and stone henges at Deacon's Garage is now a meeting place for bikers.

2300-800 BC — The Bronze Age

Copper and gold were the first metals to be used in Britain, followed by bronze, which is a copper alloy with tin. Bronze is harder and more durable than copper providing more advanced technology and allowing tools and ornaments to be made in a variety of shapes. Flint and stone were still commonly used for many objects during this period.

Bronze Age discoveries in the Thames Valley were not as common as findings in the of Iron Age when hillforts were established, but a number of hoards of various Bronze Age artefacts, such as swords, shields, axes and spearheads, have been found throughout the Thames Valley. A particularly well preserved bronze shield found in the river at Wittenham near Day's Lock is on display at the Ashmolean Museum.

There are at least two Bronze Age landmarks that are still visible:
- Cock Marsh, a field on a flood plain along the river in Cookham, is home to four circular Bronze Age burial mounds and was later used as a burial ground by Anglo-Saxons. The largest barrow had a diameter of 90 feet and would have been around 8 feet high with the mound still clearly visible today. Excavations in 1874 found the remains of a woman accompanied by what was left of a funeral feast in the largest mound, with one of the smaller barrows containing the remains of a child. The elaborate nature of the mounds suggest that they may have been the family of a local chieftain.
- A Bronze Age burial site was found at Brightwell Barrow near the Wittenham Clumps in Brightwell-cum-Sotwell. It was a bowl shaped burial ground at the top of a hill that was later covered with a clump of trees in the 1800s as was the fashion for landscape architecture at that time.

Below: Bronze Age burial mound at Cock Marsh, Cookham with Winter Hill in the background.
Above: Brightwell Barrow now marked by clump of trees.

800 BC-43 AD — The Iron Age

In England, the use of iron for weapons and tools gradually replaced bronze in the period from 800 BC. The technology to produce the more plentiful iron required furnaces with much higher temperatures for smelting and other advanced purification processes. During the Iron Age, people generally lived in small settlements and farms, constructing large enclosures which were defended with banks and ditches. Remains of significant Iron Age hillforts are still visible at the Wittenham Clumps, Taplow Court, and Whitchurch Hill, all overlooking the River Thames. As tribal groups developed across England, boundaries became important and the Thames provided a natural boundary.

The Iron Age hillfort overlooks the river at Whitchurch Hill that has been known in recent centuries as Bozedown Camp. Remnants of the earthen walls can still be seen on the sides of the hill that is now home to a large Alpaca Farm. In 1953 there were finds of pottery and other items dating from the early Iron Age. One hand axe found at the fort is now in the British Museum. An artist's depiction showing what the fort may have looked like was recently developed by the Chilterns Hillfort Project.

Above right: Artist's depiction of Bozedown Camp. Overhead view towards the Thames and Reading. Artist: Mark Gridley, © Chilterns Conservation Board.

Below: Bozedown Iron Age hillfort at Whitchurch with shadows of ramparts clearly visible. It is a favourite grazing place of the local alpacas that are clearly amendable to climbing the hill.

Protective ditches can still clearly be seen surrounding Castle Hill on the Wittenham Clumps and at the Dyke Hills at Dorchester-on-Thames. It is thought that the focus shifted from Castle Hill to the enclosure at Dyke Hills on the other side of the Thames during the late Iron Age period. The enclosure continued to be used during the Roman period. The impressive double banks and ditch completed the great enclosure with the River Thame on one side and the River Thames on the other two sides as it makes a bend in the river. Crop marks have revealed that the enclosure is full of walls, pits, and circular houses set along roads. The enclosure still has only had limited archaeological excavation but has produced one of the densest concentrations of Iron Age coins in Britain.

Above: A view of Wittenham Clumps at Dorchester-on-Thames with Dyke Hills Iron Age earthworks in the foreground. The three hills in the distance from left to right are:
- Brightwell Barrow —where a Bronze Age burial site was discovered
- Two Wittenham Clumps on the right: Castle Hill Iron Age fort to the left and Round Hill on the right.
- The two Dyke Hill ridges provided a protected enclosure for settlements, initially during the Iron Age, but the enclosure was also used by Roman settlers.

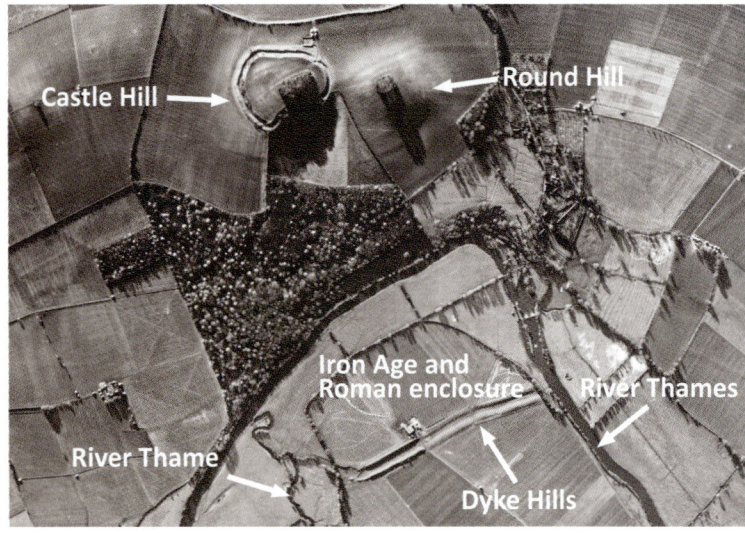

Below: An RAF surveillance photo from 1943 that shows the Wittenham Clumps and how the Dykes Hills enclosed the area between the Rivers Thame and Thames. Photo ©Historic England Archive. USAAF Photography.

43-410 AD, Roman Britain — Julius Caesar's first successful crossing of the Thames happened during his second expedition to Britain in 54 BC, having been unsuccessful in his invasion attempts the year before. The exact location of this crossing is not certain, but Caesar's own commentaries on the war stated 'the river was passable on foot only at one place and that with difficulty', making historians believe that the Roman army may have crossed the Thames at a ford at Brentford, West London. Caesar successfully defeated a number of local tribes and may have passed through parts of the Thames Valley on his way towards St Albans, but then returned with his troops to the continent the same year. Caesar's invasion seems to have opened Britain up to trade with the Roman empire, but there was no further settlement of Romans in Britain until 90 years later when Emperor Claudius staged a full scale invasion in 43 AD.

The Thames Valley is dotted with Roman settlements, villas, major potteries, and sites where coins and other artefacts were discovered, being used as a crossroads between other major Roman centres.

The largest Roman towns in the area were Alchester to the north of Oxford, just below Bicester, and Silchester (Roman name Calleva), in Hampshire, about 10 miles south of Reading.

- Both Alchester and Silchester are now abandoned towns, but Silchester was the more significant site with an impressive one and a half mile circumference stone and flint wall built in the 3rd century. It has been the site of extensive archaeological excavations by the University of Reading since 1997 and many of the findings are the subject of a dedicated exhibition at the Reading Museum, located in Reading Town Hall.
- Silchester (Calleva) was present in the Iron Age prior to Roman invasion and was thought to be the capital of the Atrebates tribe that probably migrated from the region of Belgium in northern Gaul. Atrebate coins and other artefacts have been found that pre-date Roman occupation. The Thames is thought to have acted as a border between Atrebates to the south and the Catuvellauni to the north that included Verulamium, now St Albans. The Calleva city walls and large Roman amphitheatre are still visible and the site is open to visitors during daylight hours, free of charge.

Dorchester-on-Thames continued to be a hotbed for early settlers during the Roman period with its strategic location on the Roman road between Alchester and Silchester.

- Apart from Alchester, Dorchester was the only walled Roman town in Oxfordshire. About a quarter of the old Roman town in Dorchester is still accessible for archaeological digs as it sits on the site of the town's community allotments. Residents from the village have been participating in archaeological digs at the allotments most summers since 2008, working with experts from Oxford University's School of Archaeology.

Roman Roads and other notable settlements in the Thames Valley. Map courtesy of Oxford Archaeology.

Dorchester-on-Thames was a key crossroad for number of Roman roads:
- The road north to Alchester via Berinsfield gave access to a strategic crossroads with the Cirencester to St Albans road.
- Beyond Alchester, the road goes to Towcester (Roman name Lactodorum) where it joined the ancient Watling Street between London and the north of England (now the route of the A5).
- Another road goes due south from Dorchester towards Silchester, crossing the Thames at or near Streatley. The name of the village of Streatley comes from the Latin name "Stata" for road. The Ridgeway possibly acted as a separate route from Streatley towards a Roman temple at Lowbury Hill near Aston Upthorpe.
- A Roman road from Dorchester to Henley is thought to have passed through Nettlebed and Bix, along the Fairmile Road and crossed a ford in the river at what is now the Phyllis Court Club.

Two elaborate mosaics were discovered by workers building the Great Western Railway in 1838 that were part of a Roman villa near Beale Wildlife Park at Pangbourne. The site of the villa was by the Thames river crossing in the Goring Gap near Brunel's railway bridge. Fortunately, someone made a rough drawing of one of the mosaics before the GWR workers, known as navvies, carried on with construction of the railway and the mosaics were destroyed. Mosaic experts from the Reading Museum created a reconstruction of what the mosaic may have looked like as part of the *Time Team* archaeological television show in 2001.

Another villa was found and excavated on the opposite side of the river from Beale Park at Gatehampton. This crossing is by a ford in the river where there was a ferry for many years and is the same crossing mentioned earlier where Neolithic hunters were thought to have trapped animals trying to cross the river after the last Ice Age.

Buried treasure – Before the advent of modern banking, valuables were often buried in hidden hoards, the equivalent of stuffing money in a mattress, or perhaps more like a buried treasure. Some of the most valuable archaeological finds in recent years have been rediscovering lost hoards, often by amateur metal detectorists.
- An incredible Roman hoard was found by metal detectorist Bill Darley in 1995, near the Oxfordshire town of Didcot. Whilst hoards of bronze and silver coinage are relatively common from Roman Britain, this hoard instead consists of 126 solid gold coins known as aurei.
- The Treasures Act of 1996 makes it a requirement for detectorists to report all finds of treasure to authorities in a scheme that is managed by the British Museum. Local museums have to right to acquire all finds and may offer a reward equal to the market value of the find which is normally split equally between the finder and the landowner.

Excavation at Silchester by Reading University archaeologists.

Conservationist cleaning the mosaics at the Roman villa in North Leigh situated along the Evenlode River that is a tributary of the Thames.

Above: There is still a path along the old Roman road north of Dorchester-on-Thames. The path heads north through Berinsfield and passes through the east side of Oxford via Blackbird Leys and the Cowley Mini car factory.

Below: The Roman road heading out of Berinsfield towards Oxford.

A hoard of rare gold Roman coins found by an amateur detectorist in Didcot, now on display at the Ashmolean Museum.

2. 410 - 1066 AD: Anglo-Saxon Britain — Christianity, King Alfred and the Vikings

5th-7th century – West Saxon community in the North Thames area

Historians now recognise that the general area of South Oxfordshire was the heartland of the Gewisse tribe of Saxons. The Gewisse are thought to be the descendants of Germanic West Saxons who captured the area after the end of Roman occupation and contributed to the formation of the Saxon Kingdom of Wessex.

Saxon hall — Long Wittenham was a site of significant Anglo-Saxon remains found in the 1890s including several burial sites around the village dating from 608-679 AD. The outlines of a number of buildings were discovered through the use of crop marks where different growing patterns revealed buried buildings. This was more recently aided by aerial photography using LiDAR imaging to outline a large group of buildings. The Sylva Foundation obtained a grant to reconstruct one of the largest buildings near the village from 2016-2018.

Early Christianity — Pope Honorius sent Birinus to Britain as a missionary in 635 AD to convert the Anglo-Saxons to Christianity. Birinus was successful in converting Cyneglis, King of the Gewisse. King Oswald of Northumbria acted as godfather to Cyneglis, as Oswald had previously been converted and sought to marry the daughter of Cyneglis. The two kings then granted land at Dorchester-on-Thames for the establishment of a cathedral church. Birinus became the Bishop of the West Saxons. Dorchester was to remain a regional cathedral city with a diocese of varying size and influence at least up through the end of the Anglo-Saxon period in 1066. The Anglo-Saxon cathedral was thought to be made of timber on the site of today's Dorchester Abbey building which was constructed in 1186.

Left: St Birinus baptising West Saxon King Cyneglis. From stained glass window at St Birinus Catholic church in Dorchester.

Left: A reconstructed Saxon building in Long Wittenham. Archaeologists from Oxford university believe that the building found near this site was too small to be a Great Hall, but unusually large for a normal house and built with timber that was reserved for important buildings. The reconstructed building was appropriately opened in 2019 by HRH the Countess of Wessex.

Previous page: Cyclists on the King Alfred's Way 350 km cycle route at Tan Hill over the Vale of Pewsey near Avebury.

650-727 — St Frideswide

Legend has it that St Frideswide, the patron saint of both Oxford City and Oxford University, was the daughter of a King of Mercia, the sub-king of the upper Thames region within the overall kingdom of Mercia.

- Part of the legend relates to her being pursued by a Saxon prince seeking her hand in marriage despite her wishes to lead a monastic life. Frideswide ran off into the wilderness to escape her suitor with two other nuns. The prince pursued her and eventually followed her back into Oxenford, as it was called back then, where the prince became blinded upon passing through the city gates.
- According to William of Malmesbury's account written in 1125, Frideswide later forgave and healed the prince.
- Frideswide may have spent her time in the wilderness at Frilsham, near Yattendon, in Berkshire. Frideswide and her companions discovered a small ivy-covered pig-sty that they made into a small chapel. They lived off the land for some three years, drinking from a well which appeared when Frideswide had prayed for water. There are many tales of Frideswide's healing miracles, including returning the sight of a blind girl with water from the well and kissing a man suffering with leprosy who was healed immediately. Some believe that 12th century documents refer to a different Berkshire town of Bampton, as opposed to Yattendon, as the place where she spent her time in the wilderness; however there is a church dedicated to St Frideswide in Frilsham dating back to at least the 12th century and also a well of spring water in the nearby woods, long referred to as Frideswide's well.
- After the episode with her suitor, Frideswide lived happily at Oxford for many years. She retired to quiet seclusion at Bisney, by Port Meadow in Oxford, where she built a small chapel. She prayed for water once more, this time to St Margaret, and a spring appeared, known locally as Treacle Well. The well is said to heal those who drink from it or who pray there. The well also has links to the Treacle Well from Alice in Wonderland and can still be seen in the grounds of St Margaret's church in Bisney.
- After her death in 735 AD, her remains were held in a shrine where many came to visit to pray including one of Henry VIII's wives Catherine of Aragon — unsuccessfully praying in hope of giving birth to a son.
- Cardinal Thomas Wolsey and Henry VIII established Christ Church College on the site of St Frideswide Priory in 1525, and made it the diocese cathedral for the newly established Church

St Frideswide praying in a pig-sty during her period in the wilderness. From the stained glass window at Christ Church Cathedral.

St Frideswide Shrine, reconstructed from the original St Frideswide Priory, in the Latin Chapel at Christ Church Cathedral, Oxford.

of England. Remains of the previous Frideswide shrine were later recovered and now form part of the reconstructed shrine that can still be seen below a stained glass window that tells the story of her life. The location of the bones of Frideswide is still somewhat of a mystery, but they are thought to be in an unmarked location somewhere in the floor of the cathedral.

Left: St Margaret's church in Bisney. The Treacle Well can be seen in the lower left of the picture behind the church by the bench.

Below Left: St Frideswide's well at Frilsham.

Below right: Stained glass window at St Frideswide church in Frilsham.

7th century barrow at Taplow

Taplow is the site of Tæppa's Mound, the burial site of an Anglo-Saxon chief, located on a prominent hill overlooking the river near Maidenhead. The mound was excavated in 1883 by three local amateur archaeologists who uncovered a hoard of treasures including military gear such as a sword, three spears, two shields, drinking horns, and an elaborately braided gold belt buckle. It was the most lavish Anglo-Saxon burial site known until the discovery of the ship burial at Sutton Hoo in Suffolk in the 1930s. The finds were donated to the British Museum where some of them remain on display.

Like Dorchester-on-Thames and Gatehampton described earlier, Taplow is an example of a Thames Valley 'persistent place' though the ages:

- It sits on the top of an Iron Age hillfort that was positioned on the only hill in the area offering long-distance views over the Thames.
- The mound is unusual in that it is located in a Christian graveyard dating to the 7th century and still used by St Nicholas church today.
- The mound is now also on the grounds of Taplow Court, a grand Elizabethan manor house built in the 16th century. As described later, it became the home of Lord Desborough of Maidenhead, an important local and national figure.

Above: Elizabethan Taplow Court, built on the site of Tæppas Mound.
Below: Tæppas Mound, the Anglo-Saxon burial ground on the site of a former Iron Age fort overlooking the Thames at Maidenhead — showing the gold Saxon belt buckle discovered there.

7th–10th century — Anglo-Saxon kingdoms

England consisted of a number of different Anglo-Saxon kingdoms during this period, with the Thames Valley split between Mercia and Wessex. The River Thames generally acted as the border between these two kingdoms, making it an important strategic boundary. Mercia controlled land north of the Thames and Wessex controlled the area south of the river although there were a number of changes to the borders over the years.

Places like Cookham and Pangbourne were under the control of Mercia during some periods despite being south of the river, whilst Dorchester, north of the river, was originally a Wessex settlement.

- The monastery at Cookham was a bone of contention between the two kingdoms. An archaeological excavation performed near Cookham Holy Trinity church in 2021 confirmed that the monastery was run by the powerful King Offa of Mercia during the 770s. The excavation confirmed that Offa's Queen Cynethryth retired to a religious life as abbess of Cookham Abbey after Offa's death in 796 AD. There are other earlier historical accounts of Cookham changing hands between Mercia and Wessex prior to 750 and then later becoming a fortified stronghold under King Alfred of Wessex by the 880s.
- Pangbourne is first mentioned in historical records in 844 when land was granted from the Bishop of Leicester to Berhtwulf, the King of Mercia, whose image is still shown on the village sign. Again, despite Pangbourne being just south of the river in Berkshire, the grant was to Mercia, not Wessex. Berhtwulf later granted the estate at Pangbourne to Ealdorman Æthelwulf who led a victorious battle against the Vikings at nearby Englefield in 870. Ealdorman Æthelwulf was killed four days after the victory at Englefield fighting the Vikings at Reading alongside Alfred of Wessex who was born in nearby Wantage. The fact that Ealdorman Æthelwulf from Pangbourne was supporting Wessex

Anglo-Saxon Kingdoms circa 800 AD. The borders of these kingdoms changed significantly over the Anglo-Saxon period, eventually forming the first united England.

Angel in the cemetery of Cookham's Holy Trinity church.

in the battle against the Vikings indicates that the land at Pangbourne may have been transferred to Wessex before the battle or that Mercia and Wessex were fighting together against the Vikings.

- As described earlier, control of Dorchester Cathedral, which was to the north of the Thames, was originally part of the West Saxon kingdom. The area moved to control by the Kingdom of Mercia after a battle in Bensington, the old name for Benson, in 779 when the powerful King Offa of Mercia defeated the West Saxon King Cynewuld.
- A rare set of 200 Anglo-Saxon silver coins showing the Kings of Wessex and Mercia together was found in a hoard in Watlington, outside of Henley-on-Thames. Discovered by amateur detectorist James Mather in 2015, the 'Two Emperors' penny shows Kings Alfred of Wessex and Ceolwulf of Mercia seated side by side below a winged figure of victory. The image on the coins suggests an alliance between the kingdoms of Wessex and Mercia, probably after the Battle of Edington in 878 where Wessex won a decisive victory over the Vikings. The treasure was valued at £1.35m by the independent Treasure Valuation Committee. The Ashmolean Museum raised the money required to pay the reward for this rare finding of King Alfred coins. They received a £1.1 million grant from the Heritage Lottery Fund and raised the rest from member donations. The coins are now on display at the Ashmolean Museum. It is understood that Mr Mather split the reward with the landowner.

Mercian King Bertwulf and a Viking ship can still be seen on the Pangbourne village sign. Viking ships would have passed along the river through Pangbourne from their bases in London or Reading. The sign also shows a book with the title of *"Wind in the Willows"* in honour of former resident Kenneth Grahame.

848-899 — King Alfred the Great of Wessex

Alfred was born in Wantage, Berkshire, in 848 AD — a son of the Thames Valley. His father was the highly respected King Æthelwulf of Wessex who had developed a strong alliance with the neighbouring Kingdom of Mercia after defeating them in major battles. Alfred became king in 871 following the death of his older brother King Æthelred. Alfred was to became one of the most famous kings in British history, becoming the only English king to be referred to as 'Great'. Even though this moniker was given to him posthumously, there is much justification for his reputation as one of England's greatest leaders.

- Alfred promoted literacy and education, arranging and participating in the translation of important texts from Latin to Anglo-Saxon, now known as Old English, in topics ranging from history, geography and philosophy. He is said to have personally translated large parts of the Bible.
- He established the first united Anglo-Saxon legal code, that included the laws from the kingdoms of Mercia and Kent as well as reforms of his own.
- He sponsored the development of the Anglo-Saxon Chronicle — a patriotic history of the English from the Wessex viewpoint that also detailed and celebrated Alfred's many great achievements. The Chronicle, initially written by Alfred's friend Bishop Asser, was the first documented record of English history and is the reason we know so much about Alfred and his reign. The history in the Chronicle was added to and expanded until the time of the Norman Conquest.
- Alfred was probably best known for his bravery and leadership in preventing Wessex from being defeated and ruled by Danish Viking invaders. In 871, the year Alfred became King, Wessex was the last remaining Anglo-Saxon kingdom to be free from Danish rule.
- By the time of his death in 899, Alfred ruled over a combined Wessex and Mercia and was referred to as the leader of the Anglo-Saxon people, if not quite a united England. Alfred's eldest son, Edward the Elder, and then Edward's son Æthelstan, achieved Alfred's vision of forming a united Anglo-Saxon England by defeating the Vikings across the country and gaining the respect of the other Anglo-Saxon kingdoms. Æthelstan is considered by most historians to be the first true King of a united Anglo-Saxon England.

Right: King Alfred's statue from 1877 at his birthplace in Wantage.

The first major Viking battles with Wessex were in the Thames Valley at the start of Alfred's reign. Reading was first mentioned in history when the 'Viking Great Heathen Army' set up camp there where the River Thames intersects with the River Kennet. Ramparts across the third side of the triangle would have formed a secure enclosure in a similar manner to Dykes hills at Dorchester-on-Thames. The Anglo-Saxon Chronicle documents details of three major battles in the Reading area during a 10 day period starting in late 870.

Battle of Englefield — The Saxons were initially victorious at a smaller battle, more of a skirmish, outside of Reading at Englefield near Theale. On the 31st December 870, local Ealdorman Æthelwulf, who was from Berkshire and probably based at Pangbourne, led a team of soldiers that attacked a large Viking party that were on a foraging and reconnaissance mission from their camp at Reading. Æthelwulf was successful in killing the two Viking earls who were leading the party and many Viking soldiers. Badly shaken, the Vikings scattered back to Reading. Lord Richard Benyon, whose family has owned Englefield Estate since the 18th century, understands that the site of the battle was in fields just to north of Englefield House where old maps show the battlefield on what is known as Old Deer Park.

Battle of Reading — Hearing the news of the victory, King Æthelred of Wessex and his brother Alfred quickly led their larger Wessex army from their royal base in Winchester to Reading to seize the advantage within four days. The Vikings prevailed in the major battle at Reading on the 4th January 871. Local Ealdorman Æthelwulf was killed in the battle but Wessex King Æthelred and Alfred were able to escape.

Battle of Ashdown — Four days after the battle of Reading, the great Viking army was defeated by Æthelred and Alfred in another major battle at Ashdown just up the river from Reading. Many details of the battle of Ashdown are described in the Anglo-Saxon Chronicle, but the exact location of the battle is not clear. Most modern historians now believe that it took place in the Berkshire Downs, previously known as Ashdown, by the ancient Ridgeway trail near Streatley and Moulsford. Some have placed the battle site at Kingstanding Hill just above Moulsford or Lowbury Hill by the Ridgeway towards Aldworth.

The following account is based partly on Asser's history of Alfred's life, partly from oral history passed down in Aston Tirrold, and partly based on speculation of modern historians.

- The Viking army may have travelled in boats up the Thames from their camp at Reading to Streatley or Moulsford and then marched west along the Ridgeway towards the strategic town of Wantage. Alfred biographer Justin Pollard believes that they may have walked up an ancient road from Reading such as the Tuddingway, or the Roman Road between Silchester and Dorchester.
- To match the strategy set by the Vikings, King Æthelred and Alfred split their force into two armies, one led by Æthelred to fight the Danish Kings with Alfred leading a second army to fight the Danish Earls. The Wessex army may have camped at a fortified Wallingford after the Reading battle and then King Æthelred's army set up camp at Blewburton Iron Age hillfort near today's Aston Tirrold, with Alfred's army based at Kingstanding Hill above Moulsford. Both were within easy access of the Ridgeway trail.
- The Vikings would have been spotted by the Saxons making their way along the top of the Ridgeway from the Saxon's vantage point on Kingstanding Hill. It is said that Æthelred was attending mass on the morning of the battle and refused to fight the Vikings until the service was finished as it was important that God was on the side of the Saxon army. Alfred decided that the urgency of the situation meant he could not wait and started without him.
- The key strategy for both the Saxon and Viking armies at the time would have been to form shield walls to defend against an attacking army. Asser described Alfred's decision to close down his shield wall and attack 'like a wild boar' without waiting for support from his brother.
- Æthelred's army later outflanked and ultimately defeated the Danes in what was considered a major victory for the Saxons.

Alfred is also remembered at the King Alfred's Head in Wantage.

33

Above: Site of a Viking battle? Some have suggested Reading's Kings Meadows as a probable site of the Viking battle with Wessex, as it sits near the confluence of the River Thames and River Kennet as described in the Saxon Chronicle. The rivers would have protected a Viking camp on two sides. The remaining side would have been protected by Viking-made ramparts and perhaps Plummery Ditch that is no longer visible due to development. The ditch ran through what is now Kings Meadows, previously connecting the two rivers, and was used as a Royalist defence during the Civil War.

Left: Near the mouth of River Kennet in Reading where it meets the Thames. The once iconic gas tower shown in the photo was finally dismantled in 2022 to make way for a new 130-flat development.

- King Æthelred died of battle wounds a few months later and Alfred became the new King of Wessex by Easter. As King Alfred the Great, he would hold off advances from the Vikings to make Wessex the only Anglo-Saxon kingdom to remain free from Viking control.

Local artist Anna Dillon and aerial photographer Hedley Thorne have studied the Wessex landscape and work together on exhibitions focussed on the former Wessex Kingdom. They both support this version of events for the Battle of Ashdown.
- Hedley is part of a history podcast called "Wessex Ways" that explores the ancient history of the area.
- Anna's mother Judy Barradell-Smith is a local historian from Aston Tirrold and gave weight to the oral tradition that was passed down over the centuries, which she in turn passed on to Anna.
- Examples of Anna's and Hedley's work can be seen on the facing page.

If you would like to explore the route of the ancient sites where the battle is likely to have occurred, you can follow it on an Ordnance Survey map such as the one on the facing page. You may want to approach it from the Ridgeway trail starting in Streatley or perhaps via a circular pub walk from the The Bell Inn at Aldworth.

Three Men in a Boat author Jerome K. Jerome also acknowledged the historic importance of this area of the Thames and mentions the battles of Vikings and Anglo-Saxon warriors that took place at Reading and Ashdown.

> One does not linger in the neighbourhood of Reading. The town itself is a famous old place, dating from the dim days of King Ethelred, when the Danes anchored their warships in the Kennet, and started from Reading to ravage all the land of Wessex; and here Ethelred and his brother Alfred fought and defeated them, Ethelred doing the praying and Alfred the fighting.
>
> Jerome K. Jerome – *Three Men in a Boat*, 1889

The view from Kingstanding Hill over Starveall Farm towards the Thames at Moulsford.

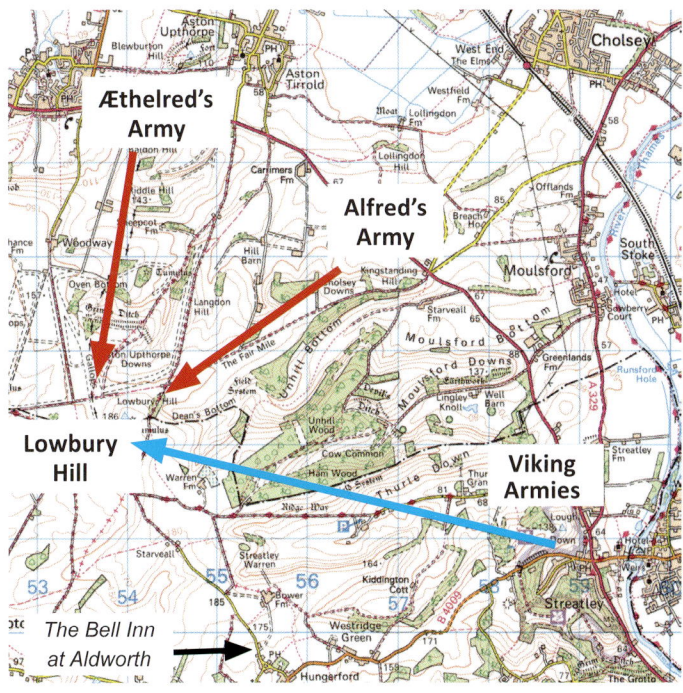

Above: Diagram of possible Ashdown Battle movements towards Lowbury Hill and the Ridgeway. © Ordnance Survey Maps.
Above left: Painting by Anna Dillon of the Fairmile ancient road leading from Kingstanding Hill towards Lowbury Hill. This is thought to have been the former route of the Ridgeway via Moulsford.©Anna Dillon.
Left: Aerial photo by Hedley Thorne of Lowbury Hill, former Roman and Anglo Saxon fort near the Ridgeway trail and possible site of the Battle of Ashdown. The outline of the square building can still be seen as can the round barrow where remains of 'Lowbury Man' were found. ©Hedley Thorne.
Below: Artist Anna Dillon and aerial photographer Hedley Thorne at Lowbury Hill where they believe the battle of Ashdown was fought.

880-914 creation of burhs

King Alfred established a number of fortified towns, know as 'burhs' throughout the kingdoms of Wessex and Mercia to defend against Viking invasions. The word 'borough' comes from the Old English burh, meaning fortress. His idea was that no one in Wessex should be more than 20 miles away from a fortified town to flee to and defend against a Viking invasion. Alfred's burhs were towns created from scratch, with a precisely laid out grid of streets, combining urban and military functions, and capable of accommodating hundreds, or even thousands of soldiers and citizens.

- By 914, Oxford, Wallingford, Cricklade, and Cookham (on Sashes Island at the site of today's Cookham Lock) are all mentioned in a Burghal Hidage document and are thought to be examples of settlements Alfred established by 880. In Wallingford, remains of the original fortifications are still visible today on the Kinecroft in the centre of town where the Bunkfest annual music festival is now held.
- Even though Oxford was known to be in Mercia, it is thought to have been established as a burh under King Alfred or his son Edward. Given Alfred's strong interest in scholarship, there were Victorian-era theories that he may have even instigated the founding of Oxford University, although this theory has been largely disproven.
- Dorchester-on-Thames was not chosen for establishment as a burh despite its importance as an Anglo-Saxon Cathedral town, as well as its continued importance from Roman and Iron Age periods. This could be because Wallingford and Oxford were on the rise as more strategic locations by then, or it could just be a matter of Wallingford and Oxford already being less than 20 miles apart and there was no need for an additional burh at Dorchester to defend against the Danes. The result of being passed over as a burh appears to be the start of the relative decline of Dorchester throughout the middle ages compared to Wallingford and Oxford that were to grow in strategic importance, especially after the Norman Conquest.

Children playing on the Anglo-Saxon ramparts that can still be seen surrounding the Kinecroft open space in the centre of Wallingford.

Left: Crowds on Wallingford's historic Kinecroft during the annual Bunkfest music festival.

Below: An offshoot of the Thames at Odney Common in Cookham with Holy Trinity church in the background. Sashes Island, that was originally set up by King Alfred as a fortified burh, is on the other side of Cookham Lock from Odney Common, but is now private farmland that is not accessible to the public.

Anglo-Saxon settlements under King Æthelred the Unready —978-1013 and 1014-1016

Thanks to the success of predecessors King Alfred and his successors in defeating the Vikings and uniting the country, King Æthelred the Unready reigned over a united Anglo-Saxon England. The nickname 'the Unready' was given to him posthumously and more accurately translates into him being 'ill-counselled' during his reign. Æthelred's actions led to a resurgence of Viking invasions that ultimately resulted in the Vikings taking full control of England in 1013 when Æthelred fled to Normandy and was replaced by the powerful Viking Sweyn of Denmark. Æthelred returned to rule after Sweyn's death in 1014, but upon Æthelred's death in 1016 he was succeeded by King Cnut of Denmark. Æthelred spent fortunes paying money to Vikings either as a bribe to leave England or to protect the country as mercenaries. This led to the introduction of the first equivalent of income tax to pay either the Vikings or local Wessex soldiers, along with harsh measures to extract wealth by local sheriffs.

Whitchurch-on-Thames is first recorded in 990 as having 10 hides of land being owned by Æthelred's thegn Leofric of Hwitecyran (Whitchurch) who later had to forfeit the estate for fomenting rebellion amongst the king's soldiers and for adultery and other unspecified misdemeanours.
- A hide was an English unit of land measurement intended to represent the amount of land sufficient to support a peasant family, which was traditionally about 120 acres.
- A thegn was an Anglo-Saxon warrior or nobleman roughly equivalent to a medieval knight in service of the king.
- Whitchurch presumably had a 'white church' at the site of today's St Mary the Virgin church.

Cookham is first mentioned in 997 where the Kings of Wessex held a Witan (the equivalent of an Anglo-Saxon parliament) called by Æthelred. Attending the Witan were one arch bishop, three bishops, two aldermen, three abbots and numerous lords from the West Saxons, Mercians, Danes and English. The village of Cookham was probably established in the 8th century after an Anglo-Saxon monastery was founded there. The old abbey church was probably the basis of the present parish church which shows signs of Anglo-Saxon work near the altar.

St Brice's Day Massacre, Oxford – As part of his disputes with the Vikings, King Æthelred ordered a massacre of all Danish men on St Brice's Day in 1002, held on the 13th of November. Some of the Danish men near Oxford sought refuge in St Frideswide's chapel, but the townspeople ended up burning it to the ground, killing the men inside.

Over 1000 years later, in 2008, archaeologists discovered the remains of at least 34 young men, most beheaded or burned and unceremoniously dumped in a ditch on the grounds of what is now St John's College.
- Radiocarbon dating showed that the bones dated from AD 960 to 1020, the late Anglo-Saxon period. According to analysis by the Museum of Oxford in 2022, it seemed probable that this mass grave might be archaeological evidence of the St Brice's Day Massacre of 1002.
- The skeletons were all of fighting age men, ranging from their late teens to mid-thirties and were unusually tall for the period. Analysis of atomic variations within the bones revealed that the men's diets consisted largely of fish and seafood, which was not typical of the Anglo-Saxons, strongly suggesting that these were the remains of Vikings.

Inset: St Giles, Oxford, outside of St John's College, where archaeologists believe they have found the remains of St Brice's Day Massacre from 1002. Opposite Page: View of the old mill house and St Mary's church in Whitchurch-on-Thames.

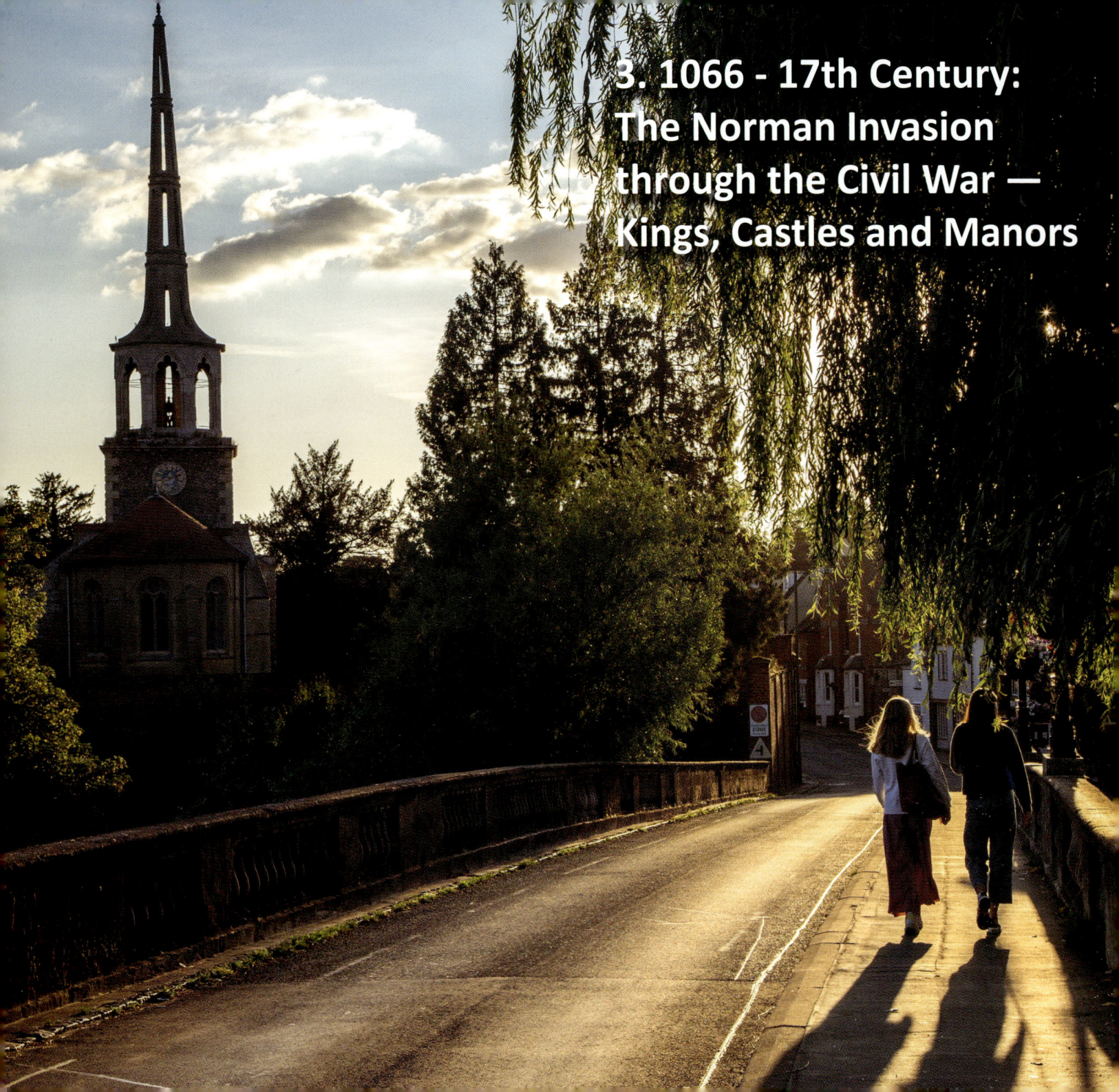
3. 1066 - 17th Century: The Norman Invasion through the Civil War — Kings, Castles and Manors

1066 — William the Conqueror

Following the Norman defeat of the last Anglo-Saxon King Harold at Hastings, the new King William the Conqueror set about establishing control over his kingdom through the construction of Norman style castles at strategic locations around the country. In the Thames Valley he saw that important castles were established at his home base in Windsor and at Wallingford and Oxford.

Wallingford Bridge

Wigod, the Lord of Wallingford, was a known Norman sympathiser and welcomed William. Just after William's invasion at Hastings in the south of England, William was blocked from crossing the Thames at London, but Wigod invited him to cross the Thames at Wallingford allowing his conquest of England to proceed, implying that Wallingford had a bridge by that time. As a gesture of thanks for the town's cooperation, William granted the town an extra hour of curfew in 1069, extending it from 8pm to 9pm. The clock on Wallingford's church tower still chimes at 9pm every evening in honour of this favour from William the Conqueror almost 1000 years later.

Image of William the Conqueror lifting his visor to reveal his face at the battle of Hastings. From the Bayeux Tapestry – a full replica of the tapestry can be seen in the Reading Museum.

Above: Wallingford town centre with the clock tower of St Mary-Le-More that still chimes the curfew bell at 9pm every evening almost 1000 years after the curfew was extended by William the Conqueror.
Preceding page: Wallingford Bridge today, site of William the Conqueror's first crossing of the Thames.

A model of what Wallingford Castle may have looked like at its height in the 1330s can be seen at the Wallingford Museum. The Thames and the bridge over the river can be seen on the far left side. ©Wallingford Museum.

Wallingford Castle — One of King William's knights from Normandy, Robert D'Oilly, married Wigod's daughter, Aldgytha. On William's instructions, Robert D'Oilly began to build a massive castle at Wallingford which was to dominate the town's history for the next 600 years, until its destruction after the Civil War.

D'Oilly became one of the principal landowners in Oxfordshire, with holdings in several other surrounding counties. He became Lord of Wallingford and later passed his title and manor to Miles Crispin who marred his daughter Maud. Both Crispin and D'Oilly are listed in the Domesday Book as owners of large areas of land in Berkshire and Oxfordshire, including Wallingford, Goring, Pangbourne and Whitchurch.

Windsor Castle — William the Conqueror captured the manor of Old Windsor, just a couple miles downstream from today's Windsor that continued to be his main base. He had a motte and bailey style castle built to guard the Thames from invaders starting in 1070 that was considered finished just before his death in 1087. The castle evolved over the centuries to become Windsor Castle as we know today.

- The motte and bailey castle design was brought to England by the Normans. The 'motte' was a large hill, or mound of earth that was often artificially created with a moat around it. On top of the mound was a fortified 'keep' with a protective wooden wall and tower at the top. The 'bailey' was a large flat yard beneath the motte that was also protected by a wooden fence. The bailey was the centre of domestic life and contained a variety of buildings including halls, kitchens, stores and stables. The Round Tower at the centre of Windsor Castle today is on the site of the original motte with a lower bailey and an upper bailey still forming the structure of the castle.
- The castle has been used by nearly all reigning monarchs since the time of William's son King Henry I (1100–1135). Henry held court at the castle for the first time in 1100 and was married at the Castle Chapel in 1121.

Oxford Castle — The town of Oxford had been stormed in the Norman invasion resulting in considerable damage and William directed Robert D'Oilly to build a castle in the town following his work building the castle at Wallingford. Although it was never the size of Wallingford or Windsor, it was an active county castle throughout the medieval period, and continued as a country gaol and prison until 1996.

Above: Remains of Wallingford Castle today.
Right: The original motte of Oxford Castle is still visible as is St George's Tower behind it.
Below: Artist's impression of what the initial motte and bailey Windsor Castle would have looked like. Image: Royal Collection Trust, © His Majesty King Charles III 2023. Illustrator: Bob Marshal.

1086 — The Domesday Book

Once King William had sufficiently secured domination of the country, he parcelled up the land to his loyal henchmen to run their local manors and fiefdoms. By 1086 he was ready to conduct a survey of the land and its residents to understand what he had conquered including its value for tax purposes. The resulting Domesday Book is the first comprehensive documentation of life in England, including details of over 13,000 settlements at the time.

After the Norman invasion, all land in England was owned by the monarch with tenants-in-chief being those who managed feudal land on behalf of the king. Under feudalism, the king was the only true 'owner' of land in England, and was thus the ultimate overlord. The Domesday Book lists the Lords or 'tenants-in-chief' for each town and village who may have been given the land to run on behalf of the king. William is listed as the tenant-in-chief in cases where he either managed the land himself or had not allocated it to another lord. This period of the Middle Ages in which lords of manors ran vast rural estates is where villages often first developed as communities of workers supporting the manor. The system started in Anglo-Saxon times, but was first fully documented in the Domesday Book. Feudalism and the power of the kings was gradually phased out over the centuries and replaced by capitalism and private land ownership, although there are still vestiges of the feudal system left in parts of Britain.

Nearly all of the towns and villages included in the book were part of one or more manor, normally with a manor house where the lord of the manor lived. The lord was responsible for the well being of his workers, with the exception of the spiritual guidance which was provided by the priest of the parish.

The table on the facing page shows a number of prominent Thames Valley settlements included in the Domesday Book in order of population at the time.
- The book lists Oxford and Wallingford as being amongst only 18 towns in England that had a population of over 2000 people at the time, although the actual population of the towns does not appear in the records. The population of some households was not included in the Domesday count, but the reasons remain a subject of historical debate.
- Small holders owned an average of 5 acres with perhaps a share in the village's plough team.
- Many Thames Valley villages had mills and fisheries. Mills were listed as assets of generally about one pound.
- The mills in Pangbourne and Whitchurch continued to produce flour until the early 1900s.
- Abingdon is listed as having no population, which was the case for some towns.
- Iffley, Headington, Walton, Cowley and Holywell, are listed as separate settlements but all became part of Oxford by 1929.
- Slaves, more commonly known as feudal serfs, clearly did not own any land and belonged to the lord. Ælfric of Eyshan describes the life of an unfree ploughman at the end of the 10th century. "He must rise at dawn and labour all day for fear of his master, however harsh the weather, until an acre or more has been ploughed. Oh the work is hard, yes the work is hard, because I am not free."

Since the time of the Domesday Book, growth and development of towns and villages across the region has not always been consistent and steady. Some settlements, such as Dorchester-on-Thames, that had been of strategic historical significance for thousands of years, were overtaken in population growth by other towns in more recent centuries. The table on the opposite page shows that towns such as Reading, Oxford, Windsor, and Maidenhead have seen significant growth since 1086, whilst the relative size of others has diminished, including Wallingford, Marlow, Dorchester-on-Thames, Bray and Benson that had been listed as some of the most populous settlements in 1086.

Settlement	Population 1086	Population 2021	Value	Lord(s)/Tenant-in-Chief	Small Holders	Slaves	Plough Teams	Mills
Oxford	>2,000 (18 reported)	170,798	£242	King William, Oxford Canons of St Frideswide, Robert D'Oilly	0	0	15	1
Wallingford	> 2,000 (66 reported)	8,455	£73	King William	0	22	0	0
Dorchester-on-Thames	153	991	£77	Bishop of Lincoln (St Mary)	42	5	52	5
Cholsey	137	4,388	£64	King William	100	15	9	0
Marlow and Little Marlow	107	14,644	£40	Bishop Odo of Bayeux, Miles Crispin, Walter of Vernin, Queen Matilda	39	5	34.5	1
Reading	102	203,808	£63	King William, Abbey of Battle	38	0	60	3
Bray	80	9,416	£10	King William, Alwyn	7	7	26	6
Benson	69	4,801	£86	King William, Thodric	32	5	24	2
Hambleden	68	1,332	£35	Queen Matilda	9	9	27	1
Cookham	67	5,771	£38	King William	31	4	23	2
Aston Tirrold and Upthorpe	54	566	£24	Tir: Robert of Mortain, Up: Reinbald of Cirencester	15	12	13	0
Taplow	52	2,389	£712	Bishop Odo of Bayeux	32	2	15	0
Hurley	47	2,012	£8	Robert D'Oilly	1	6	3	1
Nunham Courtenay	45	208	£13	Richard of Courcy	0	10	17	1
Caversham	43	11,411	£20	Walter Giffard	13	2	13	1
Streatley	36	1,069	£26	Geoffery de Mandeville	11	7	16	1
Goring-on-Thames	33	3,436	£15	Robert D'Oilly	2	10	10	1
Whitchurch-on-Thames	32	841	£20	Miles Crispin	7	5	15	1
Crowmarsh Gifford	27	1,327	£20	Walter Giffard	11	4	5	2
Windsor	26	31,563	£15	King William	2	2	11	1
South Stoke	25	518	£12	Bishop of Lincoln (St. Mary)	5	1	8	0
Eton	23	5,123	£8	Robert D'Oilly	1	6	3	1
Pangbourne	17	3,277	£6	King William, Miles Crispin	10	0	3	2
Checkendon	15	523	£3	Alfred, nephew of Wigot	3	4	2	0
Ipsden	11	341	£2	Reginald the Archer	5	0	3	0
Maidenhead	10	67,374	£2	Giles, brother of Ansculf	4	0	3	0

1121 – Reading and Dorchester Abbeys

King Henry I, son of William the Conqueror, ordered the construction of Reading Abbey in 1121. In its heyday the abbey was one of Europe's largest and holiest royal monasteries.

- Henry chose a spot on high ground in the middle of town by the River Kennet. The location allowed both the Kennet and the Thames to be used to transport stone to build the abbey. The major roads leading to Reading would make it easy for pilgrims to visit the abbey.
- The abbey also held over 230 relics including what was believed to be the hand of St James the Apostle. Pilgrims would visit the relic at Reading and start the Camino de Santiago (St James Way) from Reading, across the English Channel at Southampton and ultimately to Spain, where the remaining relics are buried. A shrivelled human hand was found in the abbey ruins during the abbey demolition work in 1786 and is now held in St Peter's Catholic church in Marlow. The hand has since been analysed by historians at Oxford University and found to be from a different era from St James, so unlikely to have been from the time of Christ, but still obviously more than 1000 years old and subject many thousands of pilgrimages to Reading in the middle ages.
- After Henry I died in Normandy in 1135, his body was returned to Reading Abbey and buried under the then incomplete altar.
- A slightly smaller but still quite grand abbey was founded and built in **Dorchester-on-Thames** between 1140 and 1350 as a branch of the Augustinian Order. This was built on the site of the original St Birinus Anglo Saxon Cathedral, which by this time had been replaced by Lincoln as the diocesan cathedral.

Henry I holding a model of Reading Abbey.

A major project to refurbish the remains of Reading Abbey for visitors was completed in 2018.

Canon John Urdis of St Peter's church in Marlow is now the custodian of the hand of St James the Apostle, first brought to England by Empress Matilda in 1125.

1102-67 – Empress Matilda, Lady of the English

Henry I's daughter Matilda had an eventful life where she became Empress of the Roman Empire at the age of 15 and then fought an 18 year war against her cousin Stephen de Blois over who would succeed Henry as the ruler of England. Matilda used the Thames Valley as her base for this war, known as 'The Anarchy'. The terms of the succession of her son Henry II were finally agreed at Wallingford Castle in 1153.

- Matilda was born in England along the Thames at Sutton Courtenay in Berkshire in 1102 to King Henry I and his wife Queen Matilda (known as Maud), who was born of Scottish royalty.
- At the age of eight, Matilda left England to marry King Henry V of Germany as arranged by her father Henry I, although the formal wedding did not happen until she was 12, which was considered a suitable age at that time. This strategic alliance was seen as important to bolster the legitimacy of Henry I's Kingdom, which at the time included England, Normandy and other regions that are now part of France.
- Upon arrival in Germany, Matilda earned the title of 'Queen of the Germans' at Mainz on St James' Day. One of the treasures at the royal chapel was the mummified hand of St James the Apostle, a holy relic.
- Matilda became 'Empress of the Roman Empire' when Henry V was anointed Emperor in Rome in 1117, although we now call it the Holy Roman Empire, an area that covered a large portion of central Europe and Northern Italy.
- After Henry V's untimely death in 1125, Matilda left Germany, returning to Normandy, along with her imperial regalia and the valuable relic of the hand of St James the Apostle. She later brought the sacred relic to England and had it kept at Reading Abbey that was being built by her father Henry I.
- Matilda became Henry I's heir to the throne after his oldest son William was killed in a tragic shipwreck. Henry held a special court in Windsor where he demanded his subjects swear an oath to support Matilda as his only legitimate heir. As there had never been a female heir to the English throne before, many only agreed reluctantly under pressure from the king.
- Henry then brokered Matilda's re-marriage to a much younger Geoffrey Plantagenet, Count of Anjou, which was a strategically important region of France just south of Normandy. Geoffrey was 13 and Matilda 25. Despite initial difficulties, they eventually had three sons, including the future Henry II who would form the start of the House of Plantagenet dynasty that ruled England for over 300 years.
- Upon Henry I's death in 1135, Matilda's cousin Stephen of Blois contested her accession to the English crown, and managed to secure support for his coronation as king with the backing of many powerful English barons and bishops. Matilda was unable to contest this, as she was engaged in Normandy giving birth to her third child. Pregnancy and child birth was still very dangerous at this time and the survival of the mother was not always assured.
- Matilda refused to accept the decision to make Stephen king quietly. With the help of her half brother, Robert Fitzroy, Earl of Gloucester, Matilda returned to England after a few years and gained control of the southwest of England. Matilda and Robert controlled as far east as the Thames Valley, with Wallingford and Oxford castles acting as key strongholds nearest to London.
- Matilda ultimately defeated Stephen's armies and had him imprisoned, but she was never successful in being crowned due to Stephen's still loyal followers in London. Matilda was called 'Lady of the English' but never formally became Queen of England.
- Matilda was later forced to release Stephen from prison and 'The Anarchy' continued. At one point Stephen captured Oxford and surrounded Oxford Castle where Matilda was based, attempting to starve her out. Matilda famously escaped from the castle in the middle of a cold winter's night, dressed in white robes for camouflage and crossed a frozen River Isis. She was able to flee to Abingdon with a handful of knights, and then on to the safety of Wallingford Castle.
- As the war dragged on to a stalemate, Matilda's son Henry and Stephen eventually reached an agreement at Wallingford Castle in 1153 (later ratified as the Treaty of Westminster) that allowed Stephen to remain as king, but ensured that Henry would succeed him following his death. By this time Henry was 20 years old, had been promoted to Duke of Normandy, and was clearly in the ascendant.
- Henry II became king a year later following Stephen's death. Henry II rewarded Wallingford for its assistance in the struggle by giving the town its royal charter in 1155.

12th century, The Swan Upping

The earliest records relating to royal swan ownership indicate that by around 1186, the reigning monarch was entitled to claim ownership of any unmarked mute swans swimming in open water. At the time, it was desirable to own swans because the young birds, cygnets, were highly valued for food and often served at special banquets and feasts. It may be difficult to understand why the Royal Family still carries on with an 800 year old exercise of counting the swans in the 21st century when it seems the money could be better spent on fixing potholes or stopping sewage outflows into the river. The tradition has persisted despite some attempts to have the crown's ownership removed in the 1970s.

According to David Barber, who has been the Royal Swan Marker since 1993, the role today is about conservation of the welfare of the swans on the nation's rivers and the education of children about the river and the ecology of the swans.
- Mr Barber had suggested a change in the role prior to his appointment in 1993. Instead of being 'Swan Keeper', the roles of 'Swan Marker' and 'Swan Warden' were established, the latter being filled by Professor Christopher Perrins, who has a scientific background in ornithology and focusses on evaluating the heath of the swans.
- Mr Barber took over from the previous Royal Swan Keeper, Captain John Turk of Cookham, who had followed in the

The Swan Uppers at Marlow heading out in the morning refreshed after breakfast at the Compleat Angler Hotel.

footsteps of his father. The Turks based the swan upping team at their boatyard near Cookham bridge, featured in one of Stanley Spencer's paintings. Mr Barber bought Turk's boatyard in 1982 and still runs it as DB Marine boatyard, now on the Buckinghamshire side of the river opposite Cookham. The boatyard serves as Mr Barber's Office where the Swan Upping uniforms, flags and other equipment are stored.

The swans are normally counted in the third week in July during the 79 mile Swan Upping journey that takes five days. It originally took place between London and Henley, but the journey now begins at Sunbury and ends at Abingdon.

- The counting takes place when the parent birds are moulting feathers and less likely to fly away and the grey cygnets are still too small to fly.
- When a family of swans is spotted, the Swan Uppers cry 'All Up!' and begin approaching the swans, gradually surrounding them by the boats until the birds can be lifted up out of the water.
- The uppers check their health and then weigh and measure the swans to assess their growth rate, recording it for future trends.
- The Swan Uppers travel in six traditional wooden skiffs, two each for the Crown, the Vintners and the Dyers with each boat flying the appropriate flags. They all dress in uniform: red for The Crown, blue for Dyers, and white for Vintners.
- The Vintners received their rights to own swans on the Thames under King Edward IV in 1472 and the Dyers in 1545. These two companies, together with the Crown, still perform the Swan Upping each year. Originally, the two Companies made their own marks on the birds' beaks — one nick for a Dyers' bird and two for a Vintners'. The Crown's swans were left unmarked. Rings and tags are now used instead of marking the beaks.
- The Vintners and Dyers continue to be two of the most important Livery Companies of the City of London acting as trade associations for their industry. The Vintners' Royal Charter initially allowed them to sell certain types of wine without a license. The Dyers Company is responsible for trade in dyeing clothing.
- The crew members work with the Swan Warden to check the health of the birds. Since WWII, swan numbers started to fall dramatically from a maximum of 76 breeding pairs with cygnets on the London to Henley stretch, to only 7 in 1985. Research was initiated that showed lead poisoning from swallowing fishing weights was a major factor in the decline. Most lead weights were banned in the late 1980s, after which the swan population steadily increased again with 50 breeding pairs with cygnets in 2010.
- In 2023, the Swan Upping counted only 94 cygnets, down from 155 in 2022. The decrease was due to the spread of the Avian Flu. Mr Barber said that this is the worst drop he has seen in the 31 years as Royal Swan Keeper, but also notes that infections seem to be down since then.
- Mr Barber agrees that the river is more polluted in recent years from more frequent raw sewage discharges from sewage plants such as the one at Little Marlow, upstream from Cookham, however he is quick to point out that he has never seen a case of a swan dying from polluted water.

Left: Members of the Dyers Guild — actually Thames Watermen paid for the week's work by the Dyers Guild — at Goring Lock.
Below: Capturing the swans and cygnets for weighing and measuring. The Swan Warden Christopher Perrins is seen pointing in the centre. The Royal Swan Marker, David Barber, is standing on the right.

12-13th century – bridges over the Thames — By this time, a combination of wooden and stone bridges over the Thames existed at Oxford, Abingdon, Wallingford, Caversham, Henley-on-Thames, Maidenhead, Staines and Windsor, most of which were previously ford crossings. These were supplemented by ferries at Newnham, South and Little Stoke, Goring, Whitchurch, Lower Caversham, and Lashbrook in Shiplake.

Robert d'Oilly, builder of Wallingford and Oxford Castles, also commissioned a stone causeway across the marshes to the south of Oxford leading up to a bridge at Folly in 1085. The causeway, completed in 1091, was probably built along the route of an earlier Anglo Saxon causeway leading to the river crossing at Folly, but the crossing was likely to be a ford at that time. The ford at Folly is thought to be where Oxford gets its name, originally called Oxenford, from Oxen crossing the river there. The Norman causeway, referred to as Grand Pont, ran along the stretch of road from St Aldgates at Christ Church College, over the Folly Bridge and down Abingdon Road to where the Redbridge Park and Ride car park is now. You can still see some of the many drainage archways from the Norman causeway such as those shown below on Abingdon Road between Folly Bridge and Western Road.

Below: Norman drainage archways from the 11th century causeway beneath Abingdon Road near Folly.
Right: A sunny summer's day at the *Head of the River* pub at Folly Bridge. The pub is located near the finish line of the Oxford Intercollegiate rowing competitions with the winning teams being crowned 'Head of the River'.

1214 – Oxford University

The precise origins of the university are unclear, but despite King Alfred's connections to Oxford and his academic leanings, later conjecture that it was founded by him in the 9th century are unlikely to be true. We know that there was a school of philosophy in Oxford by 1095 that was set up by French scholar Theobald of Étampes. Another key date was 1167, when Oxford developed rapidly after Henry II banned English students from attending the University of Paris following a quarrel with Thomas Becket. At that time, the only other universities in Europe were in the long established cities of Paris and Bologna, so having university status placed on this small town on the Thames of about 4000 residents was significant.

In 1214 the university organisation became more formal and was headed by a chancellor at which point it is generally considered to have become a university. Robert Grossetetest (1168-1253) was a distinguished theologian, scientist and general scholar that is normally credited with being Oxford's first chancellor. Courses at Oxford initially included theology, law, arts (rhetoric and philosophy) and medicine.

- The 13th century was a time of frequent rioting between town and gown (general residents of Oxford vs. students) making the establishment of the first halls of residence for students a matter of practical student safety. These began as private halls, run for profit, where the students took meals together in a common dining room. As the university started gaining rich benefactors, a new institution called the college was formed. Colleges were basically endowed halls, established by charter and owning their sites. As all students were priests or in some religious order at that time, the colleges were often set up by wealthy churchmen to support studies of poorer priests.
- Students and alumni of Oxford colleges still like to debate which is oldest and the exact dates of their founding but it is generally agreed that the first colleges were formed between 1249 and 1264, with University, Balliol and Merton Colleges being the oldest. Exeter, Oriel and Queen's were established by 1341.
- It was following serious town and gown rioting in 1209, resulting in the deaths of several residents and students, that some disgruntled teachers from Oxford went off to form Cambridge University, making Cambridge an offspring of Oxford and Oxford the slightly older of the two.
- One of the grandest colleges in Oxford is Christ Church. It was originally founded as *Cardinal College* in 1525 by Cardinal Thomas Wolsey (inset photo), who was Archbishop of York and Lord Chancellor of England under King Henry VIII. Wolsey built the college on the land of St Frideswide Priory that he had closed down. He used funds from the priory and other closed priories to build the college. Wolsey fell out of favour with Henry VIII before the college could be completed, and the king had the college renamed *King Henry VIII's College* in 1532. When the King broke with Rome in 1546 as part of the Reformation, Henry designated the large college chapel as the cathedral of the recently created Diocese of Oxford, and renamed the college as *Christ Church*. The cathedral still serves this dual role today and there are still normally three services a day that are open to the public. The college served as Charles I's Royalist Headquarters during the Civil War in the 1640s, and after the war, Dean John Fell led the refurbishment and completed the construction of the college. Fell asked Christopher Wren to design the elaborate Tom Tower that stands out along St Aldgates and remains one of Oxford's most distinctive landmarks. The tower gets its name from Great Tom, a bell rescued from Osney Abbey that had been named after Thomas Becket.

Above: Christ Church College outside of the old Deanery where Charles I was based during the Civil War. Inset: College founder Cardinal Thomas Wolsey.

- It was not until 1920 that women were admitted as full members of the University. By 1986, all of Oxford's male colleges had changed their statutes to admit women.
- As with Cambridge, Durham and other 'collegiate' universities, student life at Oxford revolves around individual colleges as opposed to any central university administration. Students generally live in college accommodation, eat in the college dining hall, and are assigned a college tutor who meets with small groups of students to discuss their studies. Students may or may not attend course lectures for the university classes they take, but they do need to attend weekly sessions with their college tutors in small groups, generally with only one or two other college students. The students are expected to have in depth discussions about their ideas and opinions on the weekly readings allowing the tutor to guide them and monitor the student's progress.
- As of 2023, the university was comprised of 39 colleges. Given the college-focus of Oxford, the central university facilities are generally limited to the main Bodleian Library, St Mary's the Virgin church, the Sheldonian Theatre for ceremonial gatherings, and the Examination Schools on the High Street for tests.
- The Bodleian Library dates back to at least the 14th and 15th centuries. Today it is comprised of several buildings in the Broad Street area including the Radcliffe Camera and New Bodleian Library that was rebuilt from 2011-15. As of 2023 it held over 13 million printed documents much of them stored in underground shelves. It is one of six legal deposit libraries in the UK that may request copies of all new books. It is second in size only to the British Library. The Bodleian's breadth of treasures is priceless — it includes three original versions of the Magna Carta, a copy of the Gutenburg Bible that is though to be the first major printed book, and a copy of the first printed version of 39 of Shakespeare's plays from 1623, known as the First Folio.
- As of 2022, the total endowment of Oxford's colleges and the university overall was estimated to be close to £8 billion, a similar amount to Cambridge which are by far the largest endowments for UK universities. In the US, there are about a dozen top universities that exceed this level, including Harvard University, that had world's largest endowment as of 2022 of around $50 billion (£39 billion).
- The University of Oxford is still regularly ranked as one of the top five universities in the world and each of the 39 Colleges has a long list of world famous alumni that very few universities could come close to matching. It is difficult to fully describe the influence that Oxford graduates have had on the world, but a few facts will give you an idea. As of 2022, Oxford graduates have included:
  - 30 British Prime Ministers —most recently Rishi Sunak, Boris Johnson, David Cameron, Theresa May, Tony Blair, and Margaret Thatcher.
  - 100 Members of Parliament
  - Countless other heads of state of government around the world

- 73 Nobel Prizes awarded in Chemistry, Economics, Medicine, Literature, Peace and Physics
- 170 Olympic medallists.
- Notable authors have included C.S. Lewis, J.R.R. Tolkien, Aldous Huxley, Oscar Wilde, T.S. Elliot, John Betjeman, Lewis Carroll, Jonathan Swift, Samuel Johnson, and Graham Greene.
- In the world of science, Albert Einstein and Stephen Hawking are normally associated with the universities of Princeton and Cambridge, but they were also students at Oxford Christ Church and University College respectively.

Below: An Oxford scene at the Radcliffe Camera reading room.
Right: Gargoyles protecting Magdalen College.
Opposite page: Punting on the River Cherwell under Magdalen Bridge.

Depiction of King John signing the Magna Carta under pressure from the Barons at Runnymede. Historians have pointed out that King John used his royal seal to approve it and didn't actually sign the document.

1215 — The Magna Carta

King John and 25 powerful barons agreed to the terms known as the Magna Carta, the Latin term for 'Great Charter', in 1215. The location was a water meadow along the south bank of the Thames at Runnymede near Windsor. It is thought that the location was chosen as it was equidistant between the king's castle in Windsor and Staines, where 25 powerful barons were gathered to pressure him to agree to the terms. The barons were aggrieved at the high taxes that the king extracted from them to fund his unsuccessful wars abroad in his ancestral lands in France.

- King John's father, Henry II, had introduced extensive judicial reforms, establishing the authority of the royal courts, laying the foundations for the future system of justice in England. In contrast, King John had regularly abused the justice system to suppress his opponents and to extort revenue from the barons.
- The Magna Carta established for the first time the principle that everybody, including the king, was subject to the law.
- Most of the 63 clauses granted by King John dealt with specific grievances relating to his rule, however, buried within them were a number of fundamental values that challenged the autocracy of the king.
- Most famously, Clause 39 gave all 'free men' the right to justice and a fair trial, judged by a jury of their peers. *"No free man shall be seized or imprisoned, or stripped of his rights or possessions, or outlawed or exiled, or deprived of his standing in any other way, nor will we proceed with force against him, or send others to do so, except by the lawful judgement of his equals or by the law of the land".*
- Some of Magna Carta's core principles were echoed in the United States Bill of Rights in 1791, the UN's Universal Declaration of Human Rights in 1948 and in many other constitutional documents around the world. The first memorial to the Magna Carta at Runnymede was established by the American Bar Association in 1957.
- Amongst the many demands included in the document was the need to remove the king's fish weirs along Thames and other rivers. This is thought to have been an effort to restore fish to the river to support local fisherman and also to improve commercial navigation on the river.

Windsor Castle from the 12th-19th centuries

The castle's easy access to London and proximity to royal hunting grounds made it a popular location for royalty over the centuries. The original Norman motte and bailey castle built by William the Conqueror in 1086 has been consistently enhanced by British monarchy for almost 1000 years to where is it now one of Europe's grandest palaces and, in recent centuries, it has been the main home and place of business for British monarchy along with Buckingham Palace.

The castle has such a long history of change and development that I will only touch on a few of the more notable monarchs that have left their mark on the castle:

- **Henry I (1100-1135)** — was the first king to hold court in the original motte and bailey castle in 1100. Windsor is also where Henry summoned his nobles to in 1127 to swear allegiance to his daughter Empress Matilda as his heir.
- **Henry II (1154-1189)** — was responsible for converting the castle into a palace, building two separate sets of royal apartments within the fortified enclosure: a public or official State residence in the Lower Ward and a smaller private residence on the north side of the Upper Ward for his own use. He also started the replacement of the wooden walls with stone and rebuilt the round tower.
- **King John (1199-1216)** — seems to have spent a lot of time in Windsor by evidence of his agreeing to the Magna Carta at nearby Runnymede. After he decided to backtrack on his agreement with the barons a few months later, asking the Pope to annul the document, rebel barons declared war, enlisting the support of the King of France. As part of the First Baron's War, Windsor Castle withstood a three month siege that only ended after the King fled to the east of England, dying of dysentery in October 1216. The regents of his heir, the nine-year-old Henry III, confirmed their support for the agreement and the new king even issued his own version of the Magna Carta in 1225.
- **Henry III (1216-1272)** — completely rebuilt Henry II's buildings in the Lower Ward and added a large new chapel all around a courtyard with a cloister on the site of what was to was to become St George's Chapel. His children took residence making it a family home for the first time.
- **Edward III (1327-1377)** – spent £50,000 in the currency of his time, transforming Windsor from a military fortification into a gothic palace that was considered the greatest palace of the age.

Artists impression of Windsor Castle by 1208 at about the time of the signing of the Magna Carta. The upper, north Ward on the right is still the location of the Royal private apartments, with the south, lower Ward on the left, housing the public State Apartments. Image: Royal Collection Trust, © His Majesty King Charles III 2023. Illustrator: Bob Marshal.

Under the direction of William of Wykeham, Bishop of Winchester, he created a large palace containing areas for both official business and private use.

- **Order of the Garter** — Edward III created the Order of the Garter to honour the bravery of knights during his campaign against France. Edward was inspired by the tales of chivalry from the legend of King Arthur and intended the members of the Order to be a kind of Knights of the Round Table equivalent. Amongst the first to receive the honour was Edward's son, the Prince of Wales — also known as the Black Prince due to the colour of his armour. They used the chapel built by Henry III in the lower ward that became St George's Chapel to honour the first Knight Companions of the Order of the Garter in 1348. As the reputation of the Order grew with time, the chapel was further developed into its present grand architecture by successive kings. Annual ceremonies of the Order of the Garter continue to be held at

Above: The Copper Horse statue of George III.

Below: View of the castle beyond the Long Walk, established under Charles II.

Windsor every June. Membership of the Order is still is the country's is the oldest and most senior Order of Chivalry.

- **Henry VIII (1509-1547)** — had a great affinity for Windsor. He became King at the age of 18 and was known as a charming extrovert with a passion for outdoor sports in his youth. Of the many songs that he wrote by his early 20s, one song called *Pastime with Good Company* was very popular, describing his youthful energy and activities: "At Windsor we hear of him exercising himself daily in shooting, singing, dancing, wrestling, casting of the bar, playing at the recorder, flute, virginals, in setting of scenes and making of ballads." Henry built the main gate to the castle's Lower Ward that sill bears his name and a timber terrace along the north side of the Upper Ward, from where he could watch the hunts in the park below.
- It was around the time of Henry VIII, in the early 1500s, that nearby **Wallingford Castle** started to fall into a state of disrepair and was cannibalised to support the remodelling of Windsor. Barges with pieces of stone and lead taken from Wallingford Castle could be seen being shipped downstream along the Thames to help with the building work at Windsor Castle. Wallingford was later restored in the years leading up to the Civil War to defend against Parliamentary forces.
- **Charles II (1660-1685)** — led a major restoration of the Windsor following the difficult Civil War period where the castle was used by the Parliamentary army for various activities such as housing prisoners and the poor. Many pieces of valuable artwork, tapestries, books and furniture were confiscated and sold. The castle itself was nearly sold by Parliament as 'surplus to requirements' — only being saved by one vote! Charles II spent much time hunting stag and walking in the park and had the famous Long Walk, 3-mile avenue of trees planted.
- **George III (1760-1820)** — appointed architect James Wyatt to transform the exterior of the Castle into a more medieval appearance and also made many changes within the castle. The king, Queen Charlotte, and their daughters, tended to stay at the now demolished Queen's Lodge that was just near the castle along the Long Walk. In 1800, Queen Charlotte was the first to introduce Christmas trees to England from her native Germany, displaying one at their home in Windsor.
- **The Copper Horse** — The statue of George III at the top of the Long Walk, known as 'The Copper Horse', was commissioned by his son King George IV during the first year of his reign. According to King George the IV, the statue shows the king dressed in a classical Roman toga, on a horse without stirrups, with his hand pointing towards his favourite residence, Windsor Castle. The plane in the photo on the previous page is a reminder that the castle is now on the direct path of many flights from Heathrow removing just a bit of its mystique.
- **George IV (1820-1830)** – started his reign in the period following the victory at Waterloo, where according the historian A.L. Rowse, the nation had 'a sense of triumph after twenty years' struggle with Revolutionary France and Napoleon, emerging from it as the first nation of Europe —indeed at that time in the world'. George IV's coronation was the most lavish on record. The king commissioned the building of the Royal Pavilion in Brighton and remodelled Buckingham Palace. Parliament willingly granted the king £150,000 for work on Windsor Castle that ultimately cost £1 million. Jeffry Wyatville, nephew of George III's architect James Wyatt, was chosen to give the castle the more imposing appearance it has today, inside and out. His comprehensive renovation included doubling the height of the Round Tower, re-clothing the exterior in massive masonry, creating the George IV entrance leading to the Long Walk, and ultimately making the castle what it is today.
- **Queen Victoria (1837-1901)** – was not a fan of London and preferred doing business at Windsor. She became very closely associated with Windsor Castle, especially after the death of her beloved Prince Albert. After the comprehensive work done by her uncle George IV, she had very little reason to make further changes, but it is said to have reached a social highpoint under her reign.

Below: Statue of Queen Victoria near the main entrance to Windsor Castle next to a Christmas tree, such as the one first brought to England at Windsor in 1800 by Queen Charlotte.

1440 – Eton College was founded by King Henry VI as a charity school to provide free education to 70 poor boys who would then go on to King's College, Cambridge. Henry took Winchester College as his model, visiting on many occasions, even borrowing its statutes, its headmaster and some of its scholars to start his new school. Eton is well-known for its history, wealth, and notable alumni, known as 'Old Etonians'.
- It is one of only three public schools, along with Harrow (1572) and Radley (1847), to retain the boys-only, boarding-only tradition, which means that its boys live at the school seven days a week.
- Like Oxford, Eton has educated prime ministers and other world leaders, as well as Nobel laureates, Academy Award award-winning actors and generations of British and international aristocracy. The 20 prime ministers it has produced include David Cameron and Boris Johnson, who were both famously also at Oxford University together. Princes William and Harry were also students.

Eton College students crossing the street by the main library.

1479 — The Tuddingway was a significant medieval route between Wallingford and Caversham along the Thames that likely had Anglo-Saxon origins and still exists as a bridle path.
- Today, parts of the route coincide with both the Thames Path and the ancient Ridgeway in places between the Goring and Wallingford. From Whitchurch, it follows Hardwick Road and though Hardwick Estate to Caversham.
- The stretch from the east gate of Hardwick Estate to Mapledurham was the subject of an inquisition in 1479 that determined that only packhorses should be allowed to use the route as it was not suitable for wheeled vehicles. Despite this ruling, it evidently remained a significant throughway at least through the 18th century.
- Whilst the stretch is certainly not used for large vehicles anymore, and is still known for being muddy in winter months, it is increasingly popular with both walkers and two-wheeled mountain bikers including those using the King Alfred's Way cycle route that passes through the stretch!

Cyclist Mark Dunstan on the controversial muddy stretch of the Tuddingway between Mapledurham and Hardwick Estates.

1539 – Dissolution of Reading and Dorchester Abbeys

Following the English Reformation, papal authority was abolished and the Church of England was established under King Henry VIII. When Reading Abbey and other Catholic organisations were abolished, the monks were evicted and forced to find new work and all the abbey's silver, gold, textiles and art were shipped to London to add to the king's treasury.

The last Abbot of Reading, Hugh Cook of Faringdon, resisted the king's right to close the abbey and was subsequently arrested on the road to Pangbourne as he tried to flee to his country home at Bere Court. He was tried and convicted of high treason and then hung, drawn and quartered in front of the abbey church. The abbey was later mostly destroyed under the rule of Henry's son Edward VI.

Nearby **Dorchester Abbey** escaped demolition following the Reformation due to the generosity of Sir Richard Beauforest who paid Henry VIII the £140 value of the lead on the chancel roof, avoiding the need for it to be pillaged. The building has undergone extensive refurbishment in recent years and continues to act as the spiritual centre of the village, hosting concerts, festivals and other events. It is open to the public and has a very informative museum about the history of the area. The Dorchester Museum and tea room is open in the summer months and is well worth a visit.

Above: Dorchester Abbey today.

Below: Image of Hugh Faringdon before his execution at Reading Abbey. ©Reading Museum.

1527 — Hardwick Estate

Set at the edge of the Oxfordshire Chiltern Hills along the river across from Pangbourne, the 900 acre estate and former manor house was mentioned in the Domesday Book, and has been owned by only two families in the past 500 years. Hardwick was owned by the Lybbe family from 1527 and was later run by the Canadian-Scottish financier Sir Charles Day Rose who was a tenant since 1877, finally purchasing it in 1909. The estate continues to be owned and managed by the Rose family.

- As with other manors in the area, the Lybbes had Royalist sympathies during the Civil War and the house was attacked and pillaged by Parliamentary forces.
- The Lybbe family welcomed King Charles I to bowl at a pub on Collins End at Hardwick Estate while he was being held prisoner by Oliver Cromwell's army during the Civil War. An excerpt from Mrs Philip Lybbe Powys' diary reads: "King Charles the First was prisoner at Causham Lodge, and bowled in Collins End Green, 9th July 1648, attended by a troop of horse of Colonel Rossiter's". Causham Lodge was on the site of today's Caversham Park, where there is still a Victorian-era mansion that was used by BBC Monitoring from 1943-2018. Charles was tried and executed within 6 months of his visit.
- Collins End is on the top of a Chilterns Hill at the back of Hardwick Estate. There was an inn at Collins End, afterwards called the King's Head. The house where the original inn was is now called Holly Copse. The pub was moved to nearby Goring Heath c1870 on the road to Reading. It became known as the

Hardwick House, situated on the Thames at Whitchurch.

King Charles Head at the new location until it closed in about 2010. It is now a private residence with the same name.

- Shortly after purchasing Hardwick House in 1909, Sir Charles Day Rose was made '1st Baronet of Hardwick House in the Parish of Whitchurch in the County of Oxfordshire.' This award was for his services to the Liberal government under Prime Minister Asquith and Chancellor of the Exchequer Lloyd George. Sir Charles was the Liberal MP for Newmarket from 1903-1913, advocating progressive policies and advising on the motor car tax regime where the revenues raised would be used for the building of a national road network.
- Rose created a stir with his passion for horse racing, automobiles, aeroplanes, real tennis and literary house parties. He used the grand Tudor-style stables as a stud farm for breeding race horses. Sir Charles and *Wind in the Willows* author Kenneth Grahame both worked as bankers in the City of London and it is thought that Grahame attended some of Rose's parties at Hardwick. A strong case can be made that Sir Charles was a model for Mr Toad.

Like Blenheim, Mapledurham and Englefield Estates, Hardwick is still actively managed as a diverse agricultural estate with vestiges of its feudal past still evident. The vibrant Hardwick community is the subject of a chapter in Part 2.

Above: The King Charles Head Pub before its closure in about 2010.
Below: Hardwick horse stud farm.

1558 — Englefield Estate

Located outside of Theale near Reading, the house was built at the site of the Anglo-Saxon battle with the Vikings in 871. In 1558, it was purchased by John Paulet, 5th Marquess of Winchester, who defended Basing House against Parliamentarian attacks during the Civil War. After Oliver Cromwell won the war in 1645, Paulet was imprisoned in the Tower of London for high treason. His property was returned to him after the Restoration of King Charles II in 1648, at which time he retired to Englefield House.

- The house was passed on to the Benyon family through marriage in the 18th century and has been home to the Benyons ever since.
- Numerous members of the Benyon family have represented West Berkshire as Conservative Members of Parliament over the years. Sir William Richard Benyon, was MP from 1970 until 1992, and his great-great grandfather was former Conservative Prime Minister Lord Salisbury.
- Richard Benyon, now Lord Benyon, was most recently Conservative MP for Newbury and West Berkshire from 2005-2019. He had his Conservative whip removed in September 2019 along with 20 other Conservative MPs by Prime Minister Boris Johnson after voting against the government on a key Brexit vote. Johnson then nominated Benyon to be a life peer in 2020. Lord Benyon served the government with his expertise in agricultural affairs in his role as Minister of State for Biosecurity, Marine and Rural Affairs in Defra from 2022 as he had done previously.
- Englefield is still very much run as a functioning estate, where Lord Benyon and his family live and manage the 14,000 acres of woodland and farmland that includes 600 residential and commercial properties. In addition to historic Englefield House, there is a deer park, cricket ground, and polo club. Gamekeepers manage field sports and conservation on the estate, especially for fishing and for pheasant and partridge shoots. Like nearby Mapledurham Estate, it is often host to film crews using it as a location for dramas such as *The King's Speech*, *X-Men: First Class*, and *The Crown*.

The neighbouring village of Englefield lies within the grounds of the estate and has vestiges of feudal life also seen at other estates described in this book. In the late 19th century, Richard Fellowes Benyon restored both the house and the village as a model estate

village, modernising existing cottages and farm buildings and significantly improving St Mark's church that is shared with those living on the grounds of the estate. The village improvements provided residents with amenities such as a swimming pool, soup kitchen and a new school. Like Mapledurham, Hardwick Estate, Blenheim Palace and Culden Faw Estate in Hambleden, Englefield Estate still owns and rents out all 50 homes in the village and a further 25 in rural locations in the parish. The Estate also owns the village hall, shop, garden centre and the estate yard by the village.

Above: Englefield Village Stores and Tea Room.

Lord Benyon speaking on agricultural policy in 2023.

1604-1920s — Whitchurch manor houses

Ownership of the Manor of Whitchurch-on-Thames changed hands many times over the centuries and the house itself has changed location a few times. After 1604, when King James I sold the manor, it was owned by four main families — the Whistlers, the Gardiners, followed by John Foster and the Howard family.

- Prior to 1604, the Whitchurch Manor remained in royal hands dating back to Anglo-Saxon times. Notable owners included Edward the III's gallant son, the Black Prince, noted earlier for his role in the Order of the Garter at St George's Chapel in Windsor. After being held by various queens as dower and to other royal servants through the centuries, King James I granted it to his Chancellor of the Exchequer Sir George Home in 1604 who sold the manor to the John Whistler of Gatehampton in Goring the following year.
- The Whistler family were Lords of the Whitchurch Manor from 1605 to 1789. They built Walliscote House not far from the river near the mill and St Mary the Virgin church as the manor house in about 1656. They later moved the manor house from Walliscote House to Whitchurch House on the High Street as of 1712. A separate timber-framed house on the High Street that is now called Manor House, was built by the Whistlers as the farm house for the manor farm, and previously called it Manor Farm.
- In 1792, Whitchurch Manor was sold to Bristol-based, West India merchant, Samuel Gardiner who built the Palladian style mansion house Coombe Lodge as the new manor house, to the west of the village. Several generations of the Gardiner family owned the manor.
- In the 1880s, John Foster, a new owner of the estate along with manorial rights, enlarged and remodelled the house, changing the name from Coombe Lodge to Coombe Park. The main part of what was left of the estate, Coombe Park, was sold to businessman Charles Edward Howard in 1898. The Howards were enthusiastic race horse owners and breeders. After 1920 they extended the property to 670 acres that included what is now Beale Park on the Pangbourne side of the river. The manorial rights were broken up in the 1920s.
- During World War II, Coombe Park was requisitioned as a rest and recuperation centre for United States Air Force personnel following bombing raids on Germany. A similar country house used for US troops for recuperation is featured in the 2024 television series *Masters of the Air*.
- As described later, Coombe Park was also requisitioned to host a camp with Nissen huts to house troops for bridge building training operations in Pangbourne in 1943. According to local historian Peter Hawley, a villager at the time said that the owner of Coombe Park, "Teddy" Howard, only found out about the intended military use when builders began digging foundations on his property. Apparently, Whitehall failed to get the requisition papers through to him. Tragically, Mr Howard is said to have been so distressed at this news that he died of a heart attack.
- After the war, Coombe Park was dilapidated and large parts of it was torn down and remodelled. The Howards sold the estate, but some members of the family continued to live as tenants at Coombe Park and some Howard family members still live in the village near the site of Walliscote House that was also in need of replacement after the war.
- Coombe Park remains a private estate, being sold to a new owner David Paine in 2018 when it had a price guide of £10 million after languishing for a number of years under the previous owner. In 2023, plans were approved to demolish the current house, replacing it with a new grand Palladian-style mansion.

Walliscote Lodge in Whitchurch is the last remaining vestige of an early Whitchurch manor house, Walliscote House. Sally Howard, seated on the left in red, is part of the Howard family who were the last owners of Whitchurch Manor, then centred on nearby Coombe Park. Sally now lives in a new house on the site of the former Walliscote House and members of her family continue to live in the village. On Sally's right, seated, are Diana and Rodney Cole, long-time owners of Walliscote Lodge. Sally's children, Amber and Selby are standing. Selby is married to Nicola Armstrong, seated on the right. They also live in the village with their three children Florence, Daisy and Mabel.

Above: There is a long tradition of jumping off the Whitchurch Bridge and swimming in the river despite the risks involved and a growing awareness of sewage outflows in the river.

Left: The Whitchurch Village Green is the perfect setting for a cricket match on a summer's day just below the Chiltern Hills.

1612 – Mapledurham House

The village of Mapledurham was listed with two manor houses in the Domesday Book —Gurney, which was the larger manor that now forms Mapledurham village —and Chazey, a smaller manor that still has remnants towards Caversham off of The Warren road. The large country house and surrounding village now known as Mapledurham today was built by Sir Michael Blount starting in 1608 and completed by his son Sir Richard in 1612.

- Sir Michael meant this to be a grand home expressing his status as a high official of Queen Elizabeth I, such as his roles as High Sheriff of Buckinghamshire, and later Oxfordshire and Lieutenant of the Tower of London. The house is built in the classic Elizabethan E-shape architecture.
- Like Englefield House and Hardwick House, the property was sequestered during the Civil War, but returned to the family in 1660 after Charles II's restoration.
- Alexander Pope became a frequent visitor from 1707-1715 to court the two daughters Martha and Theresa, until they went to live in London.
- St Margaret's church in the village has Norman origins and is still used for weekly Church of England services for the community. It is unusual in that it has a private, closed off section of the church for use by owners of the manor since the 14th century called the Bardolf aisle. As the owners have been Catholic for many centuries, this is a rare example of a Catholic aisle within an Anglican church.
- The house and grounds remain in the Blount-Eyston family to this day making it one of the longest continuously-owned manor homes on the country. John Joseph Eyston was the owner from 1960 until his death in 2019. He worked to restore the house, using it as a family home until his death in 2019. He is survived by his wife, Lady Anne, her children, Edward, Katharine and Mary and seven grandchildren. The house is still owned by the family who live in the area, but it is not clear if any of family members live there at the moment. The estate is managed by Savills Estate Management.

Mapledurham House.

- Mapledurham Estate still has a feudal feel to it as it owns most of the homes in small village who see the estate as their landlord. Other enterprises on the estate include a dairy farm, various crops, and green energy projects including a large anaerobic digester that is powered by methane from cow waste and a hydro-powered electricity generator from the old mill on the river.
- The grounds are also used to host concerts, fairs and other events, and are frequently used for films and television shows such as *Midsomer Murders*. Mapledurham was famously the site of a village invaded by Germans in a fictitious WWII attempt to assassinate Winston Churchill in the 1976 film *The Eagle Has Landed*.

Right: Mapledurham Mill, background image for Black Sabbath's first album cover.
Below: Red Kites at Mapledurham known to follow ploughs in South Oxfordshire for access to fresh worms.

1642-1646 — English Civil War

More than 400 years after the Magna Carta, England was still struggling to define the limits of the king's power. By this time, England had a Parliament, but they were not democratically elected and had very limited powers — the main one being to approve any new taxes.

- King Charles I believed that the king should have absolute power as his divine right and even dismissed Parliament for 11 years to avoid their meddling in his 'personal rule'.
- Things came to a head in 1642 with the start of the first English Civil War. The battle lines were drawn between the Royalists — known as the 'Cavaliers', who supported Charles I's right to rule as he wished, and the Parliamentarians — known as the 'Roundheads', due to the short cropped hair styles used by many Puritans. The Parliamentarians favoured a constitutional monarchy and later called for the abolition of the monarchy altogether.
- I'm sure that it wouldn't be a spoiler for many readers to learn that the Parliamentarians eventually won the war, secured power over the country and had King Charles I executed.
- Oliver Cromwell was an MP and committed member of the Parliamentary army who was swiftly promoted — first to second in command of the Eastern Association army, followed by a further promotion in 1645 to second in command of the newly formed main Parliamentary army, referred to as the New Model Army. After the war, Cromwell, and later his son, became 'Lord Protector' of the newly established Commonwealth of England, Scotland and Wales, a role that was somewhat equivalent to the formal role of king, but with some constitutional limitations.
- It is also no secret that Britain as a Commonwealth didn't last too long — the monarch was brought back after only 11 years of 'Protectorate' rule with the 'Restoration' of King Charles II in 1660.

Like many parts of the country, the Thames Valley had split allegiances during the Civil War. Indeed, it was the main base for both the Royalist government and Parliamentary army.

- Wallingford and Oxford Castles remained Royalist strongholds for the duration of the war with their significance declining dramatically after the Parliamentarian armies secured victory.
- Windsor Castle was used by the Parliamentary army as a military headquarters and was one of the many prisons for Charles I.
- London was under control of the Parliamentarians from the start of the war and King Charles I chose Oxford as his headquarters during the war, being based in Christ Church College.
- The entire city of Oxford became the seat of the Royalist government. Charles and his court was based in the Christ Church deanery, an old section of the college still used by the Dean of the college. His Queen Henrietta Maria lodged at neighbouring Merton College. The Privy Council was based in Oriel, and Parliament met at the grand Christ Church dining hall. Magdalen College became an artillery park and tailors stitched uniforms in the astronomy and music schools.
- Oxford, as a walled city, and Wallingford Castle, were refortified to support the king and were not captured until the very end of the war in 1646. The centre of Oxford had natural defences on three sides from the conjunction of the rivers Cherwell and Thames at the south border of the city. Ramparts were made to the north.
- Charles was forced to leave Oxford in 1646, which was soon besieged. The city held out until the 24th of June when the garrison of 3000 men including the king's nephews, Prince Rupert and Prince Maurice, were allowed to march out of the city with full honours.
- Oxford Castle was largely abandoned after the Civil War, but it continued to serve as the county gaol. The prison finally closed in 1996 and is now the site a Malmaison Hotel and other shops and restaurants.
- Wallingford Castle was one of the last Royal strongholds to be captured. Thomas Fairfax ordered his troops to besiege Wallingford in 1646. After 16 weeks of battle and protracted negotiation, an honourable surrender of the Royalists to the parliamentarians, similar to that at Oxford, was agreed. Wallingford Castle was taken over by Parliamentary forces and used as a prison, but in 1652, Cromwell's Council of State decided it was too great a risk to remain. They ordered its total demolition. Wallingford's period as a Royal stronghold had come to an end.
- Windsor Castle survived the tumultuous period of the English Civil War. It escaped the fate of Wallingford and other castles in 1652 when Parliament narrowly voted to not have it destroyed. As described earlier, after the Restoration of the monarchy in 1660, Charles II rebuilt much of Windsor Castle with the help of the architect Hugh May.

Right: Christ Church College dining hall was used to house Parliament during the Civil War.

Below: Remains of Wallingford Castle — the final Royalist stronghold to surrender in the Civil War. Parliament had it destroyed after the war to ensure there would be no repeat of such resistance.

Opposite page insets

Top: Statue of Charles I outside Oxford's Botanic Garden.

Bottom: Death mask of Oliver Cromwell from the Ashmolean Museum.

4. 18th and 19th Centuries: Development of today's towns and villages — Horses, Boats and Trains

1711-1807 — Ascot Racecourse

When out riding from Windsor Castle in 1711, Queen Anne came upon an area of open heath that looked, in her words, 'ideal for horses to gallop at full stretch'. The traditional opening Royal Ascot remains The Queen Anne Stakes run over the straight mile.

- The first four-day race meeting was held at Ascot in 1768, although the meeting as it is known today only really started to take shape with the introduction of the Gold Cup in 1807.
- Each of the five days of Royal Ascot begins with the Royal Procession at 2pm, when the king and other members of the royal family arrive down the straight mile in the royal carriages, accompanied by the playing of the National Anthem and the raising of the Royal Standard. This tradition was started in 1825 by King George IV.

Below: King Charles and Queen Camilla at Ascot in 2023 just after the coronation.
Right: Fans supporting their horses at Ascot. Photos courtesy of Ascot Racecourse.

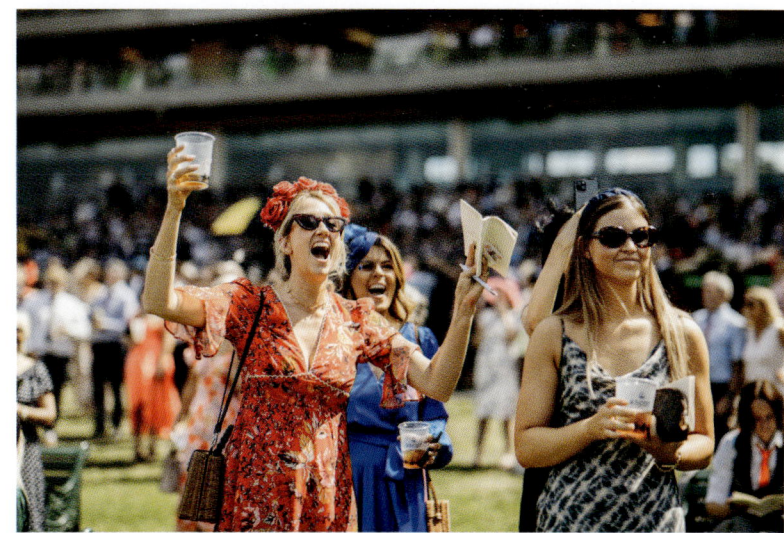

1722 — Blenheim Palace

Another legacy of Queen Anne is the grand Blenheim Palace that was built on the favourite royal manor of Woodstock that she gifted to John Churchill, the first Duke of Marlborough for his military achievements. Parliament agreed to fund the building of a suitable 'castle' but it was later referred to as a palace after the flamboyant English baroque-style design of Marlborough's preferred architect Sir John Vanbrugh. Parliament approved funding in 1705, but work dragged on until after the duke's death in 1722, and was completed by the Duchess of Marlborough who had fallen out with both the queen and architect in the meantime.

Marlborough's greatest military successes came as commander-in-chief of the army during the War of Spanish Succession for which — having been born into the gentry — he was elevated from earl to duke. His primary objective was to maintain the balance of power in Europe that suited Britain's interests. His victories over France and Germany ensured that Spain remained an independent nation following the death of their king with no clear successor. In 1704, Marlborough marched 250 miles from Holland across Germany in five weeks to defeat a larger French-Bavarian force at the village of Blindheim on the Danube River in the south of Germany. This was a pivotal win that ensured France was not in a position to challenge the allied arrangements in Europe. The battle became known as the Battle of Blenheim in England giving the palace its name. Marlborough continued his military success with a number of other notable victories after becoming a duke.

Blenheim continues to be the home of the Churchill and later the Spencer-Churchill families and successive Dukes of Marlborough. It may be best known as the birthplace of Winston Churchill who was a descendant of the 1st Duke of Marlborough. Whilst Churchill did not actually live in the palace, he and his family clearly spent a fair amount of time there. He was born at the palace in 1874 and later proposed to his future wife Clementine at the Temple of Diana in the grounds of the palace. Churchill's grave can be visited at St Martin's churchyard in Bladon, just outside the grounds of Blenheim.

In the 19th century, successive generations of the Duke of Marlborough's family struggled to cover the great costs of maintaining the palace, when the family were forced to sell some of the valuable paintings and other artefacts, including a priceless Reubens gifted to the 1st Duke of Marlborough from the City of Brussels as thanks for his war efforts. Fortune returned to the palace thanks to the 9th Duke of Marlborough's marriage to an American railroad heiress, Consuelo Vanderbilt in 1895. The duke apparently negotiated with his wife's parents a suitable price for the honour of her becoming a duchess. The multi-million dollar deal included preferred shares in their train company and a guaranteed income for life for both partners. The story is reminiscent of a plot in *Downton Abbey*, but is not unusual for country houses in the 19th and 20th centuries.

Since the Second World War, the practice of opening private grand homes to the public has become common, with some — such as Blenheim — proving quite successful. It was first opened to the public in 1950 and as of 2020, it had nearly 700,000 visitors per year. A tour a Blenheim Palace in 2023 starts at £28, and is generally over £100 for a family day out.

- Blenheim and many other country houses in England, such as Chatsworth House in the Peak District, are becoming increasingly popular family weekend destinations, especially during the summer months and around Christmas. They have become very sophisticated in their offerings that include high tea, adventure playgrounds for children and a gift shop with a growing number of products, ranging from Blenheim Christmas ornaments and hampers to countless premium gifts such as Blenheim-branded bottled water, beer and gin.
- Beyond visits to the palace and access to the grounds, the palace is a very popular place for a growing number of annual events including a 'Nocturne Live' summer concert series with big name artists, BBC Countryfile Live shows, a highly regarded triathlon, and a growing number of "Christmas at Blenheim" events. Tickets for these events are not cheap and generally sell out.
- Blenheim received over £22 million in income in fiscal year 2022/23 from visitor admissions, events, merchandise and water business sales and other grants and donations. This includes a revenue stream for using the palace as a filming location which netted £1.7 million in 2022. This was in a year when visits were still down from the peak following COVID but were expected to reach a new peak of 750,000 in 2023. All this means that Blenheim is in a healthy financial state, allowing it to invest an average of about £4 million a year in important restoration and renovation activities as part of a $40 million, 10 year project. It is also able to reacquire selected pieces of artwork that may have been sold in the past and purchase other new works such as some of Winston Churchill's paintings.
- As if all this weren't enough, Blenheim Estate acquired a housing development company, Pye Homes, to develop new homes on land near the estate. The estate received planning permission from West Oxfordshire District Council to build 209 homes and 67 homes had been completed by 31 March 2022. Sales of new homes generated £11.2 million by the end of 2022 with another £9 million projected to be received over the next few years. Their goal is to raise £45 million from these housing sales to 'conserve the World Heritage site'. They also have a goal to build 300 high quality, affordable homes at 40% below the going market rate.

Blenheim was selected as a World Heritage site in 1987 by the United Nations Education, Science and Culture Organisation. The list now includes over 1000 sites around the world, such as Yellowstone Park in America and the historic centre of Florence in Italy. It is considered a coveted designation that helps to attract tourists from around the world and also includes an obligation on national governments to support preservation of its heritage. Downsides of the designation can include a burden of bureaucracy to provide management plans and report on progress along with the risk of attracting over-tourism as has been seen in some cities in Italy such as Venice.

Opposite page: Blenheim triathlon.
Below: Carriage racing at Blenheim.

1839 — Henley Royal Regatta

The Henley rowing competition was established 10 years after Oxford and Cambridge competed in their first boat challenge in Henley in 1829.

- Its success is partly due to the straight stretch of the river that is so amenable to racing. Nestled between the base of the Chiltern Hills to the northwest and the Berkshire Downs at Remenham to the southeast, it is also a beautiful setting for the annual event. The river at Henley forms a straight course of 1 mile and 550 yards (2112 meters), from the bottom of Temple Island upstream towards Henley Bridge.
- It became the Henley Royal Regatta (HRR) in 1851 when Prince Albert became the first royal patron. Since his death, every reigning monarch has agreed to be the patron.
- The course has been used for the Olympic rowing competitions when it was held in London in 1908 and 1948. In 2012, the Olympic rowing was held at Eton College's man-made rowing lake at Dorney.
- Marlow resident and Olympic champion Sir Steve Redgrave became Chairman of the HRR in 2015 and continued this role through the 2024 season.

Right: Oxford Brookes 4-man crew celebrating their win at the finish line.
Below: Oxford Brookes 8-man crew celebrating with the tradition of throwing their cox into the river.

Clockwise from top left: Sir Steve Redgrave, HRR Chairman, greeting a member of the Stewards Enclosure; a traditional lunch break picnic in the car park; HRR umpires officiating a race; Henley with a Pimms.

The Coaching Age: 17th – 19th centuries

The growth of stagecoaches along the London to Bath Road, now the A4, meant that towns such as Hounslow, Slough, Maidenhead, Reading, Theale, Woolhampton and Speen at Newbury were important staging posts. The road was one of the busiest roads in the country when trips to Bath were made fashionable for therapeutic reasons following Queen Anne's visits between 1688 and 1703.

- The first stagecoaches ran at about 5 miles per hour, but steady improvements in coach design along with road improvements ultimately increased speeds to up to an average of 10 miles per hour by the 1800s.
- A coach company in 1667 advertised getting to Bath from London in 3 days, 'God permitting':
    - *'FLYING MACHINE. All those desirous to pass from London to Bath, or any other Place on their Road, let them repair to the 'Little Savage' on Ludgate Hill in London, and the 'White Lion' at Bath, at both which places they may be received in a Stage Coach every Monday, Wednesday, and Friday, which performs the Whole Journey in Three Days (if God permits) and sets forth at 5 o'clock in the morning.'*
- At its peak, in 1834, a survey recorded 823 horse drawn vehicles passing through Maidenhead every two weeks, more than any other town in England. This led to the growth of Maidenhead as a favourite first stop out of London providing inns, taverns, alehouses and the like. Old coaching inns can still be seen along the A4 such as the Shire Horse, Horse & Groom and many other pubs along the A4.
- The Old Bear Inn was one of many inns at Maidenhead, and owed some of its prosperity to the unwillingness of travellers from London to venture across Maidenhead Thicket at night, just to the west of the town. It was best to travel that portion in the morning with the full light of the day!
- Highwaymen, typically on horseback with a gun, flourished on the Bath Road until the early 1800s. At the Maidenhead Thicket, highwaymen had plenty of hiding places and escape routes. I often wondered why the road verges were so wide and grand by the Thicket Roundabout on the A4. It appears that this stems back to the Coaching Age where the trees closest to the road were consistently cut back to reduce the element of surprise from rogues coming out of the thicket!

- Highwayman William Hawkes was known to work the area. Whilst there is no solid evidence, it is said that the most famous highwayman, Dick Turpin, used the Dew Drop Inn at Littlewick Green as his usual stomping ground. The pub had an underground room where Turpin could hide his horse, Black Bess, when in need of shelter after an escapade on Maidenhead Thicket. Turpin was also alleged to have an aunt in Sonning whose home he would use as a hideout.

Opposite page: The A4 (Bath Road) at the Maidenhead Thicket. The trees are still set back significantly from the road to reduce the element of surprise from highwaymen attacks.
Left: The Bear in Maidenhead, former coaching inn.
Top Left: The Dew Drop Inn at Littlewick Green — still a remote location in the woods and a good hideout for highwaymen.
Above: The Horse & Groom on the A4 outside of Reading is over 300 years old and still a traditional coaching style pub and a good place for a family meal.

1786-1840 — Bridges supporting the coaching trade

- 1786 — **Henley's** iconic 5 arch stone bridge (shown below) was built to replace a wooden bridge that had been in place since the 12 or 13th century. A toll was required for almost 100 years until the £10,000 debt was paid off.
- 1792 — The first timber bridge across the Thames at **Whitchurch** was built by a group of residents. Prior to that there was a long-standing ferry. The ferryman was compensated for the loss of his business by a payment of £350. The Whitchurch Bridge Act of 1792 requires a bridge to be provided in perpetuity, owned and operated by the bridge company, with powers to collect tolls to pay for the bridge. Unusually, these powers are still in force, making it was one of the last remaining privately owned toll bridges in the country. It was replaced by a second wooden bridge in 1852, and iron bridges in 1902 and 2013-14. The toll bridge replacements in 2014 cost £6.2 million. This was double the original estimate and was used as justification to increase the price of tolls from 40p to 60p in 2015 . The increased construction costs were blamed on delays due to heavy rain and flooding the winter of its building.
- 1827 — Today's **Folly Bridge at Oxford** is likely to be the site of the ford over which oxen pulling carts across the Isis gave Oxford its name. The stone bridge was built along a Norman stone causeway through the marshes along what is now Abingdon Road.
- 1832 — **Marlow's** present suspension bridge was completed to replace a wooden bridge further downstream which collapsed in 1828. The suspension bridge was designed by William Tierney Clark using the same design as the larger Széchenyi Chain Bridge that was later built over the River Danube in Budapest in 1849.
- 1837 — The first wooden bridge across the Thames at **Goring and Streatley** was established to replace a ferry. The new bridge, combined with the arrival of the train in 1840, paved the way for the area to become a fashionable riverside resort with new substantial middle and upper class houses.
- 1840 — The first wooden bridge at **Cookham** was built by a Mr Freebody to replace the ferry. Two more elegant and robust designs by Brunel were rejected by the Cookham Bridge Commissioners as being too expensive. In addition to the bridge building costs, the commissioners needed to pay £2565 to compensate the ferry company for loss of trade, however the new wooden bridge was so unreliable that the ferry continued to trade when the bridge was out of use. It turns out that Brunel was right in the end — the bridge was in a bad state within 20 years and replaced with an iron bridge by 1870. For 107 years a toll was payable — ceasing in 1947 when Berkshire County Council bought the bridge from its private owners.

Opposite Page: Dragon Boat racing at Henley Bridge.

Left: The project to replace the Whitchurch Bridge in 2013/14 took almost a year and was 50% over budget due to flooding along the Thames that winter.

Below: Marlow suspension bridge and the Compleat Angler Hotel on a winter's evening.

1838-1866 — The Great Western Railway

In many ways, the Great Western Railway (GWR) put the Thames Valley on the map. By connecting Maidenhead, Reading, Oxford and many other Thames Valley towns and villages with quick and easy access to London Paddington, the GWR changed everything.

- The railway marked the start of a period of rapid growth due to the popularity of visiting the river in the Thames Valley for recreation and the possibility of commuting to London for work.
- Given the significantly reduced travel times offered by trains, stagecoaches from Reading to London were all but shut down within a few years of rail service starting in 1840.
- The railway also greatly reduced commercial activity on the river and connecting canals. The Kennet and Avon Canal had finally been completed in 1811 after almost 100 years of work. In the end, its main period of commercially viability was only about 30 years. By 1852, unable to compete with the railway, the Kennet and Avon Canal was sold to GWR for £210,000 — one fifth of its original cost. Reduced trade on the canal continued for some time but it was a loss making enterprise by the 1870s and all but closed down by 1900.

The GWR was initiated and built by a wealthy group of London and Bristol merchants to provide a way to ship goods between London and ports in Bristol. This was partly to stay competitive with ports in Liverpool that were aided by the Liverpool and Manchester Railway that had opened in 1830.

Isambard Kingdom Brunel, known for his ground-breaking engineering work (literally) on the Thames Tunnel in London and Clifton Suspension Bridge in Bristol, was appointed chief engineer. Brunel was an energetic and persuasive man who was determined to make the GWR one of the engineering wonders of the Victorian Age.

- Brunel's original vision was that passengers could travel directly from London to New York with one ticket. They would take the train from London to a port in west Wales, and then directly board a Great Western ship to New York. He later designed and built three ships that were influential in British naval design, but his vision of connecting the railway to New York never materialised.
- Brunel had also envisaged a future route to the European continent via a terminus in London south of the Thames at Vauxhall. That vision had to be altered as well when his plans were vigorously opposed by local landowning MPs, leading to the less controversial location at Paddington Green.
- Over three months in 1833, Brunel surveyed the entire route of the line between Bristol and London personally, on horseback, along with two assistants struggling to keep up with his furious pace.
- He decided that the GWR should take a route from Bristol north of the traditional coaching towns of Hungerford, Marlborough and Devizes to avoid the steep Wessex Downs in Wiltshire. Instead, he followed the Vale of the White Horse and then the Thames Valley into London via the Goring Gap. This route provided the low 1-in-1000 overall gradient that he was seeking, but made it a longer, indirect route between Reading and Bath. The relatively flat gentle gradient he planned for the length of the line enabled maximum speed while keeping running costs down and supporting passenger comfort.
- Some questioned the route passing through a largely unpopulated area of the Vale of the White Horse, but the board approved the route as it achieved its primary objective of getting freight between London and Bristol quickly and had the added benefit of offering convenient connections to Oxford and Gloucester.
- The selected route from Bristol had the tracks first reaching the River Thames at Cholsey, then followed the river to Reading, and on to Maidenhead and London. The route through the Thames Valley via the Goring Gap was the only viable route that achieved the low gradient, winding between the Berkshire Downs and Chiltern Hills.

It took two attempts to get Parliament to approve an Act authorising the GWR route between London Paddington and Bristol's Temple Meads. The Act was finally approved in 1835 after Brunel endured 11 days of vigorous cross-examination from landowners and other parties questioning the bill.

- The formidable Eton Headmaster, Dr Edward Hawtrey testified that Eton College would be ruined by the railways, stating that it would 'destroy the classical tradition'. He declared that Homer, Virgil, and Horace would be thrust aside in favour of dangerous

Inset: Isambard Kingdom Brunel statue at Paddington Station.

thoughts of Rousseau and Voltaire. Even worse, 'the boys themselves would take advantage of the short interval of their play hours to run up into town, mix in all the dissipation of London life, and return before the absence could be discovered'. Dr Hawtry's influence led to a concession that prevented the company from building a station within 3 miles of Eton College.

- Once approved, Brunel and GWR pushed to get the railway completed within 5 and a half years. Service to Maidenhead, Reading and some other locations were opened in even less time, with the full route to Bristol completed by 1841.

The design of the Maidenhead railway bridge proved to be one of many controversial design decisions made by Brunel. At the time of construction, and still today, the bridge has two of the widest and flattest brick arches that have ever been built anywhere in the world.

- The arches, at 128 feet wide, with a rise of only 24 feet 3 inches above the river, were designed by Brunel to comply with the combined requirement from the Thames Commissioners to provide sufficient height to allow boats to navigate beneath it combined with the need to keep the crossing relatively flat to keep the gradient of the line as low as possible.
- Many thought the bridge would be unstable, with well-known critics vociferously predicting that the bridge arches would collapse even before the first train passed over them. To mollify critics, Brunel left wooden supports in place on the bridge even after it was operational, however, he had actually lowered the support structure enough so that they were not actually bearing any weight and made no difference. When flooding later washed

Members of the Maidenhead rowing club pass under Brunel's railway bridge at Maidenhead.

away the wooden structure leaving the bridge standing unaided, Brunel once again proved the critics wrong. The bridge still stands today and has supported several upgrades over the years including recent electrification and track changes to support the Elizabeth Line.

Brunel was a man who wanted to carve his own path and didn't like following other men's lead. He controversially chose a wide gauge track of 7¼ feet for the GWR that varied from the more common 4 ft 8½ in gauge used in other parts of the UK at the time. Brunel's analysis showed that his broader gauge was the optimum size for providing both higher speeds and a stable and comfortable ride for passengers. The wider gauge also allowed for larger wagons and thus greater freight capacity. Whilst he may have been correct from a technical perspective, it proved to be too late to change the emerging default standard for the narrower gauge. In 1846, Parliament formed a commission to standardise railway gauges that ruled in favour of the narrower gauge and the GWR broad gauge tracks had to be phased out over the next 50 years. In retrospect, Brunel's insistence on the broader gauge proved to be a costly and time consuming mistake.

- The route also included a controversial 3 km tunnel through Box Hill, between Chippenham and Bath, the world's longest train tunnel at the time. Again, many said it couldn't be done or was too dangerous. Naysayers worried passengers would suffer from the smoke in the tunnel, the train would accelerate to dangerous speeds due to the steep incline, or it was just too long for passengers to be trapped in a dark tunnel. The construction of the tunnel did end up delaying the opening of the full line, but in the end, Brunel proved critics wrong again.

The initial route to Maidenhead opened in June 1838 but included no station at Slough due to the restrictions demanded by Eton. The GWR got around this by still serving passengers at Slough without a station. Fortunately for residents of Slough and Windsor, it seems that thinking had moved on by 1838, as Eton College requested a special train to take its scholars to London for Queen Victoria's coronation on 28th of June. Slough was given its own station by 1840.

- Queen Victoria tended to spend weekdays at Buckingham Palace and weekends at Windsor and the train seemed a better option than horse and carriage. The queen was the first British Monarch to use a train, travelling between Slough and London in 1842. GWR had built a special rail car for royalty complete with silk hangings, Louis XIV sofas and a rosewood table. The train was driven by chief locomotive engineer Daniel Gooch, assisted by Brunel. The ride seemed to be a hit with the Queen. She wrote her Uncle King Leopold of the Belgians that day saying "I am quite charmed by it. By railroad from Windsor in half an hour, free from dust and heat." The line was extended to Windsor by 1849 thanks to royal support.

The GWR service had its teething problems but proved faster than any other train service in the country at the time, reaching speeds of 40 to 50 mph. Today trains run at up to 125 mph along the mainline route. Later expanded south of Bristol to Cornwall, west through Wales, and north via Gloucester, the hugely popular GWR came to be affectionately known as 'God's Wonderful Railway'.

Many stops and branch lines in the Thames Valley were added over the next 20 years:
- 1839 – Service extended to Twyford.
- 1840 – Service extended to Reading, including stations at Pangbourne and Goring terminating at Steventon. Coaching service was provided for the 7 mile journey to Oxford from Steventon until the branch line from Didcot to Oxford was opened.
- 1841 – Bristol Temple Meads to London Paddington service becomes fully operational.
- 1844 – Didcot service extended to Oxford.
- 1847 – Reading to Hungerford via Newbury completed.
- 1849 – Slough to Windsor branch line completed.
- 1854 – Maidenhead to High Wycombe line via Cookham opened. In 1873 the spur from Bourne End to Marlow was added, now referred to as the Marlow Donkey after the locomotive that used to run on the line.
- 1857 – Twyford to Henley GWR branch was added with stations at Wargrave and Shiplake.
- 1866 – Moulsford to Wallingford branch was added, known as the Bunk. This line and Wallingford Station were closed in 1959.

Right: Josh and Joe, two young train enthusiasts demonstrate model steam engines at Didcot Railway Centre.
Below: The Windsor branch line from Slough that was added after Windsor and Eton were originally excluded from the GWR route. The only stop is at Windsor.

1846 — WH Smith

The well-known British newsagent started in London but the family settled in the Henley area after it became successful by taking advantage of the railway boom. William H Smith Jr, the grandson of the newsagent's founder, joined the family business in 1946.

- William Jr and his father began opening news-stands on railway stations, starting with Euston in 1848. William Jr used the newsagent business success to launch a political career, becoming an MP in 1868 and later First Lord of the Admiralty during the Disraeli Administration.
- The family lived in the country house Greenlands that sits along the river at Henley-on-Thames, before moving to the nearby village of Hambleden. Greenlands is now the site of the Henley Business School, becoming part of the University of Reading in recent years.
- The widow of William H Smith Jr became the 1st Viscountess Hambleden in 1891 as a tribute to the family shortly after William's death. The Smith family owned most of the idyllic village of Hambleden, which has been the site of numerous films and television shows such as *Chitty, Chitty, Bang Bang, Band of Brothers* and *Sleepy Hollow*.
- In 2007, the family sold their property which consisted of most homes and businesses in the village and the surrounding Culden Faw Estate to Swiss Financier Urs Schwarzenbach for a reported £38 million. Members of the WH Smith family still owned and lived in the Manor House in Hambleden until the 4th Viscount Hambleden passed away in 2012.
- The current 5th Viscount Hambleden, William Henry Smith, now lives in Switzerland with his long-term partner Frida Lyngstad, the singer in ABBA.
- WH Smith also has a surprising connection with Pangbourne. As a relatively small village, WH Smith is one of the few national chains represented on its High Street. The shop was first opened in 1937, before the Honourable David Smith became the Governing Director of WH Smith from 1948 to 1972. He lived in Pangbourne with his wife Lady Helen at Bere Court, the old Manor House. As they both liked to visit the shop, he made a stipulation that the shop should remain indefinitely despite the town's small size.

Below: Greenlands — former home of WH Smith along the river at Henley — now the Henley business School.   Inset: WH Smith Jr.

Summer of 1858 — The Great Stink and the story of London's sewerage system

London was often referred to as 'The Big Smoke' during the industrial revolution from the excessive amount of coal burning, but in the summer of 1858, the mighty River Thames became known as 'The Great Stink'. Residents of London, including leading politicians, became disturbed by the foul smell emanating from the Thames and there were legitimate concerns that it was a cause of recent deadly cholera outbreaks. The smell was exacerbated by the heat wave that hit the metropolis in June where the temperatures averaged 34–36°C (93-97°F).

- In 1858 the newly built Houses of Parliament, located along the Thames, had to be closed due to the smell. Curtains soaked with a mixture of chlorine and lime where hung in the windows to little effect. They even considered temporarily moving Parliament to Oxford or Henley.
- The cause of the smell was clearly the ever increasing amount of raw sewage being dumped into the river, which was also the source of much of London's drinking water.
- Concerns about pollution in the river had been growing for several years, but the Great Stink ended up being the crisis that finally forced Parliament to take action to address the issue.

Whilst the Thames pollution problem was most evident in London, there were similar issues with pollution and cholera outbreaks in Oxford, Windsor and other areas. Prince Albert's death from typhoid in 1861 was said to have been caused by poor sanitation in waters around Windsor Castle, where he is said to have delighted in bathing and swimming. The issue of raw sewage being dumped into the Thames is still an issue across the Thames Valley today, so it is worth exploring how the issue was originally dealt with by Victorian engineering in London.

- Household sewage in England had traditionally been treated with private or locally shared cesspits. Whilst these had their own sanitation issues, they did not generally affect river quality except for cases where there were leaks from properties near a river or other water source.
- Sewage really only began flowing into local rivers that then fed into the Thames after the introduction of the modern flushing toilet, originally known as the water closet. According to a report to London's chief sewerage engineer John Bazalgette:
    - *We believe that the introduction of water closets (WCs) in the metropolis, to any extent, may be dated from the year 1810, from which time until 1830 their increase was only gradual; but since 1830 the increase has be very rapid and remarkable. The number of cesspools which have been disconnected is not far short of 200,000.*
- A further stimulus was provided by the Great Crystal Palace Exhibition of 1851 where 827,000 people used WCs installed at Hyde Park, many of them for the first time.
- Not only were more people using WCs in London, but there were more and more people in London. In 1801, there were still less that 1 million people in London — by 1861, the population had almost tripled to 2.8 million.
- Whilst WCs were seen as an improvement to sanitation at each home, it had a growing impact on pollution of the Thames and the tributary rivers leading into it. According to Victorian sewerage builder Thomas Cubitt:
    - *Now sewers have been very much improved, scarcely any person thinks of making a cesspool, but it is carried off at once into the river. The Thames is now made a great cesspool instead of each person having one of his own.*

So how to solve the problem? Between 1848 and 1855, the government had set up a series of Metropolitan Commissions of Sewers to study the problem and propose solutions, but still the problem continued. The Commissions were comprised a number of prominent civil engineers including Joseph Bazalgette, who initially served as the assistant surveyor of the sewers in London, later becoming Chief Engineer of the Water Management Board (WMB), the body set up to deliver the new sewerage system.

- At one point there were at least 137 proposals submitted to the commission with differing ideas on how to clean up the river.
- The main strategy they came up with was to develop a series of tunnels that would intercept the sewage across London and release it near the mouth of the Thames downstream and east

Satirical view of the Thames 'Monster Soup' from Punch Magazine from 1858.

of the main London Metropolis where there was no danger of it flowing back into the city.

- There were many suggestions related to finding a way of reusing the sewage by converting it into agricultural fertiliser.
  - One challenge to this approach was that it would require sewage channels to be separated from rain water run-off channels. Bazalgette and others favoured combined channels as being more pragmatic and cost effective. Combining the two channels is generally not an issue as long as the system had sufficient capacity to handle extra rainwater in peak rain periods. This is one of the main problems with the system today as the tunnels and treatment plants do not always have enough capacity during peak rain periods, requiring emergency raw sewage discharges into the river.
  - Another challenge was the expense of moving the sewage for agricultural use. Newsagent WH Smith made a proposal that involved conveying sewage by rail. One idea was to create a sewage pipeline along the rail lines.
- The design that was ultimately approved was a series of intercepting sewage channels — one network in North London, and a separate system for sewage south of the river. The North London channels were diverted to an outflow to the river at Barking and the South London channels sent the sewage to the river at Crossness. Major sewage plants are still based at these two locations.
- Part of the success of Bazalgette's design was that he sized the system for a population of up to 4.5 million inhabitants which allowed 50% capacity for growth at the time. London's population eventually peaked at close to 9 million in 1941, so the system has required many expansions and improvements over the years, but the core system is still in place.
- One of the main reasons for the lack of action until 1858 was the absence of a unified government in London with the authority to carry out such an ambitious project. Apart from the core City of London, the 2 million people living in what is now metropolitan London were governed by 90 separate parishes and precincts, normally led by church vestry committees that included a mix of local vicars, some elected members, and many 'principal inhabitants' who often had seats passed down over generations.
- By 1858, after more than 10 years of work to develop a design, and with the MWB governance in place, work had still not started. The Great Stink crisis gave the final impetus for

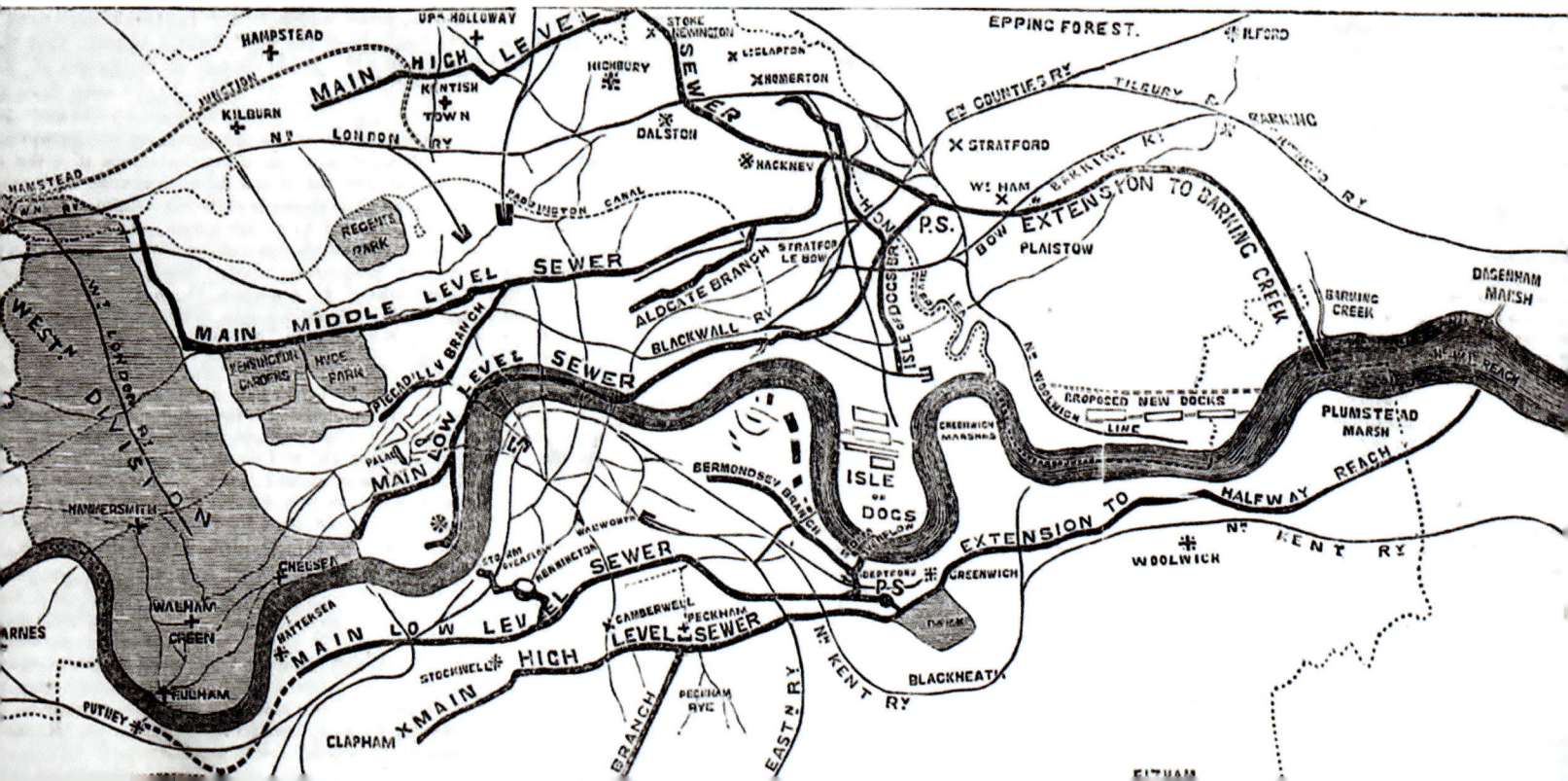

Baguette's design for London's intercepting sewage channels that effectively collected the sewage from existing sewers and dumped it in the Thames east of London. The North London Sewers reaching the Thames at Barking and the South London sewers at Crossness.

Parliament to do what was needed to make it happen. Benjamin Disraeli, in his role as Leader of the House and Chancellor of the Exchequer, introduced legislation in July 1858 "for the purification of the Thames and the main drainage of the metropolis". He lamented how "that noble river" had become "a Stygian pool reeking with ineffable and unbearable horror". The Act empowered the MWB to start the work, including guaranteeing the required £3,000,000. The law was passed in a record 18 days giving Bazalgette (pictured on the right) and the MWB the ability to finally start work.

- The massive project was then delivered within the next 10 years to great acclaim from the press and general public. Sewage outflow for South London at Crossness started in 1865, and north London outflow at Barking started in 1868. Lavish celebrations were held with guests including the Prince of Wales, Members of Parliament, Archbishops, and many foreign dignitaries and royalty. Members of local vestry committees were treated to tours of the facilities for many months after their opening. After the Crossness facility for South London was completed on time, Local MPs proposed that Bazalgette receive a £6000 bonus, although this was never approved. He did receive a knighthood for his contributions in 1874.
- The greatest benefits from the new sewerage system has to be the lives it saved from disease. Between 1831 and 1855, there had been three major cholera outbreaks in London, the worst being responsible for over 14,000 deaths. This stopped after the introduction of the new sewage tunnels. The final cholera outbreak was in 1866 just as the sewage project was nearing completion. This outbreak only affected a localised area of East London. By this time the South London tunnels had been completed, but the affected area of East London was not operational.
- It wasn't until the 1880s that treatment of the sewage was deemed necessary before being discharged into the Thames. When the outflow points were set up at Barking and Crossness, these were considered to be remote and sparsely populated areas. By the 1880s these areas were already becoming substantial suburbs of London and there were reports of severe poisoning and deaths from the polluted water. Sewage treatment facilities were eventually established and the sludge — the part of the sewage that remains after treatment — was shipped to Hole Haven near Canvey Island where it was dumped into the Thames Estuary. The practice of shipping of sludge remained until 1998 when European directives came into force that prohibited such practices. Incineration of the sludge carried out at Barking and Crossness now generates the electrical power needed to power the sewerage plants.

Today, London's sewerage system is owned and managed by Thames Water. During periods of heavy rainfall, many sewers and sewage treatment facilities still get overloaded and Thames Water are allowed to discharge raw sewage at 57 overflow points along the river in London. Whilst this problem also affects many parts of the Thames Valley, a solution for London, called the Tideway project is in the works.

The £4.3 billion Thames Tideway project, due to be operational by 2026, will effectively be an overflow extension to Bazalgette's Victorian London sewerage system. At the core of the Tideway scheme is a 7.2m (24 ft) diameter tunnel, running 23 km (16 miles) under the length of the Thames to capture sewage runoff to avoid it going into the Thames. The overflow will be stored in the tunnel and the shafts leading down to it, until it can be transported to the newly expanded Beckton Sewage Treatment plant at Barking in East London where it will be treated before being discharged to the Thames. The tunnelling phase was finished in 2023 with overall construction due to be completed in 2025. There are currently thought to be about 60 discharges per year and the target is to reduce this to 5. The Tideway tunnel will still be subject to future capacity constraints due to changing weather patterns from climate change and a growing population in London, but will clearly make an improvement to the quality of the water in the Thames in London once it is in place.

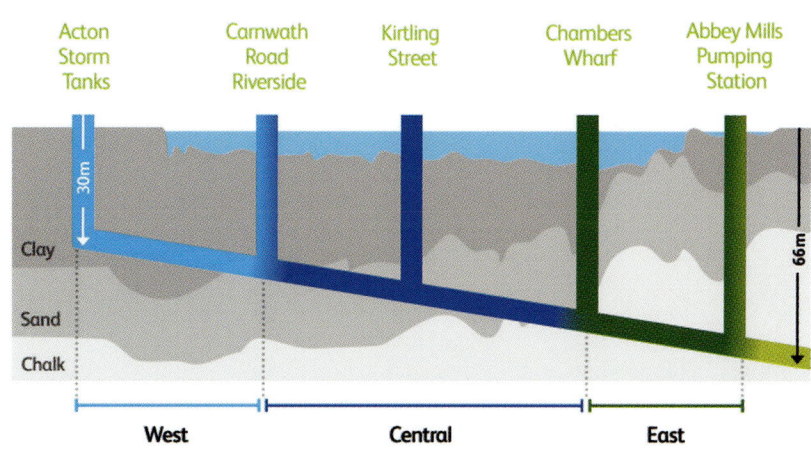

Side view of the Thames Tideway Tunnel project.

1867 — Taplow Court and Lord Desborough

William Grenfell, who later became Lord Desborough, lived an extraordinarily active and productive life, especially for his day. He lived at Taplow Court near Maidenhead, originally a part of the Cliveden Estate that was sold in the 1850s to the Grenfell family. The family were Lords of the Manor for many years and William inherited Taplow Court in 1867.

Lord Desborough was a true man of the Thames. 'Nobody has a closer connection with the Thames,' the *Derby Daily Telegraph* reflected upon his death in 1945. 'He had swum in it, rowed on it, represented it in Parliament, lived by the side of it, spent hours fishing in it, administered it and measured it.'

Today we might call him a renaissance man and a bit of an adrenaline junkie. He was a multi-talented athlete, member of Parliament for three different districts and had a long and productive career of public service. Locals called him "Willy" and considered him a genial and popular man — clearly someone who could 'get things done'.

- He excelled at cricket while at Harrow and rowed in the Boat Race against Cambridge for Balliol College in Oxford. In 1877 he rowed in what turned out to be the only dead heat (tie) in Boat Race history. The following year, he served as president of the Boat Club and rowed in the crew that won by ten lengths.
- Just a few of his more notable sporting achievements after graduating from Oxford included:
    - Acting as President of the 1908 Olympic Games in London.
    - Winning the Thames punting championship for three successive years (1888-90).
    - Rowing a boat of eight crew across the English Channel, acting as the stroke (lead rower).
    - Sculling the London-Oxford stretch of the Thames with two others in twenty-two consecutive hours.
    - Rowing in the Grand Challenge Cup eight-man crew race at Henley Regatta while serving as a member of the House of Commons — later becoming a long serving Henley Regatta Steward.
    - Climbing the Matterhorn by three different routes.
    - Swimming the pools of Niagara Falls twice in the supposedly calm water between the thundering falls and the undertow.
    - Winning a silver medal as part of the British fencing team in the Athens 1906 Olympics.
    - You get the idea…

His political career included serving as a Liberal MP for Salisbury and Herefordshire, and then later as a Conservative MP for the Wycombe district in Buckinghamshire.

- In 1905 he was awarded a peerage as Baron Desborough of Taplow, a title which he took from the old 'hundreds district' of Desborough in Buckinghamshire.
- He was president of the Thames Conservancy Board from 1904 to 1937.
- His family estimated that he served on up to 155 committees at the same time. A few examples include being president of the Marylebone Cricket Club, the Lawn Tennis Association, and Amateur Athletics Association.

- In later years he was a generous benefactor to the Maidenhead area, founding the Maidenhead Boat Club and the Maidenhead Golf Course. As of 2024, the golf course is planned as the site for a major new housing development. He rented land for Grenfell Park to the town for a peppercorn rent and twice acted as Maidenhead Mayor. His name will be familiar to those living in the area from such places as Grenfell Park, Grenfell Road, The Lord Grenfell Pub, Desborough Park and Desborough School.
- Ettie Desborough, Lord Desborough's wife, played a prominent social role in the area and was a well-known celebrity in her day. She hosted a group of intellectuals and politicians known as 'the Souls' at the house in the 1890s to socialise and discuss philosophical issues. The group's prominent guests included Edward VII when he was Prince of Wales, H.G. Wells, Oscar Wilde, actor Henry Irving and Winston Churchill.
- They had three sons and two daughters. Tragically the eldest two were killed in WWI and the third died in a car crash. With no surviving male heirs, the barony ended with Lord Desborough.

As described earlier, Taplow Court is an Elizabethan Manor House built on the site of the Iron Age Fort and Anglo Saxon burial ground on a grand hill overlooking the Thames at Maidenhead.
- In 1913 Taplow Court was rented by Rodman Wanamaker, the U.S. Department Store magnate. After World War II, Taplow Court was owned by British Telecommunications Research, a subsidiary of Plessey Electronics.
- Since 1986, Taplow Court has been owned by the global Buddhist organisation Soka Gakkai International (SGI) that was started in Japan in 1930. Soka Gakkai UK Managing Director Robert Harrap says that members use Buddhist principles to actualize their inherent potential while contributing to their local communities and responding to the shared issues facing humankind. Most practice happens individually by chanting at home or in local discussion groups across the UK. They periodically gather at the Taplow facilities for conferences or workshops. When I met with Mr Harrap, he also cited the convenience of Heathrow Airport, the M4, and the new Elizabeth Line train as reasons for locating the UK HQ at Taplow.

Robert Harrap, UK Director of Buddhist organisation SGI, the owner of Taplow Court since 1986, standing on Taeppas Mound.

1880-1914 – Golden age of Thames boating

With the advent of the railway, and corresponding loss of river-based trade, the River Thames became exceedingly popular for sport and recreation. This period, up until the start of the First World War, is sometimes known as the 'golden age of the Thames' due to the popularity of visiting the Thames Valley for short trips to the countryside and to participate in a growing number of river regatta events.

- *Three Men in a Boat* was written by Jerome K. Jerome in 1888 at the height of this period. The book is about three friends leaving London for a holiday on the Thames by rowing boat to escape the London rat race. Whilst the humour may seem a little dated today, it was an extremely popular book at the time. It is full of stories from their journey from Kingston-upon-Thames to Oxford, and then returning back as far as the Swan Inn at Pangbourne. After two days of cold rainy weather on the way back, they decided to abandon their journey and take to the train back to London from Pangbourne Station early the next morning.
- By 1889, there were around 12,000 pleasure boats, 300 steam launches and 150 houseboats registered on the Thames.
- Maidenhead sought to make up for lost coaching trade by positioning itself as a place for Londoners to take a day trip to the country by train. Many new hotels and clubs appeared on the river front and Maidenhead began to take on the reputation later associated with seaside resorts such as Brighton. The town featured regularly in divorce courts and Mr and Mrs Smiths were a frequent entry in hotel registers.

Right: E. J. Gregory's famous painting from 1895, *Boulter's Lock, Sunday Afternoon*, that epitomises the golden age of the Thames.

Below: Maidenhead bridge near Boulter's Lock today where the Thames is quite different but still used for recreational boating.

- Boulter's Lock was at the centre of the excitement and one of the most well known riverside hotels was Skindles, opening in 1883. Skindles was later joined by the Ray Meade and Thames Hotels, also situated on the river.
- Jerome avoided the town on his famous boat trip as being too posh: "Maidenhead itself is too snobby to be pleasant. It is the haunt of the river swell and his overdressed female companion. It is the town of showy hotels, patronised chiefly by dudes and ballet girls".
- A highlight of the season was Ascot Sunday when the smart set arrived on boats and boating parties were popular. Whilst Maidenhead is no longer considered overly posh, especially

compared to neighbouring villages of Marlow, Cookham and Bray, Royal Ascot dinners and drinks evenings are still popular in the area.

- Skindles continued to be a popular restaurant for many years and was later a night club for celebrities and royalty up through the 1950s and 1970s. Well known visitors included the likes of Bette Davis, the Marx Brothers, and later Princess Margaret and Diana Dors.
- In 2014 after decades of decline in the area, Boulter's Lock was redeveloped as part of the high-end Berkley Homes housing development along the Thames, called Taplow Riverside. The development has won a number of design awards, and includes a stylish riverside pub and restaurant and a new Brasserie on the old site of Skindles by celebrity chefs Roux Brothers.
- I agree that Taplow Riverside is one of the more attractive recent new housing developments — well thought out and in keeping with the river location and history of the site, making the area an aspirational place to live again. Unfortunately, prices of the homes in this development reflect its attractiveness, with 2 bedroom apartments going for £1.1 million and 4-bedroom homes with a small garden going for closer to £2 million or more in 2024. The 4-bedroom riverside homes located next to the new Roux Brothers restaurant shown above were going for more like £3 million each in 2024.

Top right: View of the celebrity chef run Roux bothers Brasserie and new riverside homes at the former site of Skindles.

Right: Life is good on a sunny day dining on the deck of the Hall & Woodlouse gastro pub on the banks of the Thames near Boulter's Lock.

1671-1894 – Pangbourne Manor, the Church Vestry Committee and changes to local government

The Breedon family were Lords of the Pangbourne Manor since they first purchased it in 1671 until the estate was sold at a Reading auction in 1894.
- The site of the original manor house was Bere Court, the former country home of Hugh Cook of Faringdon and leaders of Reading Abbey. The house can still be seen from Bere Court Road.
- A memorial to the original lord of the manor, John Breedon, can be seen at the east end of St James-the-Less church, along with memorials to other family members over the years throughout the church.
- The first John Breedon endowed a free school at the centre of the village. The endowment continues to provide for children and young people in the village in the form of the Breedon Educational and Vocational Foundation.

Bere Court, home to the Breedon family who were lords of Pangbourne Manor from 1671 - 1894. Inset: Robert Stone, Pangbourne Miller and local councillor.

In the mid to late 19th century, church vestry committees still held both ecclesiastical as well as some secular responsibility over a number of matters in the village, although their powers were in decline. Amongst other responsibilities, the Vestry had historically been given powers to tax or tithe local residents to distribute money to the poor. Rev. Robert Finch served as Rector for St James-the-Less church in Pangbourne from 1857 and led the vestry committee. Whilst doing much for the church during his time as Rector, he was known to be a prickly character with a 'Lord of the Manor' air about him.
- The local press reported Rev. Finch's vestry meetings with headlines such as: 'Stormy Vestry Meeting' and 'Another Exciting Vestry Meeting – an inquiry to be asked for'.
- Reverend Finch was involved in court cases with a number of parishioners:
  - A shoemaker was imprisoned for six months for stealing Finch's coat and hat and an old man received four days hard labour for stealing walnuts off the Rectory lawn.
  - Finch also had an ongoing argument with a local magistrate and son of the Lord of the Manor of Tidmarsh, Robert John Hopkins. This led to a widely reported court case in 1866 where Rev. Finch accused Hopkins of 'mocking him and causing disruption of the service.' Hopkins was fined 20 shillings.

Robert Stone was a prominent Pangbourne resident who originally came to the village to work at the local mill on the Pang River.
- Mr Stone was elected churchwarden in 1890 to be on the vestry committee under Rev. Finch at St James-the-Less church. This was a time when the role of churchwarden as part of the vestry committee was clearly still an important and somewhat powerful role. Mr Stone's election posters read 'Vote for Stone and for the poor people to have coals'. His election was to be a 'A fight for the people against the parson'. His election was hailed with great cheering and he was carried in the arms of several of his supporters through the village, followed by a victory dinner at The Elephant Hotel. Robert continued to be at loggerheads with Rev. Finch in the years to come.
- The 1894 Local Government Act formally required that civil parishes be set up with democratically elected parish councils to separate the secular responsibility for managing common aspects of villages from the church ecclesiastical responsibility of the vicar. Robert became a long time parish councillor and achieved his ambition of owning the mill in 1894 after it was auctioned by the Breedon Estate, marking the end of any feudal era in the village. The old mill house is still located on the River Pang just behind the Cross Keys pub.
- In 1896 the parish council voted to have the locks on the churchyard gates forcibly removed by Robert Stone to ensure that his children could access and lay flowers at the family graves.
- Parochial church councils (PCCs) in churches later took over ecclesiastical responsibility from the vestry committee.
- Elected parish councils continue to look after village-owned open spaces and community facilities such as village halls, allotments, and cemeteries. They are also the local representatives for matters handled by principal councils such as

planning decisions, highway maintenance, and school and social care funding.

Robert's descendants continued to live in the village as prominent members of the community.
- Robert's son Percy Snr was a founding member of the Masonic Lodge on Shooter's Hill which has had members of the Stone family ever since.
- Robert Stone's grandson son Percy Stone Jr established Percy Stone shops as a family business that continued in the village until the 1990s in the same buildings on the High Street that were once home to the Breedon family-endowed school. The shop sold vegetable seeds, seed potatoes, pet foods and garden accessories. His son Richard expanded the shop in1970s into a specialist garden shop with a florist and gift shop.
- The sign for the Old Breedon School can be seen on the High Street between Nino's Italian Deli and Costa Coffee. As of 2024 Richard Stone still lived in the village and maintained an interest in the buildings and the car park behind them.

Above right: St James-the-Less church, Pangbourne.
Below left: The entrance to the Old Breedon School is between Nino's Deli and Costa Coffee.
Below right: Richard Stone clearing the footpath in the car park behind the old Breedon School.

19th and 20th centuries — Reading and the Three B's

Reading became known as a centre for doing business during the rapid growth of the 19th and 20th centuries, enabled to a large part by its role as the transport hub for the Thames Valley in the form of coaching, river and canal transport, the railway and later the M4 motorway. The most famous of Reading's industries during this period were known as the Three B's: Biscuits, Bulbs, and Beer. These companies were leaders in their respective industries for one to two centuries, but saw decline by the 1970s when they started to make way for insurance and new high tech industries.

Biscuits: Huntley & Palmer —Founded in 1822, Joseph Huntley's early business was aided by the coaching trade. One of the main calling points of the stagecoaches was the Crown Inn, directly opposite Joseph Huntley's shop in Reading. Huntley started selling his biscuits to the travellers on the coaches. Because the biscuits were vulnerable to breakage during coaching journeys, they started putting them in the now famous metal tins.

- Growth really took off with the train service in the 1840s after George Palmer was invited to join the firm in 1841 when Joseph Huntley was forced to resign from ill health. As the factory flourished, much of its output was moved to rail and the company constructed its own private rail sidings and locomotives within the factory to connect with main railway lines to London. The company provided free biscuits for first-class rail travellers from Paddington, urging them to look out for the works in Reading.
- The flour for the biscuits came from many locals mills including the mill at Hambleden lock near Henley. In the late 19th century, a barge called the *Maid of the Mill*, used to make a weekly journey with flour from Hambleden Mill to Huntley & Palmer's biscuit factory in Reading. On her return trip she carried broken biscuits for sale, cheap, to the local villagers.
- By 1900 they were the world's largest biscuit firm, employing over 5000 people, making them one of the forty most important industrial companies in Britain.
- George Palmer and the Palmer family were notable local figures in Reading who generously gave money and land to the town, including Palmer Park. The town was often known as 'biscuit town' with the Reading football team known as the 'biscuit men'. George Palmer served on the local council in Reading from 1850, was mayor of Reading from 1857–58, and represented the town as Member of Parliament. His son George William Palmer was twice elected to represent Reading, serving from 1892 to 1895 and from 1898 to 1904. The Palmer's country estate was Marlston House in Bucklebury, now home to Brockhurst and Marlston House private schools for girls and boys.

Above: Marlston House in West Berkshire, former country home to George Palmer of Huntley & Palmer Biscuits.
Below: Site of former Huntley & Palmer biscuit factory in Reading.

Hambleden Mill, now converted to luxury flats.

- Biscuit manufacturing ceased in Reading in 1976 after all production was moved to the more modern factory in Liverpool. The UK HQ for Prudential Life Insurance moved in to replace many of the factory buildings. One building was preserved, the old recreation club headquarters that was used for social housing in Reading. The Huntley & Palmer logo can still be seen on one of the former factory buildings on the banks of the River Kennet.

Bulbs: Sutton's Seed Company was established at Market Place in 1837 overlooking the Saturday vegetable and general marketplace. The business, founded by John Sutton and his son Martin expanded rapidly, earning a reputation for supplying pure, unadulterated seeds.
- The railway had an important part in bringing large consignments of seeds, bulbs, and other supplies to Reading after 1840. It was also used to send wholesale orders which were too heavy to go by mail.
- Sutton's received Royal patronage in 1858, when Queen Victoria requested Martin Hope Sutton to supply seeds to the Royal household. The company has had Royal patronage ever since.
- In 1962, Sutton's Seeds moved from the Market Place to new premises on the A4 which was then still the main London-Bath Road. It was turned into Suttons Business Park after 1976 when production was finally moved to Torquay, Devon. Suttons Business Park became the first of many High Tech business parks in the area including nearby Thames Valley Business Park and the Winnersh Triangle.

Beer: Simonds brewed at the Seven Bridges Brewery along the River Kennet from 1790. It grew to becomes a major presence along the river for almost 200 years until its closure in 1978.
- Founded by William Blackall Simonds, the brewery was managed by a total of six generations of the Simonds family. It initially grew to became a major Berkshire brewer, then expanded abroad when it started to brew India Pale Ale for export in 1834.
- Simonds saw rapid growth after the world wars, winning major contracts with the military and acquiring a number of other breweries and pubs mostly in the Southwest of England. By 1945, Simonds had completed 16 acquisitions and owned 1400 pubs.
- The brewery initially made extensive use of the river and canals for trading, and later the railway was also an important form of transport, with the brewery having its own siding off the Coley branch line.
- The Simonds family made a decision to merge with Courage in 1960, ultimately resulting in Simonds as a brand being dropped by 1970.
- The Seven Bridges Brewery was closed in 1980, and by 1999, it became the site of the Oracle Shopping Centre on the east side of Bridge Street, with a number of residential apartment building developments on the west side of the old site.
- Brewing moved to a new Courage Berkshire Brewery in 1978, at Junction 11 of the M4 motorway. The Courage Brewery on the M4 was also closed in 2010. It is now the site of the Reading International Business Park, adjacent to Green Park High Tech Business Park and Madejski Football Stadium.

Above: Suttons Business park with Oracle HQ from nearby Thames Valley Business Park in the background.
Right: Advertisement showing the Simonds Seven Bridges Brewery.

19th and 20th century boundary changes

The 19th and 20th centuries saw demographic changes that were gradually reflected in new boundaries for many towns and villages. Changes in land management from Enclosure Acts and increased commuting from the railway service gradually resulted in boundary changes from strip parishes to modern villages with central populations organised around schools, churches and local businesses.

Ancient Chiltern strip villages —Many south Chilterns villages were historically organised as long, narrow, 'strip parishes' dating back to at least Anglo-Saxon times.

- The ancient strip parishes seem to have been developed to allow residents access to different types of scarce land resources across the length of the parish. Most people lived in the low lying areas by the river with access to water for transport, fishing and mills for crop processing. The narrow parishes stretched across several miles to offer access to a range of land types, encompassing common open fields for arable agriculture, woodland leading up the Chiltern Hills provided wood for fuel and construction, and common livestock grazing land was available on top of the hills.
- Churches were normally at populated areas near the river and can still be seen in close proximity along the river in Newnham, Mongewell, North Stoke and South Stoke.
- An iron age feature called Grim's Ditch separated the strip parishes of Mongewell and Newham Murren. As of 996 AD it was referred to as 'the old way' and may have originated as a border between the Catuvellauni and Atrebates tribes prior to Roman occupation.

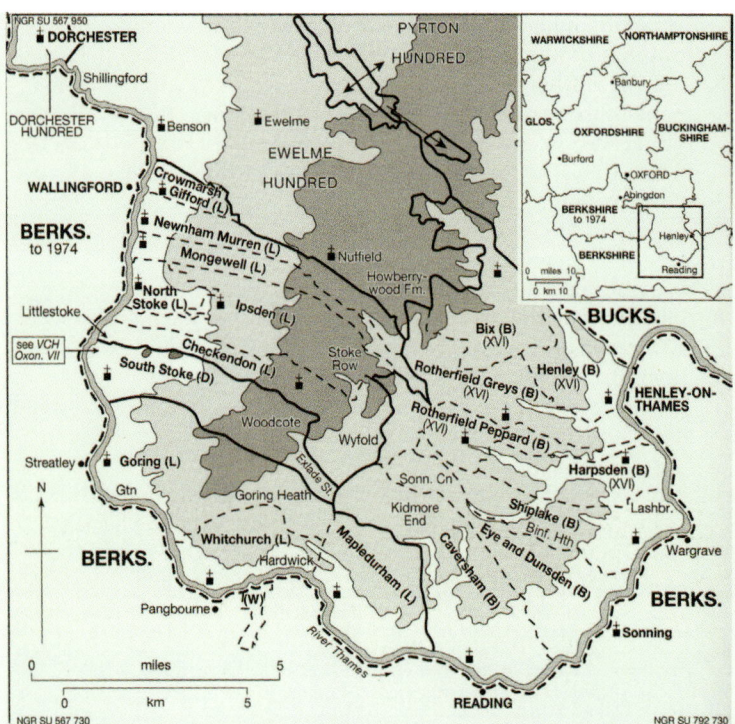

Ancient Strip parishes of South Oxfordshire at about 1845. Images on these two pages are courtesy of the Victoria History of the County of Oxford: Volume XX The South Oxfordshire Chilterns. © University of London

The ditch and earth works still stretch from near the river running up the Chilterns escarpment until at least Nuffield and may have even continued to the Thames at Henley making an enclosure at the bend of the river between Wallingford and Henley similar to the Dyke Hills at Dorchester. Grim's Ditch now coincides with the Ridgeway National Trail, and is used as a walking and cycling path, known by some of my fellow cyclists as the 'squiggly route' requiring a bit more technical skills.

Enclosure Acts — Land use changed when Enclosure Acts parcelled out previously common land to private owners that were then enclosed with fences or hedges.

- The main arguments for Enclosure Acts were to make the larger fields more productive, allowing use of modern farming methods such as crop rotation and the seed drill. Larger landowners, generally the lords of local manors, clearly benefited the most from Enclosure Acts as they received the most land to produce food in a more efficient manner. The new agricultural productivity meant fewer farmers were needed and many farm workers were forced to move to cities to find industrial work.

Grim's Ditch ancient earthworks — now a foot and cycle path on the Ridgeway.

Smaller land owners were allocated smaller plots proportionally, but some common land was still needed for poorer community members who lost their rights to previously common land.
- Each settlement needed specific Enclosure Acts approved by Parliament to ratify the reallocation of common land. Many Chiltern villages agreed Enclosure Acts quite early: Goring in 1788, Whitchurch in 1806, Goring Heath in 1812, and Whitchurch Common in 1813.
- South Stoke, which had its Enclosure Act approved in 1853 experienced a more significant impact, as it shared open fields in low lying areas that had been used since medieval times. According to local historian Vicky Jordan, Woodcote, which was part of the 'uphill' section of South Stoke parish, had 250 acres of common land that was parcelled out to new landowners to compensate for loss of access to common land. The Act included provisions for allotments, ponds, land for the poor, a recreation ground and new roads.
- The concept of common land for livestock grazing is now largely a thing of the past. Common livestock grazing is still allowed in Port Meadow in Oxford and Widbrook Common in Cookham for historic reasons and because residents have fought to keep these areas common over the centuries. They are now valued as a protection against over-development.

Population growth from the railway —The train service allowed a rapid population growth of many riverside villages with an influx of middle and upper income residents.
- In 1801 Maidenhead was still a small town of 949 residents, but by 1851 it's population had grown to 3603 and by 1901 it was 12,980.
- From 1840 to a 1901, Caversham grew as a suburb of Reading by over 440%, to a population of 7135, far exceeding that of Henley, which had historically been the largest town in South Oxfordshire.
- In 1911, Caversham moved from Oxfordshire to became part of Reading, accessing the better utilities and services that Reading could provide. Reading needed the land Caversham offered for expansion. Today, Caversham's expansion seems to have nearly reached its limit with a stark contrast between houses in the neighbourhoods on the more rural Oxfordshire side of the border. Development of 223 new homes on the site of a former golf course in neighbouring Emmer Green was initiated in 2023, filling one of the final remaining green gaps in that part of Reading. Rural villages such as Kidmore End on the Oxfordshire side fear that it is just a matter of time before they will be swallowed up by Reading's growth.
- Between 1821 and 1901, Goring and Shiplake, both served by new railway stations, grew by about 65%. Whitchurch, served by Pangbourne's station grew by 46%.

Civil parishes — The 1894 Local Government Act made it easier for strip parishes to be reorganised to more traditionally shaped

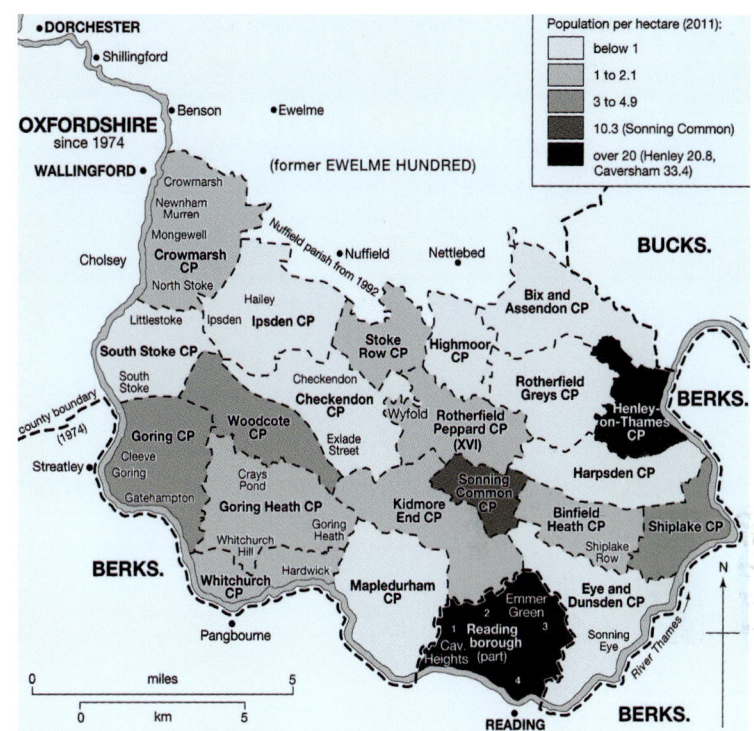

South Oxfordshire Civil Parishes as of 2020. Courtesy Victoria History of the County of Oxford, Volume XX.

villages centred around a High Street and central village population. At least four 'uphill' settlements of the strip parishes were created as Civil Parishes in 1952:
- Stoke Row was formed from the upland Chiltern Hills sections of what were previously parts of Ipsden, Crowmarsh, Newnham Murren and Mongewell strip parishes.
- The parish of Goring Heath, that includes a former commons at Whitchurch Hill, was created from 729 acres from what was the 'uphill' portion of Whitchurch-on-Thames combined with land provided from Goring.
- Woodcote was created from the uphill section of South Stoke strip parish. The village saw its growth increased significantly since WW II.
- Sonning Common's population had grown to 1400 by 1951, justifying its own parish council separate from Eye and Dundsen. During the 1960s and '70s several new estates were built, making it one of the larger villages in South Oxfordshire.
- Whitchurch-on-Thames had included 309 acres in what is now Purley and Sulham on the Berkshire side of the river as of 1878. This land was given back to Berkshire, except near the weir, where at least half of the Swan public house remained part of Whitchurch parish and Oxfordshire until 1991.

5. 20th Century to the present
— Cars, Planes and Rock Stars

1908 – *Wind in the Willows*

Author Kenneth Grahame's celebrated book *The Wind in the Willows* was influenced by his childhood memories of living in Cookham Dean. The book is evocative of country life along the River Thames, featuring the characters of Mole, Badger, Rat, Otter, and Mr Toad. As Rat famously said 'there is nothing – absolutely nothing – half so much worth doing, as simply messing about in boats'.

Grahame didn't have an easy life, but it seems he found solace in the Thames Valley with connections to Cookham, Pangbourne and Oxford.

- He was born in Edinburgh, Scotland where his mother tragically died of scarlet fever when he was five. His alcoholic father was unable to cope and sent Kenneth and his siblings to live with his maternal grandmother in Cookham Dean where he had fond memories of exploring the river environs. His uncle, David Ingles, was the curate at Cookham Dean church and would take them out on boat rides exploring the wildlife on the Thames. They lived at a grand home called The Mount for only a few years before leaving the village. Grahame moved back to Cookham Dean in 1906 as an adult with his wife Elspeth and their young son Alistair. They lived at Mayfield, now Herries Preparatory School, where he wrote the book in his spare time.
- Despite his wish to attend Oxford to study literature, Grahame's uncles decided he should follow a more traditional career in banking. He found success at the Bank of England, rising through the ranks and being appointed as Secretary of the Bank in 1898, working on writing in his spare time. He retired early in 1908, just after publication of *The Wind in the Willows*, due to ill health — most likely related to a politically-motivated shooting at the Bank, where he was shot at three times, but luckily was not hit.
- Grahame wrote *the Wind in the Willows* in 1907 in the form of bedtime stories and letters to his son Alistair, nicknamed 'Mouse'. Alistair was born blind in one eye and was plagued by health problems throughout his short life. Tragically, Alistair committed suicide whilst attending Oxford University in 1920.
- The book became very poplar in the USA. President Theodore Roosevelt was such a fan of it that he wrote to Grahame in 1909 stating that he 'read it and reread it and have come to accept the characters as old friends'. I can attest to its continued popularity in the States as both my sister and I performed in annual school plays of the book growing up in suburban Chicago in the early 1970s. My sister played the character of Mr Mole and a few years later I played the role of Tom Weasel.
- Many believe that Sir Charles Day Rose of Hardwick Estate in Whitchurch was used as a model for the eccentric Mr Toad, although other candidates have been proposed including the larger-than-life Colonel Ricardo of Lullebrook Manor in Cookham. Lullbrook Manor is now part of John Lewis' Odney Club used by the store's employees for training and retreats. Both men were the first in their villages to own a motor car with large horns on the side that went "Poop, Poop". At Hardwick Estate, the Rose family still affectionately refer to Sir Charles as Mr Toad.

Grahame lived in Pangbourne at Church Cottage, next to St James-the-Less church from 1924 until his death in 1932. In 1930, Grahame commissioned *Winnie the Pooh* illustrator E.H. Shepard to provide illustrations and had him visit the area along the Thames near Pangbourne for inspiration. Both Hardwick House and Mapledurham House are thought to have been used as models for Toad Hall. Grahame's funeral was held at St James-the-Less church in Pangbourne and he was buried at Holywell Cemetery in Oxford, sharing a grave and tombstone with his son Alistair who had been buried there as a student at Oxford's Christ Church College.

Left: The old Ditty café in Pangbourne, taken in 2006. The café was named after the 'Duck's Ditty' song that Ratty sang in the book.
Opposite page: Hardwick House, thought to be a model for illustrator E.H. Shepard for Toad Hall.

1913 – William Morris starts car production in Oxford

William Morris came to be known as the English equivalent of Henry Ford for his production of the Morris Minor and many other cars in the car factory that is now over 100 years old.

- Morris grew up in Oxford as a cycling enthusiast and started a cycle repair and sales business in the front of his parents' house at 16 James Street, Cowley. As his reputation for quality work grew, he steadily expanded the business into motorcycle and automobile repairs and sales, opening Morris Garages on Longwall Street in 1910, across from the wall bordering Magdalen College. This is where he designed and built his first prototype automobile, the Morris Oxford, known as the Morris Bullnose, in 1912.
- Needing room to expand, Morris purchased the old derelict Military Training College in Cowley that was the start of the auto plant that is still in operation over 100 years later. He used the three storey building to assemble his first order for 400 Morris cars in 1913.
- The First World War resulted in a slump in automobile sales, but Morris used his factory to secure a number of lucrative weapons contracts in addition to making cars. The factory initially made hand grenades, moving to production of naval mine sinkers (used to tether mines to the sea floor) at the rate of 2000 a week, thanks to his improved assembly line methods.
- Following the Wall Street Crash of 1929, the low cost Morris Minor —at £100— was Morris' solution to difficult economic times. The factory was modernised for the new car, becoming the largest car manufacturer in Europe. By 1937, it had produced 1 million cars and accounted for 30% of UK car sales. It continued to thrive following WW II, with another popular Morris Minor launched in 1948.
- Morris later became Lord Nuffield, named after the village near Wallingford where he settled, becoming one of the Britain's greatest philanthropists. His many gifts include endowment of Nuffield College at Oxford University. He chose his home in Nuffield partly because it was near the Huntercombe Golf Course he owned so he could enjoy his favourite sport. His former home, Nuffield Place, is now a National Trust property open to the public.
- The Cowley plant has gone through many changes and transfers of ownership since Lord Nuffield's death in 1963, but it is still a major industrial presence in Oxford. It became part of British Leyland and Rover Group and was then sold to BMW in 1994. In the 1960s and '70s it employed over 20,000 people. Today, the factory is somewhat smaller and the state of the art, highly automated, BMW Mini factory is dominated by robots, employing about 4000 to 5000 BMW 'associates'.

BMW relaunched the Mini in 2001, producing over 3 million Minis by 2016, averaging about 5000 per week. At a recent tour of the plant, I learned that despite being owned by a German company, the Mini is still very much a British made car.

- The steel for the car's frame is produced in Port Talbot, Wales.
- The steel is pressed at Mini production facilities in Swindon that produces 350 different components for the Mini body shell. The 'just in time' system means that when parts are requested at the plant in Oxford, the logistics team has four hours to get them there. Around 80-90 lorries with parts leave Swindon for Oxford each day. This doesn't include the daily deliveries from manufacturers of other components in the Oxfordshire area or other locations around the world.
- The Oxford Mini plant produces highly customised cars to meet bespoke customer requirements. Each car has a bar code and is produced to provide the specific optional features and colour schemes requested by each customer.
- Oxford is still the main production site for Minis worldwide, but some models are made in the Netherlands and there are plans for

Above: Site of Morris Garages, Longwall Street, Oxford.
Inset: William Morris with an early Morris Minor in 1928.

- The MG brand became popular worldwide, particularly in America, after soldiers discovered the car while in the UK during WW II with many veterans shipping the car to the States after the war.
- MGs continued to be built in Abingdon for 50 years, living through several parent company mergers until a until a British Leyland re-organisation resulted in the plant's closure in 1980. The devastating news of the closure came in 1979, literally a few days after the joyous celebrations held across the town marking 50 years of MG production in Abingdon.
- Production later continued under Rover with limited success. In 2005, the MG brand and was purchased by a Chinese company, who later merged with Shanghai Automobile Industry Corporation (SAIC) that still produces MGs including a number of electric SUV models as of 2024.
- North American sales accounted for more than half of MG sales after WW II, especially from 1962-1980. Classic MG sports cars are still very popular in the States with many enthusiasts making pilgrimages to Abingdon that is still considered the spiritual home of the MG.
- Visitors are still welcomed to Kimber House in Abingdon, the international HQ of the MG Car Club, housed next to the former factory's gates. There is a small museum and former employees still get together socially at least once a year over 40 years after closure of the factory.

Left: Today's highly automated Mini car factory at the Cowley Plant where manufacturing is predominantly performed by robots.
Below: Celebrating 50 years of MG production in Abingdon. Photo: Alan Davis.

a new plant in China. Both petrol and electric models are made in Oxford, but employees I spoke to believed the next generation electric models would initially be made at the China plant. In 2023 the UK Government announced a deal with BMW, said to be worth £75 million of incentives, to continue manufacturing Minis in the UK including the next generation of electric cars.

MG production in Abingdon — A special, sportier version of Morris cars, called the MG, was designed and produced by Cecil Kimber in 1924. Cecil had become manager of the original Morris Garage on Longwall Street which was still owned by William Morris and was being used as the Oxford sales and service outlet for Morris cars. The MG cars were named after Morris Garages (MG) where they were designed and initially produced.
- By 1928, the popularity of the MG line justified a new dedicated MG brand and factory being built at the site of an old leather factory in nearby Abingdon-on-Thames.

1891-1959 – Sir Stanley Spencer

Cookham's most famous son has helped to bring the charm of the village to the world's attention. Spencer's paintings depict Cookham as an earthly paradise beside the Thames. The village and its people are featured heavily in his artwork, often with an otherworldly air. His depictions of Christ's resurrection take place at the Cookham churchyard full of residents climbing out of their graves. His painting of the crucifixion brings a kind of terror to the village High Street with the villages' homes in the background.

Spencer was born and raised in Cookham, at Fernlea, on the High Street, built for his father by his master builder grandfather. Stanley was one of eight children in a musical and artistic family. His passion for painting led him to attend the Slade School of Art in London, the leading art school in London at the time, where his compatriots, including artists Paul Nash and Dora Carrington, knew him as 'Cookham', from his constant talk about the village and his habit of rushing back home for tea whenever possible.

His painting, *Swan Upping at Cookham* by the Cookham Bridge, shown below, was completed in 1919 after serving several years on the front line in the First World War in Macedonia. He started the

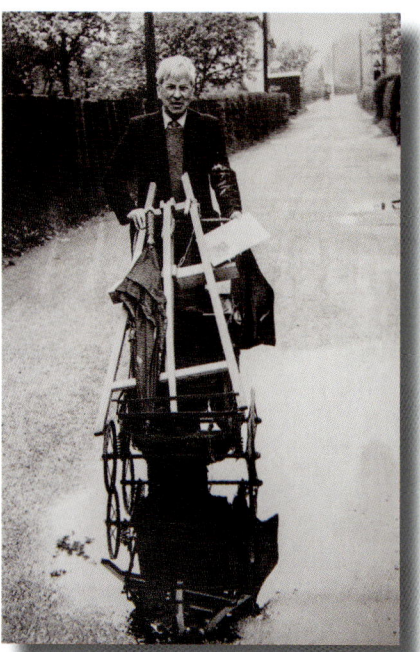

work before he left and used the thought of surviving the war and returning to Cookham to complete the painting as a source of hope.

Spencer had a sociable and ebullient personality, but was certainly quirky and unusual— definitely a village character. With two failed marriages, he was not particularly lucky in love, but had two daughters from his first marriage to his beloved Hilda. He struggled financially, depending on his art sales for his livelihood. He was known to denigrate his landscape paintings, calling them 'potboilers' to earn a living. The *Maidenhead Reporter* ran a story covering the Cookham Holy Trinity church's annual bazaar where one of Spencer's self-portraits was auctioned. Stanley had just painted it the night before and that morning. The vicar opened bidding at £1, and with encouragement s from Stanley and the vicar, that painting was sold for £11.

Spencer had some success during his lifetime, joining the Royal Academy in 1950 and earning a knighthood the year before he died, but his real fame came after his death. A retrospective exhibition at the Royal Academy in 1980 and subsequent exhibitions at the Tate and other galleries around the world sent prices for his paintings soaring. Today, Spencer's paintings typically go for hundreds of thousands of pounds with some well into the millions.

After a four year absence, Spencer moved back to the village in 1945 to Cliveden View, the small red-brick house on the High Road in Cookham Rise where he lived until his death in 1959. Spencer was well known amongst locals and could often be seen wandering down village lanes with his art supplies in a pram. Many in the village missed his presence after he was gone, but his spirit seems to lives on. The Stanley Spencer Gallery in the Cookham High Street continues to attract visitors from around the world.

Left: Stanley Spencer's painting *The Swan Upping*. Started before WWI in 1914 and completed upon his return in 1919. Photo courtesy of Tate Britain.
Above: A typical scene of Spencer wandering Cookham's streets with his painting equipment in a pram. Photo courtesy of Alamy.

1917 – Bloomsbury Group retreat in Tidmarsh — Writer Lytton Strachey and painter Dora Carrington moved to the old Mill House on the River Pang at Tidmarsh as a retreat from London life. Other members of the Bloomsbury Group helped to pay the rent and were also regular visitors. Whilst there, Dora met Bloomsbury Group author Ralph Partridge who fell in love with her. Carrington eventually agreed to marry him even though she was in love with Lytton Strachey, while Strachey was more interested in Partridge. After the wedding, the three went on honeymoon together in Venice and continued living together at Tidmarsh.

1920 - 1949 – The Kellys at the Henley Regatta

John B. Kelly, father of actress Grace Kelly from Philadelphia, was controversially banned from participating in the 1920 Henley Regatta because he worked as a bricklayer. This was considered a professional job as a manual labourer which did not comply with the HRR strict rules on amateurism. Many saw this as an attempt to prevent an American Olympic champion from winning the prestigious Diamond Single Sculls Cup. The offending references to manual labourers, mechanics, artisans and menial duties were later removed from HRR bye-laws in 1937.

The Kelly family were vindicated when Grace's brother Jack Kelly, Jr, known as 'Kell', won the Diamond Single Sculls in 1947 and 1949 at Henley. He also participated in the London Olympics in 1948 where the rowing events were held at Henley but was unsuccessful in winning a medal.

Getting to know the Kellys was a prime aim for many competitors as Jack's sister Grace was amongst the family party. This was before she found fame as an actress, but she still clearly had her movie star looks. She attended the regatta with her brother a number of times and British rowing champions Bert Bushnell and Tony Rowe both managed to secure dates with her. When she later became Princess Grace of Monaco through marriage, she returned as the regatta prize giver in 1981. In 2003, the Women's Quadruple Sculls trophy was named in her honour.

Above: Dora Carrington's 1918 painting of the Mill at Tidmarsh.
Right: 17 year old Grace Kelly, centre, at Henley in 1947 with her brother 'Kell' and sister Lizanne, right. Kell rowed for Vespers Rowing Club who are based on the Skuylkill River in Philadelphia.
Below: A plaque at the floor of the Angel on the Bridge at Henley.

Cliveden and the Astors

Cliveden was built by the 2nd Duke of Buckingham in 1666 above the river at Taplow near Cookham. The house has played host to virtually every British monarch since George I (1714-1727) and has been home to three dukes, an earl, and Frederick, the Prince of Wales. The Astors held the title of viscount. For those not familiar with the British honours system, duke and duchess are the highest hereditary peerage titles that can be bestowed by a monarch, apart from being a prince or princess, which are reserved for the children or grandchildren of a ruling monarch. The next four titles of the peerage in descending levels of rank are:
- marquess and marchioness
- earl and countess
- viscount and viscountess
- baron and baroness

Theses titles are normally hereditary in that they can be passed on to family members over generations, but now there is a 6th category called 'life peers' that is not hereditary. Since the Blair era, only life peer honours have been bestowed, with many hereditary peers being phased out.

The Duke of Westminster sold Cliveden House to William Waldorf Astor in 1893, America's richest citizen, despite concerns being raised by Queen Victoria, a frequent guest of the house.
- In 1906, William gave the house to his son Waldorf and his new American wife Nancy Langhorne, later Lady Astor.
- In 1919, after the death of William Astor, Waldorf Astor inherited his title as 2nd Viscount Astor and became a member of the House of Lords, forcing him to retire from being an MP for Plymouth Sutton. His wife Nancy Astor, now Viscountess Astor, ran for the seat at the by-election and became the first serving woman MP in British history. She was an outspoken MP for 25 years advocating women's roles in the civil service and calling for the minimum age limit for drinking to be set at eighteen. In 1945, she reluctantly stepped down after her colleagues and husband Waldorf advised her that she had lost touch with the social and cultural dynamics of the day. By this time 24 other women were acting as MPs.
- The 'Cliveden Set' was the name given to an intellectual and political group centred around Waldorf Astor and his wife Nancy Astor, in the 1930s leading up to the start of WWII. The group included many influential members of the media, including James Louis Garvin, editor of the *Observer* (which was owned by Waldorf Astor) and Geoffrey Dawson, editor of *The Times*. The group advocated the 'appeasement' of Nazi Germany and supposedly conspired to ensure that British foreign policy conformed to their beliefs. The Prime Minister Neville Chamberlain famously signed the Munich Agreement to allow Nazi Germany to annex the Sudetenland in the Czech Republic in exchange for Hitler's promise to end further territorial ambitions. Newspaper articles at the time held the Cliveden Set responsible for the events leading to Foreign Secretary Anthony Eden's resignation in January 1938. Despite their anti-war stance, the Astors invited the Canadian Red Cross hospital for wounded soldiers on the grounds of Cliveden that remained until 1985.
- Winston Churchill was said to be a periodic visitor to Cliveden, but he was clearly not a supporter of the views held by the Cliveden Set, and could, in fact, be seen as leader of the 'anti-appeasement' movement. He and Nancy Astor and were said to have had fiery exchanges as Members of Parliament. There are some famous insults that he is alleged to have made but it is not clear which ones are true. In one BBC radio interview, Lady Astor quoted Churchill as telling her, "When you entered the House of Commons, I felt like a woman had entered my bathroom and I had nothing to protect myself with except a sponge".
- In 1961, Cliveden was the source of controversy once again with the Profumo Affair. Nancy Astor's son, Bill Astor, invited a group of guests to stay, including John Profumo, British Secretary of State for War, Lord Mountbatten of Burma and the President of Pakistan. Elsewhere on the estate, Stephen Ward, a society osteopath and friend of Bill's, was staying at Spring Cottage with his guests, including nineteen year old Christine Keeler and Captain Yevgeny Ivanov, an assistant Soviet naval attaché who was also a spy. Bill and his dining companions strolled out of the house to the pool, where the married Profumo and Keeler met for the first time. The meeting sparked an extra-marital affair between the two which went on for some months afterwards. It became a national scandal after Keeler had sold her story to the papers, where she made it clear that she had also been sleeping with Ivanov at the same time as seeing Profumo. An extended investigation and trial is thought to have factored heavily in the defeat of the then-Conservative government in 1964, supposedly exhausted by scandal.

Cliveden is now a well-preserved luxury hotel and National Trust property open to the public. Situated along a lovely stretch of the Thames, Cookham-based Artist, Sir Stanley Spencer praised the area's beauty, reflecting that "you can't walk by the river at Cliveden Reach and not believe in God".

Opposite page: View of Cliveden over the river from Cookham through the hazel catkins.
Inset: Nancy Astor.

1932-1955 – J.R.R. Tolkien and *The Lord of the Rings*

Tolkien wrote *The Hobbit* and *The Lord of the Rings* whilst living and working in Oxford. These books were not just popular in the UK, but were a success in the USA and many other parts of the world, having been translated into 38 languages.

- Tolkien was Professor of Anglo-Saxon and Fellow of Pembroke College whilst writing *The Hobbit*, and then became Professor of English Language and Literature and Fellow of Merton College while writing *The Lord of the Rings*. He lived with his wife Edith and their children at 20 Northmoor Road in Oxford whilst writing *The Hobbit* and researching *The Lord of the Rings*. He later moved to Holywell Street and then to Headington before it was published.
- Tolkien recalled that he began work on *The Hobbit* one day in the early 1930s, when he was marking School Certificate Papers, and he found a blank page. Suddenly inspired, he wrote the words, 'In a hole in the ground there lived a hobbit.' In a similar manner to author Kenneth Grahame, he wrote the book in 1932 as a story to read to his three boys. A draft finally made its way to a publisher via a student who had a copy leading to the book's publication in 1937.
- Tolkien spent more than ten years writing the primary narrative and appendices for *The Lord of the Rings* sequel, during which time he received the constant support of the Inklings literary discussion group, in particular his closest friend C.S. Lewis, the author of *The Chronicles of Narnia* and many other notable books. The Inklings met during the 1930s and '40s to discuss passages of literary works that were in progress, usually held on Thursday evenings in C. S. Lewis' rooms at Magdalen College and Tuesdays at midday in the back room of the Eagle and Child Pub on St Giles in Oxford.
- Tolkien had a lifelong fascination with languages and is considered a linguistic genius by many for his ability to create his own languages for *The Lord of the Rings*. His study of Anglo-Saxon legends such as the dragon in Beowulf, and languages from the periods of Old English, Middle English, Welsh and Old Norse are thought to have influenced his names for some of the characters. Tolkien invented complete languages for the various races of men, dwarves, elves, tree ents and other creatures.
- The three volumes of *The Lord of the Rings* were initially published individually in 1954 and 55. The books had generally positive reviews, but it wasn't until a paperback version was released in the US in 1965 that sales really took off, keeping it number one on the New York Times best seller list for 8 weeks. They were a favourite of mine growing up in the States, reading them as a youth in the 1970s whilst living in New Jersey.
- The popularity of the books has been sustained over the years, especially since the release of *The Lord of the Rings* film trilogy in 2001 to 2003. Tolkien has ultimately become one of the best-selling authors in history. Estimates vary, but most put both *The Hobbit* and *The Lord of the Rings* trilogy in excess of 100 million copies sold each.
- In a survey conducted by the BBC in 2003 for 'The Big Read', *The Lord of the Rings* was voted the 'Nation's Best-loved Novel'.

99 Holywell Street where Tolkein and his family lived from about 1950 while writing *The Lord of the Rings*.

The Eagle and Child Pub Oxford, home to The Inklings Literary Club.

An inspection of Upper Thames Patrol troops, looking a bit like Dad's Army.

A WW II pillbox on the Thames Path near Goring.

World War II — Early part of the War: 1940-43

During the first World War, the need to guard strategic rail bridges over the Thames from attack was raised to the head of the Thames Conservancy at the time, Lord Desborough. As many of the lock keepers and other Conservancy members had volunteered for active service, there was a shortage of resources, so women and other volunteers were sought to look after many of the locks and guard the rail bridges. The Conservancy response for the Second World War was much more planned.

The Upper Thames Patrol was established to protect strategic areas along the Thames outside of London, from Teddington to Lechlade, in case of damage from bombing or a German ground invasion.
- Up to 5000 patrol members cruised the river and walked its banks for 24 hours a day from 1940 until November 1944.
- The patrol was divided into 5 battalions guarding different stretches of the river, each with its own headquarters, usually at a riverside pub.
- Initially their main duties were to protect the locks and weirs and ensure there was no enemy activity on the river, such as signalling to aircraft.
- From August 1940, all the bridges over the river were primed with explosives that could be detonated to prevent capture and use in the event of an invasion.

The GHQ Stop-line (General Headquarters) was a series of defensive lines set up across the country that consisted of strategically positioned concrete pillboxes, dragons teeth, and other tactics designed to defend against an expected German ground invasion. The remains of at least 6000 pillboxes are still dotted throughout the British countryside out of a total of 28,0000 that were rapidly built in 1940.
- The strategy was developed by General Edmund Ironside, Commander-in-Chief of the Home Forces, following Dunkirk, where the British army had to abandon most of its equipment and there was a need to at least slow down German forces until limited British forces could be mobilised. There was a real fear at the time that a German invasion by land involving tanks could be imminent.
- After coastal defences, the GHQ line was the next, or probably the last, line of defence designed to protect London and the industrial Midlands of England. A series of lines ran from Somerset in the west, around the south of London, up to Canvey Island in Essex and up the east coast to Yorkshire.
- This included a Blue Line that ran along the Kennet and Avon Canal to Reading and a Red Line that followed the Thames from Abingdon to Pangbourne and joined the Blue Line at Theale.
- It's hard to know how effective the GHQ Stop-lines would have been, but at the time, they were seen as a practical way of at least slowing attacks from tanks and buying critical time.

The Battle of Britain, 1940 — Instead of an invasion by sea or land, the initial hostile attacks were in the form of raids from the German Air Force, or Luftwaffe, known as the Battle of Britain overlapping with night bombing raids known as the Blitz. The Nazi attacks focussed on London, coastal areas such as Portsmouth, and some industrial centres such as Birmingham, however, isolated bombings were recorded throughout the Thames Valley. Between September and November 1940, records show that bombs were dropped at Cookham, Emmer Green, Goring Heath, Goring-on-Thames, Maidenhead, Marlow, Oxford, Streatley, Taplow, Thame, and Whitchurch-on-Thames. Whilst there were few causalities from these raids, one resulted in a person being killed in Goring and another raid killed someone in Marlow.

Devastation at Reading and Newbury — Following the Battle of Britain, there were only occasional bombing attacks in the Thames Valley, but the deadliest attack of the war came on Wednesday 10th February 1943, at about 4:30 in the afternoon, when Nazi Dornier bombers wreaked havoc in both Newbury and Reading.

- A single Dornier dropped eight bombs on the south side of Newbury resulting in 19 deaths and dozens more injured. With the sudden attack there had been no time for a warning siren, so some had assumed the aircraft was friendly and came out to see it only to be faced with machine-gun fire strafing the street. The bombs destroyed many homes and directly hit the Senior Council School, St Bartholomew's Alms Houses, and St John's church.
- At about the same time, another Dornier aircraft dropped four 500 kg bombs in Reading town centre, one of which demolished the Market Arcade on Friar Street housing the popular British restaurant chain, the People's Pantry, killing 29 people. Had it not been Wednesday, an early closing day, casualties would have been even worse. Another bomb hit the front of the church of St Laurence by the Town Hall. A total of 41 people were killed that day in Reading with a further 137 casualties being reported, including many amputations and other serious injuries. The raid was by far the worst of around 20 air attacks on Reading during the war.

Photographic reconnaissance — Intelligence gained from interpretation of aerial photography at RAF Medmenham was not as famous as the code breaking activities that were underway at Buckinghamshire's Bletchley Park, but the images provided most of the practical intelligence information required for virtually every operation. It provided insight into everything from bombing targets, to weather, troop movements and bomb damage assessment. The unit at Medmenham even discovered the V1 flying bomb sites that would later be successfully attacked. Medmenham provided extensive intelligence on targets in advance of Operation Chastise, more famously known as the Dambusters raid, one of the most iconic RAF missions during the war.

The two key airfields focussed on sending planes on clandestine photo reconnaissance flights were RAF Heston and RAF Benson. As Heston was close to London, it was subject to a number of bombing raids during the Blitz and photographic intelligence operations were moved to Benson in Oxfordshire where the flights were planned and photographs developed. Many of the photo reconnaissance missions were launched from RAF Chalgrove and Mount Farm airfield, both satellites of Benson.

- From 1941, RAF Medmenham was based at Danesfield House, now a luxury hotel at Marlow, Buckinghamshire. Known as the Central Intelligence unit, it acted as the main imagery intelligence base for the Reconnaissance and Photography Section of the Royal Air Force. The workforce grew to 1700 personnel organised into 20 sections of intelligence teams to analyse thousands of images on an industrial scale. The photo interpreters included many US and other allied personnel, especially leading up to D-Day, requiring the extensive use of temporary huts across the grounds of the estate.

Danesfield House near Marlow, home to RAF Medmenham, HQ for photo intelligence operations.

- Experts at RAF Medmenham analysed the images produced by RAF Benson throughout the war to identify strategic bombing targets. A secret map-making team of 150 experts at Hughenden Manor in High Wycombe had the task of producing the maps of the targets that the US and British bomber crews would use. Hughenden Manor, better known as the historic country house used by Victorian Prime Minister Disraeli, was close to the US 8th Air Force HQ at nearby RAF Daws Hill and RAF Bomber Command at High Wycombe.
- The task of executing the raids using these maps for the RAF fell to Air Chief Marshal Arthur 'Bomber' Harris. The USAAF 8th Airforce was commanded by General James Doolittle.
- Image intelligence operations continued at Danesfield House until they were moved to RAF Benson by 1977.

Preparations for the D-Day invasion, 1942-44

According to the Imperial War Museum, over 2 million troops from more than 12 countries were in Britain in preparation for the invasion on the 6th of June 1944. 1.4 million of these soldiers were from the United States, mostly arriving in 1943 and early 1944. D-Day preparation affected almost all parts of the United Kingdom. A large focus was on the south coast of England where troops prepared for the amphibious landing craft assault across the channel to Normandy. The Thames Valley played a number of important roles due to its strategic location. The area around Berkshire and Oxfordshire was generally not the target of German bombing attacks that were focussed on London, the south coast and midland industrial centres, yet it was close enough to the continent to act as a place to gather troops, perform critical training operations and launch the invasion from.

The organisational structure of the US troops participating in D-Day is somewhat complicated for most non-military personnel, including myself, but I will do my best to explain it for at least the US troops present in the Thames Valley leading up to D-Day. It gives you an idea of the ambition and complexity of the entire operation.

- The D-Day invasion, known as 'Operation Overlord', was led by General Eisenhower who was the Supreme Commander of the Allied Forces in Europe. This included troops from many nations, with the biggest contributions from the US, UK, and Canada. Eisenhower was primarily based in Allied Forces Headquarters London, his temporary home in Kingston-on-Thames, and in the days leading up to D-Day, he was mostly based at Southwick House outside of Portsmouth.
- US General Lewis Brereton, a colourful and controversial figure with a long military history, was Commander of the US 9th Air Force, with HQ at the royal family's country house Sunninghill Park, adjacent to Windsor Great Park in Ascot. The 9th Air Force was the US arm of the Allied Expeditionary Air Force for D-Day that had over 220,000 personnel assigned to it in the months leading up to D-Day. The 9th Air Force included around 5000 aircraft, made up of 160 squadrons. It played a crucial role in establishing air supremacy and targeting Nazi military infrastructure ahead of the D-Day invasion.
- Within the US Air Force, the 53rd Wing was responsible for paratrooper and glider operations. The 53rd Wing was split into at least 6 groups of squadrons dedicated to carrying troops and equipment, each at their own RAF airfield with specific missions for dropping troops and gliders in various parts of Normandy on D-Day.

The village of Aldbourne, outside of Hungerford where Easy Company from *Band of Brothers* was based.

The 101st Airborne Division had its HQ at Greenham Lodge mansion house at Greenham Common, Newbury. Nicknamed 'Screaming Eagle', the division consisted of a number of paratrooper and glider regiments that were assigned to different groups of the 53rd Wing. Each Regiment consisted of a number of smaller companies that could be assigned to various missions.

- The 101st Airborne Division Regiments were based along the Kennet River Valley primarily near Newbury and Hungerford from September 1943 – September 1944. Some were also in Basildon House along the Thames near Pangbourne.
- The 506th Parachute Infantry Regiment was headquartered at historic Littlecote House outside of Hungerford. This regiment included a number of companies, including E Company, also known as 'Easy Company' in the famous TV series *Band of Brothers*. Easy Company was based in the nearby picturesque village of Aldbourne to prepare for the D-Day invasions, and later returned to Aldbourne to prepare for deployment to 'Operation Market Garden' in September 1944 which was depicted in the film *A Bridge Too Far*.

Historic Littlecote House near Hungerford, headquarters for the USAAF 506th Paratroopers.

Strategic airfields — At least two dozen airfields were rapidly developed throughout the Thames and Kennet River Valleys to support the war efforts including the D-Day invasion of Europe. Several RAF bases along the Kennet Valley were handed over to the US 9th Air Force to support the 53rd Wing that was responsible for troop carrier and glider operations for D-Day. The main transport airplanes were the Douglas C-47, known as Dakotas, that either carried paratroopers directly or pulled glider aircraft full of troops and equipment. Gliders were lightweight, engineless aircraft often used to deploy troops, jeeps and other vehicles.

- The 434th Troop Carrier Group at RAF Aldermaston – opened in 1942 on the grounds of a large Victoria Manor House called Aldermaston Court. It is now the site of the UK's nuclear weapons research and development centre, described later.
- The 435th Troop Carrier Group at RAF Welford – was completed in April 1943, located between Newbury and Membury. The base is still in use and accessible via the M4 junction that states it is for 'Works Units Only' near Junction 14. It is said to be used by the US Air Force (USAF) as a munitions store for other UK and European bases.
- The 436th Troop Carrier Group (TCG) at RAF Membury – similar to RAF Heston, Membury was located by the now well known M4 service area of the same name between Junctions 14 and 15. Remnants of the runways and hangars and airfield are still clearly visible at a light industry business park now on the site.

Below: Map of strategic WW II RAF airfields along the Kennet and Thames Valleys.

Above: Eisenhower on the night before D-Day, June 1944, at RAF Greenham Common. © US Library of Congress.

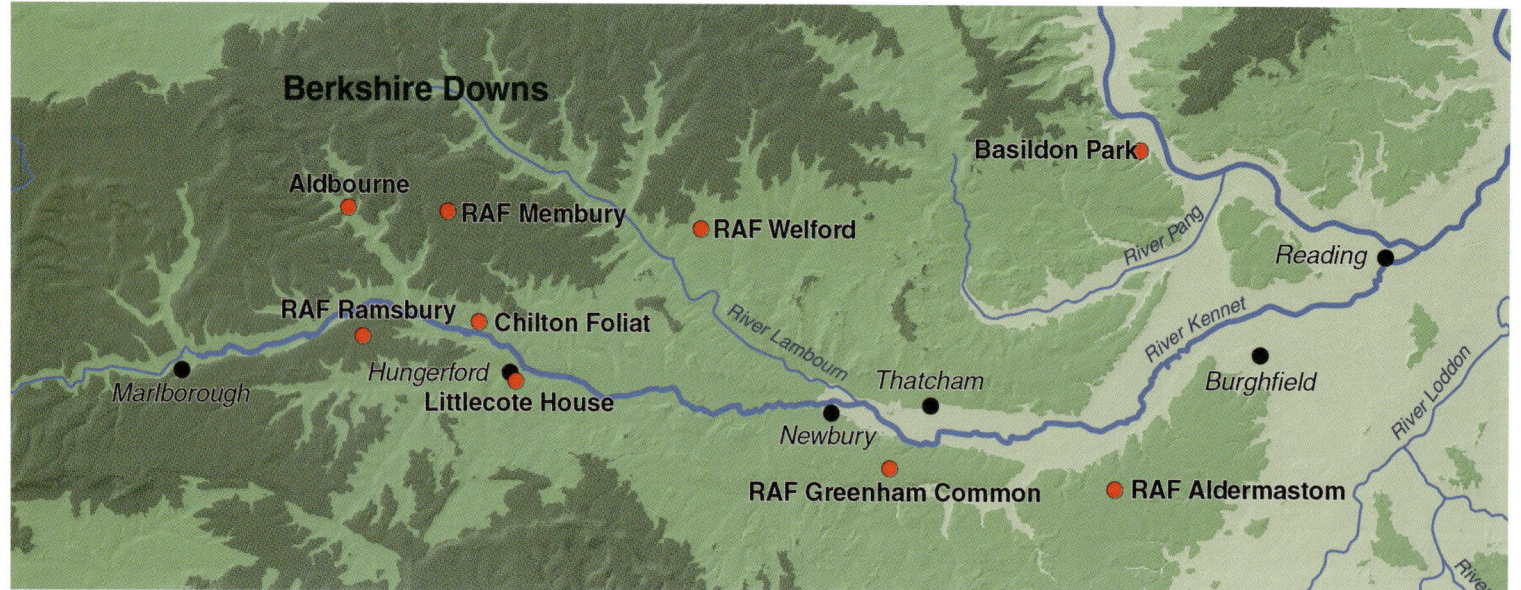

Aerial photo of RAF Greenham Common (on right) and Newbury Racecourse (on left) in December 1943 six months before D-Day. The racecourse can be seen being used as a logistics depot with rows of containers of military equipment linked to the GWR line. Photo ©Historic England Archive. USAAF Photography.

- The 437th TCG at RAF Ramsbury – built in 1942, it was returned to agricultural use following the war. What remains is now largely overgrown, but concrete foundations of former buildings and runways are still visible in some places.
- The 438th TCG at RAF Greenham Common – opened in 1942 outside of Newbury on the site of Greenham Lodge estate that had been purchased by Newbury Council in 1939.

RAF Greenham Common – The USAAF 101st Airborne paratroopers and gliders were assigned to the 438th Troop Carrier Group at RAF Greenham Common. Early in the morning of the the D-Day invasion, well before daylight, they were flown to Drop Zone A, east of St-Mere-Eglise in Normandy.
- On the night of 5th June 1944 Allied Commander Eisenhower joined Lieutenant General Lewis Brereton at Greenham Common to watch the first troops leave and give his famous "the eyes of the world are on you" speech to motivate the men before their daunting mission. The tall man facing Ike on the right, wearing the number 23 around his neck, is 1st Lieutenant Wallace C. Strobel from the 502nd paratroopers Easy Company based in Chilton Foliat (not to be confused with Easy Company in *Band of Brothers* who where in 506th Regiment located nearby in Aldbourne). Lt. Strobel survived the night and the rest of the war, dying in 1999. The 502nd jumped into Normandy with 792 men. After six days of desperate fighting, only 129 were able to make the road march back to St Come-du-Mount. Strobel was the jumpmaster for his Company who were assigned to plane 23 hence the number around his neck. He later remembered that he and Eisenhower spoke about fly fishing in Michigan along with his readiness for the mission.
- More than 80 Dakota transport planes dropped either paratroopers or pulled glider aircraft from Greenham Common that night, taking off at an average of 18 seconds per aircraft. As seen in the photo above, the Newbury Racecourse acted as a massive logistics base to support the operation linking to the GWR.
- The initial D-Day drops from Greenham saw little resistance so no planes were lost, but 26 pilots in close formation dropped paratroopers 3 miles south of target Drop Zone A due to problems with the lead pilot's radar set.

RAF Aldermaston was home to the USAAF 434th Troop Carrier Group that launched 52 Dakota aircraft early on D-Day morning pulling gliders with troops from the 101st Airbourne to Landing Zone E, just south of St-Mere-Eglise in Normandy.
- The glider's cargo included 16 anti-tank guns, 25 vehicles (including a bulldozer), 155 men, plus ammunition and other supplies. Delivery and release of the gliders was successful, but landing the gliders was difficult due to poor visibility and most crash-landed outside the intended landing zone. Despite many gliders striking a tree or ditch, most loads were successfully landed without harm. In one glider, assistant division commander Brigadier General Pratt was killed along with the co-pilot. A fictional account of the events following his death was portrayed in the film *Saving Private Ryan*. Total casualties were 5 dead, 17 injured, and 7 missing.
- Two further missions were launched from Aldermaston in the next 24 hours with additional gliders, further reinforcing the troops at Normandy.
- Aldermaston Court, the Victorian manor house located about a half mile north of RAF Aldermaston became the HQ for US 9th Air Force's Air Support Command. Led by Brigadier General 'Opie' Weyland, it became famous for the close air support it provided to General Patton's Third Army in his 400 mile gallop across France. Patton is said to have called Weyland 'the best damned general in the Air Corps'.

Many smaller Thames Valley airfields included those at Hampstead Norries, Chalgrove, Henley (Crazies Hill), Theale, White Waltham, Woodcote, Woodley, and Benson that were used for training, maintenance, logistics and many other war preparations.

Bailey Bridge building at Pangbourne with Whitchurch Bridge in the background.

Bailey Bridge building — The Thames at Pangbourne was used by the British, Canadian, and American armies to practice building temporary Bailey Bridges from 1943 to 1946. The large white house on the river by the toll bridge in Whitchurch-on-Thames, called Thames Bank (now split into three homes), served as bridge building training HQ leading up to D-Day, initially for British Royal Engineers, then for their Canadian and American counterparts.
- Exercise Spartan was carried out by the RAF using Bailey Bridges across the Thames between Reading and Oxford in March 1943. The goal of the exercise was to practice close air support for invading armies in preparation for D-Day and included the Canadian Army, the XII British Corps, and the Australian Air Force. Australian Squadron leader Peter Billyead led 12 aircraft on a simulated attack of Goring and later Pangbourne.
- The Pangbourne Working Men's Club served as a kitchen and mess hall for the multinational regiments in the months leading up to D-day. According to former club chairman Dave Wilson, "after exercising on and in the mud, muck and muddy waters of the River Thames, these soldiers had at least somewhere warm and dry to eat their meals and recover". Since about 2017 the club quietly dropped 'Working Men' from the name of the club

The Pangbourne Working Men's Club served as the kitchen for WW II soldiers working on the river during bridge building training.

A souvenir left by US Army Engineers in Nettlebed woods during D-Day preparations. The castle is the logo of the US Army Corps of Engineers.

after more than 120 years to become known as 'The Pangbourne Club'. Whilst locals still refer to it as 'The Workies', the new name is intended to be more inclusive, as membership is not limited to blue collar workers and women and families are also welcome.
- It is said that General Eisenhower came to Pangbourne to meet his old friend General Mark Clark for lunch in the months leading up to D-Day. Eisenhower was also said to be in Pangbourne for a major allied demonstration of bridge building in 1944.
- Remains of concrete foundations used for D-Day troops can still be seen in the woods near the Nettlebed Saw Mill. A small stone 'castle' was built near there replicating the logo from the US Army Corps of Engineers badge. It is likely that the camp was used by US Army Engineers as a training base, probably to practice building bridges at nearby Pangbourne.

Military use of historic homes – As so many historic country mansions were requisitioned for use during the war, it almost seems as if the US military had a penchant for choosing these grand historic homes as their base. Lt General Brereton, who chose Sunninghill Park for the US 9th Air Force HQ was described by General Omar Bradley as "marginally competent … (and) more interested in living in the biggest French chateau".

Hitler appeared to have his eye on using Blenheim Palace, just north of Oxford, as Germany's post-invasion HQ for an occupied Britain. This would have been particularly ironic given that Blenheim was Winston Churchill's birthplace and owned by Churchill's relative, the Duke of Marlborough. Thankfully, this never happened, but Blenheim did play its part in the war hosting Malvern College evacuees. It was also used by the British MI5 Intelligence Service as its base until the end of the war when it was forced to leave London.

After the War, from 1945

RAF Aldermaston became the site of the Atomic Weapons Research Establishment (AWRE) in 1950. The atomic bomb was one of the great scientific and engineering achievements to come out of WW II — also one of the most dangerous and controversial. The UK became part of the small club of powerful nations with nuclear weapon capabilities that was, and still is, seen by many as essential for national security and for preventing nuclear war.
- Clearly not everyone agreed with the UK's development of nuclear weapons. Aldermaston became the site of a number of large anti-nuclear weapon protests in the 1950s and '60s, sometimes measuring up to 10,000 participants. These protests are no longer happening but clearly the UK strategy for use of nuclear weapons is still a political issue.
- Now called AWE, the facility continues to operate as the UK's focal point for the design, manufacture, support and disposal of the UK's Trident nuclear arsenal. AWE co-operates with Los Alamos National Laboratory in the United States and other facilities including those needed to perform nuclear tests in the Nevada underground test site.

Greenham Common continued to be a strategic US Air Force base until its closure in 1992. In 1980, RAF Greenham Common was selected as one of two British bases for the US Air Force's mobile Ground Launched Nuclear Cruise Missiles. As with Aldermaston, this was controversial with Greenham Common becoming synonymous with anti-nuclear protests, the most famous being the Greenham Common Women's Peace Camp that continued

Greenham Common Women's Peace Camp in 1980s.© Bridget Boudewijn

permanent protests for 20 years. Since the base closed, it has been converted to a business park and public open space mostly used for walking dogs and cycling.

Polish refugee camps were set up in South Oxfordshire and other parts of the country after the war following their displacement by the Nazi's in 1939. Many Polish citizens had become British soldiers and then decided to stay after the war, given the Stalinist control of Eastern Europe after 1945. The UK government allowed for 200,000 Polish refugees to become British citizens in the 1947 Resettlement Act. The Polish Resettlement Corps was established to help them prepare for civilian life in Britain.

- Refugee camps were set up in Checkendon and Whitchurch in 1948. They were both self-contained communities with shops, catholic churches, community halls and cinemas. They had amateur dramatic groups, choirs and traditional Polish dance groups. The remains of some of the semi-circular Nissen huts can still be seen in the woods on the outskirts of Checkendon near the Black Horse Pub.
- A Polish church remained at the Whitchurch site and continued to be used until it became derelict and was removed in recent years. A memorial garden at the site of the Polish Catholic Church was established in 2022 that acts as a tribute to the local Polish refugee camps.
- During the war, the Checkendon camp is thought to have formed part of RAF Woodcote where the 70th Maintenance Unit was based. Remains of the Woodcote RAF unit can also be seen in the woods along Long Toll Road. After the war, but prior to it being a Polish refugee camp, the Checkendon site was also used to house Italian Prisoners of War.

Derelict WW II Nissen huts used for Polish refugee camps can still be seen in the woods at Checkendon.

Opening of the Polish Refugee Camp Memorial Gardens in Whitchurch in 2022 by former residents of the camp, Anna Szczeponek on the left who still lives at the site of the camp on Manor Road, 95-year-old Maria Kowal cutting the ribbon aided by her daughter Bronislawa Towner. Photo ©Nick Brazil.

- The Whitchurch camp was established on the site of Coombe Park Camp, originally developed for Canadian and American troops in the area participating in bridge building operations at Pangbourne. All the Nissen huts were replaced by council houses in the 1950s on what is now Manor Road. There were also four flat-roofed buildings built by the Candian Army. One of these remains, but it now has a pitched roof and is used as the Whitchurch Village Hall.

Mount Farm Airfield, located between Dorchester-on-Thames and RAF Benson, became a refugee camp for various destitute and homeless squatters living in the Nissen huts similar to other refugee camps across the country. It was eventually developed into a housing estate as the new village of Berinsfield in the 1960s.

- The name came from St Birinus who brought Christianity to the West Saxons in 671AD at the nearby town of Dorchester, followed by 'field', as the Americans called the airfield. By 1971, the town had a population of over 3000 residents. The housing mix was 75.5% owned by local authorities and only 19% owner occupied. As the national average for properties owned by local authorities was 30%, this made Berinsfield effectively a very large council estate.
- In his book *Landmark in Time*, Peter Adamson talks about the challenges the new village faced in its early years housing so many working class families. One of the early tensions was between the existing squatters who were finally moved into new homes, being resentful of those being allocated homes from other parts of the county. Another tension was between those who looked after their homes and those who were seen as

'unsatisfactory tenants', who were defined by sociologists in one study as 'rent in arrears, neglect of house and garden, and a nuisance to the community'.

- 50 years later, things at Berinsfield have moved on and the village has developed a strong sense of community but still suffers from a poor self image. The Berinsfield Neighbourhood Plan refers to a 2012 report stating the '1960s & 1970s architecture bears more relation to a run-down urban district of a town or city than to a rural village'. Adamson makes the point that Berinsfield is now a typical UK community by most measures and actually above average in terms of employment and home ownership rates, and well below average on those claiming job seekers allowance and crime rate. One of the challenges is that it sits in a rather isolated location amongst so many other higher than average income communities in the Thames Valley. According to Rightmove.com, in 2023, the average house price in Berinsfield was £274,000 whereas in nearby Dorchester-on-Thames, homes sold for an average of £930,000, and houses in Cookham, Streatley and Marlow averaged over £1 million.

Berinsfield football club scores in a home game win against rivals Compton in the North Berkshire football league — despite being in Oxfordshire since 1974.

Heathrow Airport was developed on the site of the privately owned Great West Aerodrome in Harmondsworth during WWII. The government requisitioned the airfield, ostensibly for use by long-distance military aircraft destined for Japan, although Harold Balfour, who was Under Secretary of State for Air during the war, admitted in his 1973 autobiography that it was always intended to be used for civil aviation after the war. He had used the pretext of the war needs to avoid lengthy and costly public consultation of acquiring the ideally situated global transport hub. This policy was also supported by the Labour government that came into power in 1945 after the war.

- London Airport opened in 1946 as the nation's first civil international airport. To avoid later confusion with other airports in the London area, such as Gatwick and Stansted, it changed its name to Heathrow in 1966 after the farm that used to be at the site.
- Located just south of Windsor, within easy access from Reading and the rest of the Thames Valley, it has contributed significantly to the area's growth.
- It is the busiest airport in the UK, and as of 2019, Heathrow was providing flights to over 80 million passengers.
- Construction of a third runway at Heathrow was approved by the government in 2020, but the reduction in travel patterns since the pandemic has put that in doubt.

The 1947 Flood — The Thames Valley experienced its most severe flooding of the 20th century in early 1947 after a particularly cold winter. Most of England, and the southeast in particular, had been hit by blizzards which were severe enough to freeze some reaches of the Upper Thames. The heavy snow was followed by a period of relatively warm weather, causing the snow to quickly melt on top of the still-frozen ground, giving it nowhere to drain.

- Maidenhead and Windsor were particularly badly damaged. Although there were no deaths as a consequence of the flooding, the shock was sufficient to put flooding on the political agenda.
- A number of local flood relief schemes were tried, but the Jubilee River was eventually built by the Environment Agency to reduce the risk of flooding for approximately 3000 properties in Maidenhead, Windsor, Eton and Cookham. The Jubilee River is a man-made 11.6 km stretch of river that runs parallel with the Thames to channel water from above Maidenhead to below Windsor. Originally conceived in the 1980s, the £110 million project was started in late 1990s and completed in 2002. Although it has proved successful in protecting Maidenhead and Windsor, residents of villages downstream, such as Wraysbury and Old Windsor, claim it has increased flooding for them.

Periodic flooding continues to plague nearly all villages along the river with significant floods threatening homes in 2003, 2007, 2013/14 and 2024. Despite ongoing efforts to improve drainage for vulnerable properties, when severe flooding comes, sometimes no amount of sandbags can stop the rising tide.

Below left: The normally land-based Henley Mermaid looks at home after flooding in 2014.
Below right: Wellies were the best way to get around a flooded Cookham in 2003.
Opposite: In winter months it is not unusual for the many flood plains along the river to be covered in water like these at Hardwick Estate.

1971 – The Reading Festival was originally known as the National Jazz Festival and ran in various locations around London until it found a permanent home in Reading. It was officially called the Reading Festival of Folk and Progressive Music in 1971, held on Friday to Sunday 24-27 June. Headline Acts in 1971 included Rory Gallagher, Lindisfarne, Arthur Brown, Wishbone Ash and Al Kooper. Arthur Brown came on stage hanging from a 12 foot cross at the front of the stage and pleased the crowd with his song 'Fire'. US 1950s retro group Sha Na Na were joined onstage by the Who's drummer Keith Moon who came along for the party.

The Reading Festival is the longest running popular music festival in the world, celebrating its 50th Anniversary in 2021. Now held on the August Bank Holiday weekend, with over 100,000 tickets sold every year, it has become a right of passage for many in their teens and early 20s who camp out over the three day weekend. Over the years it has changed its focus to genres such as punk, new wave, indie, heavy metal and rock. Since 1999, a second festival is held at Leeds on the same weekend with both festivals selling out rapidly due to increasing popularity.

In 1988, the festival reached a low point when Bonnie Tyler completed her set despite having trouble with some of the crowd being clearly drunk and hurling things at her and the band. Meat Loaf was on next and were hit with flattened tins and large soda bottles full of urine from the start. After the first song, Meat Loaf chastised the crowd for treatment of his friend Bonnie Tyler and then left the stage after only two numbers. They eventually returned for a third number and according to Meat Loaf's guitar player Alan Merrill "the bottles and tins came in faster and more furious at us. Meat Loaf spotted one of the culprits, a ringleader, and actually jumped off the stage and started beating one of them up. Then another, then another. All the while we're vamping on a chord, taking solos, filling time. While our fearless leader was beating up the audience". Meat Loaf then made a throat slicing finger motion for the band to cut it short and they left the stage permanently.

1968-73 – Led Zeppelin – If the D-Day invasion involved over one million yanks coming 'over here' during WWII, the British invasion of America was the 1960s and '70s in the form of pop and rock music from the likes of the Beatles, the Rolling Stones, and Elton John. Like many people growing up in America in the 1970s and '80s, I was a huge fan of British rock music. British songs from this 'classic rock' period are still widely played on American radio stations. So I was somewhat surprised to learn that one of the biggest bands, Led Zeppelin, got their start in Pangbourne, a stone's throw away from my house — and this was not even widely known in the area.

- Jimmy Page formed Led Zeppelin whilst living in a relatively small house along the Thames in Pangbourne, known as 'The Boathouse', adjacent to the historic Swan Inn pub. The story is that singer Robert Plant took the train down from Birmingham to Pangbourne to meet with Jimmy during the summer of 1968 to talk about joining his new band, a follow-on group to the recently disbanded Yardbirds. Plant agreed to join the band after spending an afternoon at The Boathouse talking about music and playing records.
- The Boathouse is where Led Zeppelin rehearsed for their first tour in Scandinavia and for their first few albums. Page came up with the

Young music fans crossing the temporary bridge that is assembled each year for the Reading festival to allow fans to cross access the festival from car parking and camp-sites on the Oxfordshire side of the river.

Jimmy Page at the Boathouse in Pangbourne with the weir and lock keepers house visible in the background, circa 1968.

famous riff for 'Whole Lotta Love' in the summer of 1968 and first played it to band members in the living room while rehearsing for their first album. The song was used on their second album, Led Zeppelin II, which they also routined at The Boathouse prior to recording the album at Olympic Studios in Barnes. 'Friends' from their third album was written on The Boathouse balcony. In his self-titled book, Jimmy Page refers to "a particularly energy about the house and it was a catalyst for everything that went on."

- Surprisingly there are no records of any noise complaints – what would the neighbours think today?
- Jimmy continued to live in the area having lived in Windsor and the village of Sonning. His daughter, rock photographer Scarlet Page, was born at the Pangbourne house and is now based in Henley.

Rock and roll valley—The Thames Valley has been a popular place for rock stars to escape to the countryside over the years making it an important part of rock'n roll history:

- George Harrison of the Beatles lived in Henley at the grand and eclectic Friar's Park mansion from the 1970s until his death in 2001. He was known to frequent his local pub, The Row Barge, including at least one occasion where he performed with his friend Eric Clapton. Harrison's widow, Olivia, still lives at Friar Park.
- John Lennon and Yoko Ono famously lived at Tittenhurst Park in Ascot where their album *Imagine* was recorded.
- Elton John lives with his partner David Furness on their 37-acre Old Windsor estate on the edge of Windsor Great Park — the site of his infamous 'white tie and tiara' balls. Elton recorded *A Single Man* and other albums at 'The Sol' studio at a former mill house on the Thames in nearby Cookham. The studio was built by his producer Gus Dudgeon in 1975 and was later owned by other local musicians Jimmy Page and Chris Rea.
- Kate Bush, known as somewhat of a recluse, lived in another old mill house on an island on the River Kennet in Theale outside of Reading until recently moving further afield to the west country.
- George Michael enjoyed village life in Goring at his country home, at yet another old mill house on the Thames called Mill Cottage, in the centre of the village until his death there on Christmas Day 2016.
- Pete Townsend, guitarist and songwriter for The Who, lived in a house on the river in Goring with his first wife. He had a private recording studio at the house and used it to write and record demo songs for the *Quadrophenia* rock opera. The house, known as The Temple, near Cleeve Lock, has since been rebuilt.
- The Spice Girls got their start whilst living in an unassuming house at 58 Boyne Hill Road in Maidenhead. They lived there for nine months in 1993-94 after being selected from about 400 applicants to an ad posted by a management company that had the idea to form an all girls band. The house was owned by one of the financiers.
- Deep Purple was one of many bands to record at Hook End Manor in Checkendon. Keyboardist Jon Lord lived at Fawley, Henley, and bassist Ian Paice still lives in the area. Trevor Horn, from The Buggles, owned and ran Hook End Manor as a studio known as Sarm Hook End for a number of years, recording bands such as the Kaiser Chiefs, Morissey, and the Manic Street Preachers. The house was previously owned by Dave Gilmore of Pink Floyd and Alvin Lee of Ten Year's who built the original studio there.
- Genetic Studios in Streatley was built in a home high on the Berkshire Downs overlooking the Thames by producer Martin Rushent. The studio was where the iconic 1981 album, *Dare*, by Human League was recorded. In 2009, a large brick mansion controversially received planning permission on the site that can now be seen from many views in the area.
- Mick Jagger lived in an historic manor house outside of Newbury call Stargroves in the 1970s. The Stones used their mobile recording studio to record key tracks at the house from *Sticky Fingers*, *Exile on Main Street* and *Its Only Rock'n Roll*.

Tributes from fans outside George Michael's home in Goring after his death in 2016.

1971 – The M4 — The M4 Motorway opened from Junction 8/9 at Maidenhead to Junction 15 at Swindon in 1971, considerably improving automobile access between London, Reading and within the entire Thames Valley area. Like the GWR coming through the Thames Valley in the 1840s, and Heathrow Airport opening after WW II, the M4 further attracted commuters from London and companies moving HQ offices to the area, especially high tech business.

1980s to the present — Thames Valley High Tech Corridor – The term 'the Silicon Valley of the UK', or 'the new Silicon Valley of ' … fill in the blank for the country/region of the world, has been used endlessly over the years. Many cities and regions in the UK can now legitimately claim to have growing high tech centres, however the M4 corridor in the Thames Valley was arguable the first and has been synonymous with high tech industries since the 1980s and '90s, remaining a high tech powerhouse today.

- High tech businesses are prevalent across business parks with easy access to the M4 in Reading, Slough, Maidenhead, Windsor, Bracknell and Newbury. Each of these towns are home to multiple business parks with global high technology firms, often acting as UK and European HQ for companies such Cisco, IBM, Dell, HP, Microsoft, Oracle, Verizon, and Huawei.
- The main reason that I came to live in the Thames Valley was to work in the mobile telecoms industry that is largely based in the area. Vodafone has a major corporate campus in Newbury, previously its global HQ, until the Vodafone Group offices moved to offices at Paddington with Vodafone UK still in Newbury. O2 plc was based in Slough until merging with Virgin Media and moving to Reading's Green Park in 2022. Mobile Operator Three was based in Maidenhead for many years before also moving to Reading's Green Park in 2023. Many other mobile telecom equipment suppliers have also been based in the area over the years including RIM Blackberry, HTC, Motorola and Ericsson.
- The first commercial Cellular networks in the UK were launched by Vodafone and Cellnet in January 1985. Vodafone's 'mobile device' was a Transportable Vodafone VT1, which weighed 11lb (5kg) and had around 30 minutes of talk time. I later worked as a programme manager for both Cellnet and Vodafone helping to deliver their first GPRS and 3G offerings working with many locally based suppliers such as Motorola, Ericsson, Huawei and Nokia.
- New emerging technology companies continue to be drawn to the M4 corridor:
    - Altitude Angels, located in Reading Town Centre, provides airspace management data and services for the fast-growing drone sector, helping drones to understand where they can fly and who else is using the airspace.
    - All.Space, also in Reading Town Centre since 2021, aims to manufacture advanced portable satellite ground terminals in Reading using an innovative optical technology.

Aerial view of Green Park in Reading. Madejski Football Stadium can be seen on the right, with the M4, Huawei Telecom and other offices on the left.

Queen Elizabeth II visiting Vodafone Offices in Newbury in 2008.

Scene at Vodafone Newbury campus.

1950s - present — Science Vale UK — If the M4 is a high tech corridor, then the area around Oxford is clearly a world leader in science-based research organisations and commercial start-ups. An area south of Oxford, known as Science Vale UK, is home to a number of science-based business parks, including Harwell Campus, Milton Park in Didcot and the Culham Centre for Fusion Energy (CCFE) near Abingdon.

Harwell Science and Innovation Centre — was established after WWII on the site of RAF Harwell. It was the first home for the secretive UK Atomic Energy Research Establishment and the Rutherford Appleton Laboratory, named after the Nobel Prize winning physicists who worked there. The campus has grown to the size of a small town over the years with its own fire brigade and police force — known as the Civil Nuclear Constabulary. By 1985, Harwell employed 6000 employees across 100 buildings.

In recent years, most of the nuclear energy research has moved to the Culham Campus and the scope of research at Harwell has greatly expanded to include cooperative efforts between commercial start-ups and government research labs. There are now over 200 space, energy, and health-related organisations based at Harwell including the UK's Space Agency and a European Space Agency research centre.

- The most imposing facility is the large ring-shaped Diamond Light Source synchrotron that forms a part of the Rutherford Appleton Laboratory. I don't fully understand how a synchrotron works, but I am told that it is a type of particle accelerator that works like a giant microscope that scientists can use to study anything from fossils to viruses and vaccines.
- In 2023, US-based Moderna Pharmaceutical, developer of one of the top Coronavirus vaccines, announced that it would develop an Innovation and Technology Centre at Harwell with the intention of working with the 'Harwell Health Tech Cluster' of over 70 companies.
- A National Quantum Computing Centre was set up by a UK government research organisation at Harwell in 2023. I also don't fully understand quantum computing so won't try to explain how it is different from conventional computing other than to say that it is based on the rules of quantum mechanics and makes use of effects that exist at the level of atoms, electrons and photons. As new technologies are developed, the centre plans to partner with companies to help them use it for new applications.

Fusion Energy—Oxfordshire has been at the forefront in developing nuclear fusion energy as part the race to find clean and sustainable sources of power since the 1950s. The standing joke is that fusion energy is always 20-30 years away from becoming commercially viable. Whether this is still the case remains to be seen, but it has taken several decades to get to the point where many commercial investors are now betting on fusion as the next big thing in power generation technology.

- Nuclear power is now valued more than ever as a low-carbon way of producing energy, so after a period of decline, more nuclear power stations are now being planned as a way of reaching global carbon reduction targets. Today's nuclear power plants use fission reactors that have the inherent risk of radiation leaks in the event of a power station accident. They also require uranium mining for fuel and have the difficult problem of how to store radioactive nuclear waste.
- Fusion reactions still generate some radioactive by-products, but these are much less severe and long-lived than those from nuclear fission. The hydrogen fuel for nuclear fusion can be derived from sea water, making fusion a potentially ideal way to meet the world's future energy needs. Fusion aims to replicate the process that takes place in the sun and stars where the intense heat at the core fuses atoms together and produces massive amounts of energy in the form of heat and light. Zeta was an early fusion demonstration project using tokamak technology started in the 1950s at Harwell. A tokamak is a device which uses a powerful magnetic field to confine ultra-hot plasma in a donut-shaped torus to produce controlled fusion reactions.
- Fusion research facilities moved from Harwell to nearby Culham in the 1960s and by the 1980s and '90s, fusion reactions were being produced with the multinational Joint European Torus (JET). Prior to its decommissioning in 2023, JET set a number of fusion energy production records. The most recent one was a sustained fusion reaction of 5.2 seconds generating 60 megajoules of energy — enough to make 600 cups of tea. This may not sound like a lot, but the results give scientist confidence that a 'break even point' is possible, where the amount of energy produced by the reaction is greater than the amount of energy needed to produce the reaction itself. A

Harwell Science Campus in Oxfordshire. Photo courtesy Harwell Press Office.

separate UK commercial fusion power plant is now being planned and targeted to be operational by 2040.

Not everyone believes fusion energy will take so long. A growing number of commercial start-ups are more bullish and are attracting attention from the world's leading investors:
- Tokamak Energy, a commercial start-up based in Didcot, has developed a compact spherical tokamak prototype at its offices at the Milton Business Park. The latest device, successfully demonstrated in 2021, has significant potential for commercial nuclear fusion. Plans for development of a prototype at Culham were announced in 2022. According to Chris Kelsall, Tokamak's chief executive: "We have moved from if it will happen to when. Investors have seen wind and solar take off and now they have to decide whether they want a seat at the table for the next big thing. It will be an industry worth trillions of dollars".
- Canadian company General Fusion, which is backed by Amazon founder Jeff Bezos, also plans to build a Fusion Demonstration Plant at Culham with a $400 million investment. The plant is due to be ready by 2025.
- The global race to commercialise fusion technology includes two other ventures in the USA with heavy venture capital backing. One company based in Seattle called Helion, raised $500 million in 2021, with $1.7 billion more promised if it hits a series of milestones. Bill Gates and George Soros are backing nuclear fusion start-up Commonwealth Fusion Systems based at MIT.

The Joint European Torus at Culham Centre for Fusion Energy. Photo courtesy Culham Press Office.

2020/2021-Coronavirus pandemic — It may now seem like a distant memory when the government made us all stay at home except for one daily outing for exercise and essential shopping and where physical interaction was limited to other members of our household. Everyone who could work from home did.

This was the cause of struggles and conflicts at the community level. The rules for social interaction changed so often that it was difficult to fully understand how to comply. Villages in rural areas suddenly became attractive locations to travel to for outdoor exercise from visitors in larger towns such as Reading, causing parking problems on country lanes, unusually busy open spaces and overflowing public bins. As a Parish Councillor, I remember debates about what type of social distancing guidance we should be posting in public open spaces, whether dogs needed to stay on leashes and whether football nets should be removed from village greens. There was even a brief period of time when Berkshire and Oxfordshire were in different tier designations making it illegal to travel between the Thames Twin Towns of Pangbourne and Whitchurch or Goring and Streatley.

One positive thing that came out of it was the formation of community groups that helped those most in need with grocery runs and prescription pick-ups at the local surgery or pharmacy. This happened in many communities such as Goring, Pangbourne, and Slough.

The Oxford/AstraZeneca COVID-19 Vaccine was approved for emergency use by the UK government in December 2021. Developed by vaccinologists at Oxford University's Jenner Institute, it was one of the first two vaccines given approval by any government in the fight against the pandemic. The university partnered with AstraZeneca PLC to develop, test and produce the vaccine initially on a not-for-profit basis.
- In contrast to other COVID-19 vaccines, such as those developed by American pharmaceutical companies, the cost was much lower, at $3-5 per dose compared to around $15-25 for Pfizer and Moderna.
- There was some controversy around the relative effectiveness of the Oxford-AstraZeneca Vaccine compared to the more expensive alternatives and also some evidence of it causing extremely rare cases of blood clots in younger people. The controversies caused some countries to stop offering it, especially in the USA and Europe.
- The low price point and ease of distribution made it a popular choice for governments in developing countries in Asia, Latin America, and Africa. As of February 2022 more than 2.6 billion doses of the vaccine had been released to more than 170 countries worldwide.

Remember social distancing, face masks and no hair cuts? Here are a few scenes around Pangbourne during Lock down.

Clockwise from top right: A long overdue haircut at the Turkish Barbers; alfresco dining and face shields at Baxter's Café; homemade sourdough bread became all the rage with social distancing and ordering through the window at artisan bakery Birch Bread.

2021-24 Film studio boom — The Thames Valley has long been a popular location for filming British period pieces in some of its idyllic locations, but growing demand for film production in the UK from the likes of Amazon, Disney, Apple TV+ and Netflix has resulted in a boom for film studio construction in the UK with several new studios under construction in the Thames Valley.

The area's scenic locations, convenience and skilled workforce has made it part of the 'UK creative cluster' that includes nearby Pinewood and Shepperton studios.

> "Britain's Thames Valley is a centre for film and television production. It has a long tradition of filmmaking with world class studios such as Pinewood, together with beautiful and varied locations all within easy access of London and Heathrow airport. A large number of crew and facilities are based in the region, contributing to the overall strength of the creative sector, a significant employer in the south east of England."
> - Gareth Neame, Executive Producer of *Downton Abbey* and Managing Director of Carnival films

Since 2021, plans for a growing number of major new studios have been announced, with many now completed or under construction.

- **Shinfield Studios** — Anyone driving along the M4 near Junction 11 cannot fail to miss the imposing new Shinfield Studios completed in 2024. Plans were approved in 2021 to open the major new film and television studio centre in Shinfield. Initial sound stages were opened in 2022, with Disney being confirmed as the first tenant. The studio complex is owned by Shadowbox Studios, an international film production company that has similar studios in Atlanta Georgia where *Godzilla: King of the Monsters* was filmed.
- **Bray Studios** is a somewhat smaller film studio between Windsor and Maidenhead that has been running since the 1950s. Originally known for its fantasy and horror films, starring legendary actors such as Christopher Lee in *The Mummy*, *The Curse of Frankenstein* and *Dracula*. Recent credits include the film about Elton John's life *Rocketman*. In 2021, it received approval for a major expansion that includes nine new sound stages, approved with an active travel friendly transportation plan including a shuttle bus to and from Maidenhead railway station. Amongst the productions being filmed there in 2023 were the Amazon series *Lord of the Rings: Rings of Power*.
- **Winnersh Film Studios** — Stage Fifty opened a campus in Winnersh with six sound stages and other facilities in 2022 just off Junction 10 of the M4. Movie credits already attributable to the studio include *The Boys in the Boat*, directed by local resident George Clooney, and the latest *Ghostbusters* sequel.
- **Arborfield Studios** was developed in 2017 to support Disney's need for a studio to film the live-action version of *Aladdin*.
- **Marlow and Holyport** — As described in Part 2 of the book, as of 2024, investors were seeking planning permission for major new studios at Marlow although initial plans were refused. Plans have also been developed for a new studio at Holyport near Windsor.

Left: Shinfield Studios near the M4 Junction 11; Above: Winnersh Studios near Junction 10;
Right: Bray Studios, a short distance from the Elizabeth Line in Maidenhead.

1996 – The Thames Path was finally opened after much discussion and planning dating back to 1948. At 185 miles (298 km), the path makes it possible to walk the entire length of the river, from its source in Kemble to the Thames Barrier in Charlton, southeast of London.

- It generally follows the route of historic towpaths for pulling barges, but there are a number of places where the path has a diversion from the river for historic reasons or to avoid some privately owned stretches. There is a diversion at Datchet around the royally-owned Home Park, for example, and the stretch from Cookham Lock at Cliveden Reach avoids Cliveden itself.
- Walking the Thames Path, either in its entirety or in selected parts, is one of the best ways to get to know the river and is also one of the things that makes the Thames so accessible and treasured today. Cycling is allowed in certain sections, but it is restricted to walkers in most stretches.

Right: The Thames Path Sign at the start of the trail at Thames Head near Kemble showing a variety of Thames Path logos seen since 1996.
Below: The Thames Path at the Hartley Steps between Goring and Whitchurch that coincide with both the ancient Tuddingway and the King Alfred's Way Cycle route. As one of the steepest stretches of the path, steps have been installed to aid walkers and a sign warns cyclists to follow the Countryside Code giving walkers the right of way. The steps were named after local resident Eric Hartley who champions walking in the area and successfully convinced the County Council to get new steps installed in 2012 after the previously deteriorated steps were removed.

2020 – The King Alfred's Way

A 220 mile (350 km) circular off-road cycle route called the King Alfred's Way was established that cuts through Reading and the Thames Valley. The route starts in Alfred's Wessex base in Winchester and follows the ancient Ridgeway trail passing near his birthplace in Wantage, crossing the Thames at Streatley and Goring, and then following the Thames Path to Whitchurch and Reading before turning south at the River Kennet where the Vikings set up camp to battle Alfred and the Wessex army.

- I have ridden the route with friends and can say, in all seriousness, that travelling this off-road route was one of the highlights of my life. More than just a series of routes through beautiful countryside, it is a pilgrimage across historic trails bringing you face-to-face with thousands of years of history, meeting other travellers along the way. You are bound to have some unusual experiences. For me, as an avid mountain biker with an interest in history, the route stitches together so many places in the region that are in my blood; the Thames Path, the Ridgeway, the South Downs Way, Old Sarum, Stone Henge, Avebury, and so much more.
- We travelled the route over three days, which is possible, but was a bit over ambitious. I would recommend doing it in a more reasonable and leisurely four or five days to take it all in. The fact that it passes right past my home in Whitchurch-on-Thames along the ancient Tuddingway makes it that much more personal to me.

2022 – The Elizabeth Line

The long anticipated Elizabeth Line (developed as the Crossrail project) become operational in 2022, connecting Reading, Twyford, Maidenhead, Taplow, and Slough directly to Canary Wharf and other stations on the east side of London via tunnels under London. The new line is expected to attract even more growth in the Thames Valley due to the improved ease of commuting to all parts of London.

The prospect of the new train line has been the cause of development of countless new blocks of flats in towns like Maidenhead and Reading for a number of years. It has also been a regular topic of discussion from residents within easy reach of the line about the anticipated boost in the value of their homes.

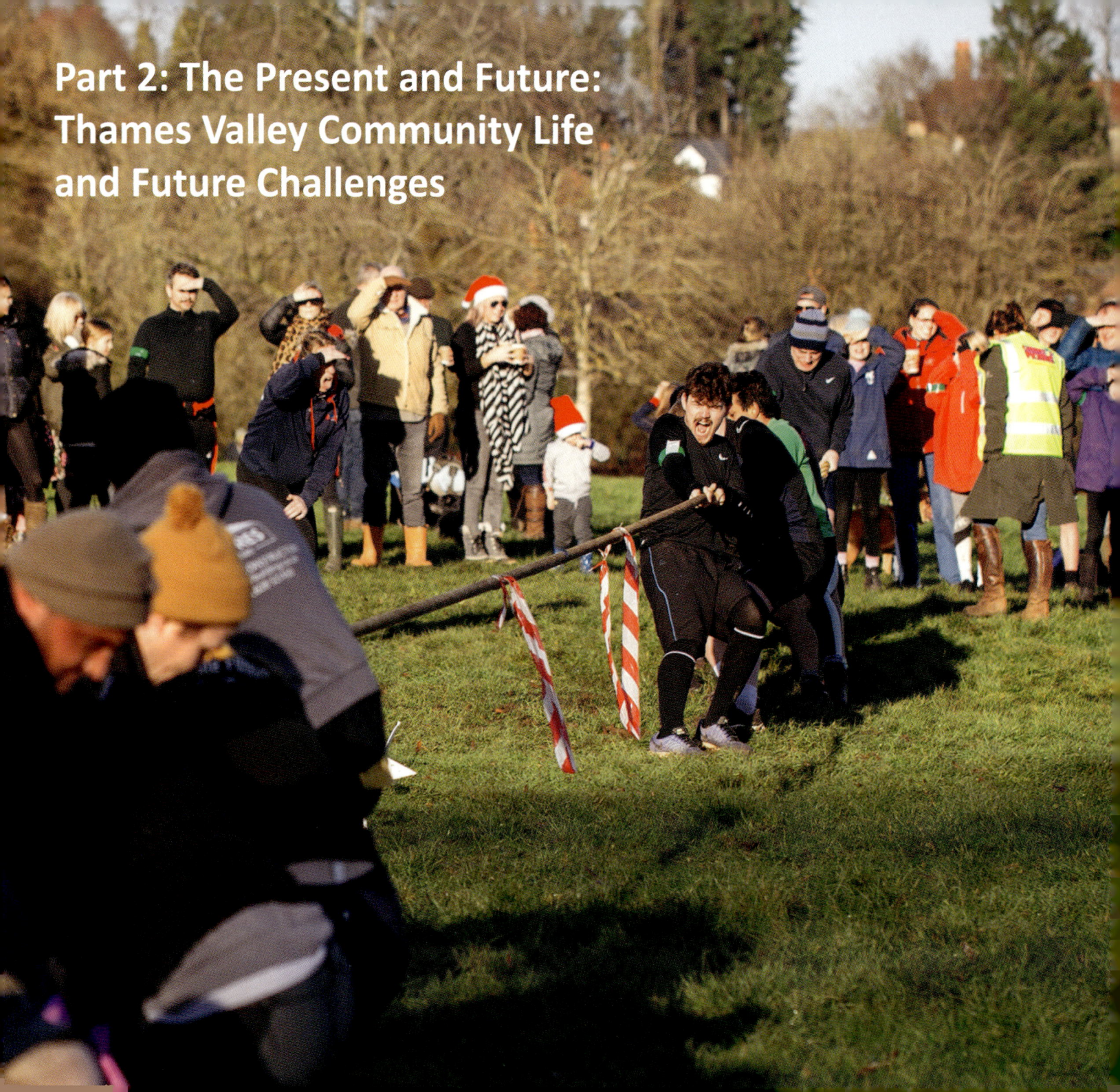

Part 2: The Present and Future: Thames Valley Community Life and Future Challenges

Now that you are acquainted the rich history of the Thames Valley, I would like to share more about what it is like to live there today along with some of the challenges I have seen communities facing in recent years. By better understanding some of the most important local issues, I hope to provide an insight into the trends shaping the area's future.

We will explore the area by taking a tour to the heart of the Thames Valley, starting at Windsor, meandering our way approximately 75 miles along river to Oxford. I don't attempt to describe every town and village in the area, but have chosen to focus on the places that are generally closest to the river itself. As I mentioned at the start of the book, the Thames Valley is only loosely defined and there are many other places that can also be considered part of the Thames Valley in the broader Thames River basin.

Some of the recurring themes I will explore include:

- **Examples of vibrant community life** — From the silly Boxing Day competitions in Cookham, to the 'semi-feudal, hippy vibe' of the Hardwick Estate community at Whitchurch, to the timeless traditions of the Henley Regatta, the Thames Valley is full of examples of vibrant community life. I will also feature grass-root community action groups on topics ranging from action against building a new film studio on the Green Belt in Marlow to community funded public toilets in Pangbourne.
- **Tension between conservation and change** – There are many examples of this tension which sometimes feels more like the 'tug of war' shown on the previous page. One of the biggest changes facing the area is need for communities to accommodate ambitious housing targets to meet growing demand. Many communities are understandably resistant to some of this change in the name of preserving and protecting the beautiful and historic areas they call home. I use Thames Valley case studies to explain many of the planning laws and processes used in England to manage these changes and to address issues such as affordable housing. These case studies highlight the determination of residents working to protect their communities and also the frustration of those advocating change, sometimes referring to those opposing the changes as NIMBYs (not in my back yard).
- **Diversity**– Many aspects of the Thames Valley are quintessentially English, so the area is not known for being especially diverse from an ethnic perspective. This section shines a light on some of its more diverse areas, such as the Oxford Road in Reading, Cowley Road in Oxford, and the rapidly growing Slough.

Opposite: Tug of war at Cookham's Boxing Day Games.   Above: Oxford's Summer 8 inter-collegiate 'bump races' held on the Isis.

1. Windsor and Eton

Thames Twin Towns — I like to call towns and villages that are divided by the river as 'Thames Twin Towns'. To varying degrees, these towns would normally be part of a single community but the strategic border of the Thames dictates that they have developed over the centuries as separate communities, in some cases in different counties. Like a number of other Thames Valley settlements, Windsor and Eton straddle the River Thames and are joined by a bridge, but have separate jurisdictions for historic reasons. The width of the river is only about 70 meters at Windsor, and in most of the Thames Valley, the river's width is closer to 50 meters or even less. In the case of Windsor and Eton, the Windsor Town Bridge has been limited to pedestrians and cyclists since 1970. Lack of direct vehicular access between the two towns adds to their separateness as Eton can only be accessed via car from roads in Maidenhead or Slough.

Unlike some other Thames Twin Towns, Windsor and Eton are at least both part of the same Royal County of Berkshire, and part of the same Royal Borough of Windsor and Maidenhead within it. Due to the presence of Windsor Castle, Queen Elizabeth II recognised the County of Berkshire as Royal in 1957, a few years after her coronation. The town of Windsor is dominated by Windsor Castle which sits on a large hill overlooking the Thames, just as the town of Eton is dominated by historic Eton College. Windsor is a much larger town, with a population of 32,000 (2021 Census). Eton and Eton Wick had a population just under 5000 in 2011. Both Eton and Windsor have vibrant pedestrian shopping districts with a broad selection of bars and restaurants catering to tourists and local residents alike.

British royalty and community life — As described in Part 1 of the book, Windsor Castle has been used as a base for the monarch of England since the time of William the Conqueror's son Henry I. Queen Elizabeth II used it as a primary residence and it is assumed that King Charles III and his heir William will continue to do so. In recent years, it has been the focal point of royal ceremonies and celebrations including state visits, royal jubilees, and royal weddings and funerals. These events are often declared as public holidays and also celebrated with community events across the country, including nearly all towns and villages in the Thames Valley.

Christmas shopping in Windsor.

Eton High Street.

- The town of Windsor has a tradition of hosting numerous street parties through its many neighbourhoods. In some cases, royalty such as Prince William and Princess Catherine may stop by as they did for a Coronation Big Lunch celebration in 2023. The photo on this page shows Prince William being given a special coronation can of beer with his father on the label called "The Return of the King".
- Windsor Castle was also the location for the extravagant Coronation Concert in May 2023, attended by King Charles, Queen Camilla, the majority of the royal family and numerous other dignitaries.
- Abingdon-on-Thames, has a long standing tradition of throwing buns to crowds from the roof of the Town Hall on special royal occasions. This is apparently the source of the British expression 'bun fight'.
- Goring and Streatley teamed up to form the world's longest dinner table that stretched over 1 km across the bridge over the Thames for the Royal Wedding in 2018 and again for the Queen's Platinum Jubilee in 2022.
- As Chairman of the Whitchurch-on-Thames Parish Council, I have been involved in organising several community celebrations on our Village Green in honour of the royal family. These included the Queen's 90th Birthday in 2016, shown in the photo on the right.

Windsor Castle and the Crown Estate — Windsor Castle and most of the parks and royal properties in the area such as Windsor Great Park are owned and managed by the Crown Estate. Windsor is considered one of the official 'Occupied Royal Palaces', like Buckingham Palace and St James' Palace that are managed by the Crown Estate. Some of the royal residences such as Balmoral Castle and Sandringham House are personally owned by the royal family and have been passed down for generations. The Occupied Royal Palaces are cared for and maintained by the Property Section of the Royal Households. According to the annual Sovereign Grant Report for 2022/23, there were 491 full-time staff working at the occupied royal palaces. Jobs include everything from private secretaries to the King, to housekeeping and catering staff for formal events, to specialist craftsmen working to preserve the historic buildings.

Above: William and Catherine at a Windsor Street Party celebrating the King's Coronation in 2023. Photo: © Martin Divisek.
Right: Villagers toasting the Queen's 90th birthday celebration in Whitchurch-on-Thames. From the left: Jennifer Bruce, Sally Trinder, Pam Wilkinson, Diana Marriot and Chris Minton.

Without digressing too much, it is worth explaining how the royal family is generally funded. Most of their income comes from revenue related to landholdings that the monarch still owns either directly or indirectly, some of it dating back to the time of William the Conqueror, making it one of the remaining vestiges of feudalism that still plays a role in British life. The Crown's landholdings include:

- **The Crown Estate** — is an incorporated public body governed by a group of commissioners that owns and manages 'the sovereign's public estate'. It is neither government property nor part of the monarch's private estate.
  - It includes an extensive and diverse range of properties across England and Wales that includes all of Regent Street and most of St James in London, the Tower of London, all the royal parks and property in the Windsor Estate, excluding the castle — and virtually all of the UK's seabed out to 12-nautical-miles. The Crown Estate plays a major role in the development of the offshore wind energy industry in the UK and generates a growing portion of its revenue from this. As of 2022/23, the portfolio of land was worth more that £16 billion and generated an annual revenue of over £442 million. In January 2023, the King announced that an expected £1 billion a year windfall from six new wind energy projects should be used for 'the wider public benefit' instead of being used as part of the Sovereign Grant.
  - The monarchy agreed to surrender the revenue from their land holdings to the government's treasury in 1760 to benefit the nation. In exchange for this, the government pays The Royal Household an annual Sovereign Grant that funds the official duties of the King or Queen and is used to maintain the official Occupied Royal Palaces, such as Windsor that are still owned by the monarch. In 2012, it was agreed that this should be calculated as a regular 15% of the Crown Estate surplus revenues. This was increased to 25% from 2017/18 as part of a 10 year programme to pay for a major refurbishment of Buckingham Palace. In 2022/23 the 25% Sovereign Grant was £86.3 million, although the King drew from reserves that year, spending £102 million during the period due to inflation and higher than expected costs for the coronation and Buckingham Palace repairs.
- **The Duchy of Lancaster** — is comprised of an estate with a portfolio of 18,481 hectares of land, properties and assets held in trust for the sovereign and is administered separately from the Crown Estate. It includes land in the counties of Lancashire, Yorkshire, Cheshire, Staffordshire and Lincolnshire as well as land at the Savoy Hotel on the Strand in London. The main purpose is to provide an independent source of income for the King as Duke of Lancaster. This income is used for the King's Privy Purse, meaning it can be used as the King's private income. A large part of it is used to meet official expenditure incurred by the King and other members of the Royal Family which is not covered by the Sovereign Grant. The King still needs to pay tax on this income. At the end of March 2022, the Duchy of Lancaster had £652.8m of net assets under its control, delivering net surplus of £24m for that year.
- **The Duchy of Cornwall** — includes around 53,000 hectares of land in 23 counties, mostly in South West England. Income from the Duchy of Cornwall funds the private and official expenditure of the Prince and Princess of Wales (William and Catherine) and is also taxed unless it is used to meet official duty expenditures. In 2020/21 the Duchy had net assets of £1.096 billion and a distributable surplus of £23 million.

Windsor Great Park and Home Park — The Crown Estate owns and manages Windsor Great Park, located south of the castle, as well as nearby Home Park, and Ascot Racecourse. Most parts of Windsor Great Park are open to the public free of charge from dawn to dusk, although there is a charge to enter The Savill Garden.

Both Home Park, located to the east of Windsor Castle, and Windsor Great Park, include a number of 'grace and favour' homes that the royal family can provide to other royal family members or privileged members of society generally.
- These include Frogmore Estate, that is the burial site of many royal family members and include Queen Victoria's mausoleum.

Frogmore House and gardens are only open to the public on selected times during the year. The property includes Frogmore Cottage that was the UK base for Harry and Meghan, the Duke and Duchess of Sussex, after they moved to California in early 2022. Harry and Meghan are said to have repaid the £2.4 million renovation costs incurred before they originally moved in. Harry and Megan vacated the cottage permanently as of summer 2023, following the publication of Harry's Memoir called *Spare*. King Charles is expected to allocate the home to another member of the royal family in the near future.

- Home Park also includes Adelaide Cottage that Prince William and Catherine, Princess of Wales have used as their primary home since the summer of 2022. Catherine is of course no stranger to Berkshire, having grown up in the area as part of the Middleton family. Her parents live in Upper Bucklebury, previously living in Bradfield Southend near Pangbourne when Catherine was younger. Her grandmother used to live in Pangbourne and she is familiar to some in the area as 'Kate' from when she used to visit her grandmother and frequent local pubs in her youth prior to her royal marriage.
- Prince Andrew lives in the Royal Lodge with his ex wife Sarah Ferguson within the Great Windsor Park although there has been some speculation as to whether he would be forced to give this up.
- Prince Edward, Duke of Edinburgh, lives with his wife Sophie, the Duchess of Edinburgh, in the 51 acre Bagshot Park, 11 miles south of Windsor in Surrey. Bagshot Park is also leased to and managed by the Crown Estate and considered part of the Windsor Great Park. Prior to the accession of Charles III, Edward and Sophie had the titles of the Earl and Countess of Wessex.

Eton and Eton College — Given that Eton College has a student population of close to 1400 and employs another 1000 teachers and support staff, the town of Eton itself, with a population of about 5000 people, is clearly dominated by the college. Eton is more or less divided into two halves:

- At the southern end of Eton is he town itself. The main thoroughfare is the historic High Street, that includes a wide range of mostly independent shops, pubs, and restaurants just across from Windsor and the pedestrian bridge over the Thames. The town of Eton is a popular destination for shopping, dining, or just strolling or cycling. It is frequented by residents of Windsor and tourists alike. There are a good number of residential homes and apartments on either side of the High Street, although the population is limited by space as the area is surrounded by the River Thames on one side, and Eton College facilities and playing fields on other sides.
- The High Street shopping district more or less ends where Eton College begins, just north of Barnes Pool Bridge. From there you can walk along the medieval streets and alleyways of Eton College, surrounded by vast playing fields. Visiting Eton is a similar experience to visiting Oxford, although much smaller and most of the Eton College grounds are not open to the public. There are Museums of Natural History and Eton Life, and a heritage tour of the Eton College that are open to the public on Sunday afternoons and certain other days. Tours can be booked at the Eton Information Centre in the High Street near the pedestrian bridge.
- During term times, you will undoubtedly come across young student boys in formal 'school dress' attire. This consists of striped trousers, black waistcoat, black tailcoat (known as a morning coat), well polished black shoes, white tunic shirts with cufflinks, Arundel collars and white ties.
- Dorney and Eton Wick are villages beyond central Eton that are adjacent to some of the College's extensive playing fields and the impressive Dorney Lake rowing facilities. The lake is 2.2km long and can accommodate 8 lanes of rowers. It is privately owned and financed by Eton College, which spent £17 million developing it with the help of some government grants. It took 10 years to complete construction and was used for the UK Olympic 2012 rowing events.

Opposite page: Stags at Windsor Great Park.
Left: The Golden Jubilee Statue of Queen Elizabeth II from 2002 at Windsor Great Park.

Eton College — When people think of Eton College, it understandably conjures images of one of Britain's most elite boarding schools for the likes of David Cameron, Boris Johnson, and Princes William and Harry. Eton has parallels to Oxford University at the other end of the Thames Valley, where many Eton students go on to earn higher educational degrees, as former prime ministers Cameron and Johnson did. Whilst much of its elite image is justified, there are growing pressures for top academic institutions such as Eton and Oxford to offer access to students with more diverse backgrounds and some things are changing.

The facilities and academic standards at Eton College are without a doubt some of the finest in the world. The fees are equally amongst the most expensive. As of 2022/23 Eton tuition costs £15,432 for each of three terms per year. With extras, this can be close to £50,000 per year, or £250,000 for the period boys attend from ages 13-18. Clearly, this is not something the average family can afford. The vast majority of Britons are educated in state schools: 94% of the population and 83% of those who take A-level exams. In contrast, state-school students made up only 57% of those admitted to Oxford in 2013.

Entrance to Oxford and Cambridge Universities used to be a natural route for the many Eton students, however top universities are now being incentivized by the UK government and other educational organisations to change admissions policies to address inequality and accept more students from less privileged backgrounds. In recent years, the number of state-educated pupils getting Oxbridge places has risen and the number gaining admission from private schools has fallen.

- In 2014, 99 students at Eton College got offers to go to Oxford or Cambridge, but by 2021 this had fallen to 48.
- During the same period, the proportion of places offered to state-school students at Oxford has risen from 57% to 68%.

Eton College offers more and more bursaries and scholarships to support families who wouldn't ordinarily be able to afford some or all of the Eton fees.

- In 2021/22, out of a total of about 1300 students, 267 boys received fee reductions, with 100 of these boys paying no fees at all. The average award was 71% of the fee.
- Approximately 14 Kings Scholarships are awarded each year. These students represent the original core of the institution founded by King Henry VI as a charity school that still provides free education to 70 poor boys who would originally be intended to go on to King's College, Cambridge.
- Kings Scholars are known as 'Collegers', with the other 1200 students, who are mostly fee paying, being known as 'Oppidans'. Boris Johnson was a King's Scholar, where David Cameron was a fee-paying Oppidan.
- King's Scholars are distinguished by the wearing of a black academic gown over the usual school uniform of a tail-coat. They share most aspects of school life with the Oppidans, including lessons and most sport, however they eat all their meals in original Eton College Hall.
- The main basis for awarding the scholarships is on a series of demanding academic examinations with several compulsory papers (English, Creative Writing, Mathematics A, Science, and General I) and at least three optional papers (French, Latin, Greek, Advanced Mathematics, or History-Geography-Divinity).
- Since 2020, Orwell Awards with full scholarships are given to up to 12 boys aged 16+ to applicants whose personal circumstance can hold back academic achievement. For example, if you are in the first generation of your family to go to university, or have refugee status. The scholarship is named after George Orwell, who studied at Eton under his birth name of Eric Blair, and was himself the recipient of financial aid as an Etonian.

Scenes around Eton College, including Eton rowers preparing to compete in the Henley Royal Regatta.

2. Slough

As you drive west from Windsor along the M4, before you reach Maidenhead, Reading and the rest of the Thames Valley, you pass through Slough at Junctions 6 and 7. Whilst very little of the River Thames actually passes through Slough, it is still very much part of the Thames Valley. With a population of nearly 160,000 (2021 Census) and a 13% growth rate since 2011, Slough is one of the fastest growing areas in the South of England.

Despite Slough's economic vitality, it is certainly not considered a quaint and picturesque part of the Thames Valley. It is famously home to the fictional Wernham Hogg paper merchants managed by David Brent in *The Office* television show created by Ricky Gervais who grew up in nearby Reading. The opening scenes of the show feature the unglamorous roundabout at the Brunel Car Park and Bus Station and the show portrays the mundane lives of employees in a typical open plan office. This negative image builds on the 1937 poem by poet laureate John Betjeman who included a harsh verse about the town "Come, friendly bombs, and fall on Slough, it isn't fit for humans now."

If Slough were to be such a miserable place, why would so many people choose to live there and why is it growing so rapidly? The main reasons seem to be the employment opportunities offered by a multitude of businesses choosing to be based there, its convenient access to London and the rest of the Thames Valley, and some of the most affordable housing prices in the region. The *Telegraph* newspaper rated Slough as the number one commuter town in the UK in 2023 for all these reasons as well as its 33 minute commute time to central London and reasonable train fares with minimal crowding.

I originally moved to the Thames Valley in Cookham in 1999 to work in Slough at mobile operator O2 (then Cellnet). Beside working there, I also used to take advantage of some of the convenient shopping at some of the large stores there such as B&Q and Dunelm.

Slough means business — The town has been home to many global and regional corporate headquarters over the years, including Blackberry phones, McAffee software, Lego, Coca Cola, Amazon, DHL, and Burger King. In 2023, O2 finally moved out of Slough after a merger with Virgin Media to Green Park in Reading, with some staff moving to offices in London Paddington.

Slough Trading Estate has been privately owned since it was established in the 1920s on the site of a large army truck depot used in the First World War. With over 350 individual businesses providing employment for 17,000 people, it claims to be the largest privately owned business centre of its kind in Europe since the 1990s. The trading estate is the site of the large Mars chocolate factory, producing Mars bars for over 70 years. When I worked in Slough, you could often smell the chocolate, particularly after Easter, when they apparently used to recycle much of the unsold Easter eggs — melting them to be used for other products.

Another claim to fame is that Slough was home to the popular puppet-based television series, *Thunderbirds*, that was filmed at APF's studios on the Slough Trading Estate between 1964 and 1966.

Left: Slough GWR and Elizabeth Line station.
Below: The Curve Library and Cultural Centre.
Opposite page: Ethnic restaurants and halal grocery shop on the High Street.

Ethnic diversity —According to the 2021 Census, Slough is one of the most culturally diverse and rapidly growing towns in the UK. Slough has a long history of accommodating immigrants:
- Welsh workers came to work at the Slough Estates in the economically depressed 1930s.
- After World War II, Slough was one of the places chosen for resettlement of Polish refugees.
- Since the partition of India in 1947, Slough has been home to more and more Indian and Pakistani communities coming to find work and to be with family members who have previously immigrated.

The percentage of people identifying as Asian or British Asian has grown from 24% of the population in 1991 to 47% in the 2021 Census.
- There is no dominant minority in Slough but those with Indian or Pakistani heritage are the two largest.
- Slough also has the highest percentage of Muslim(20.3%) and Hindu residents (7.8%) in the South East region as of 2021.
- Those identifying as Sikhs accounted for 11.3% of Slough's population in the 2021 Census making it the largest Sikh community in the South of England outside of London. There are at least three major Sikh community worship centres in Slough, known as Gurdwaras—the first formal one having been established in 1976.

I visited the Guru Maneyo Granth Gurdwara on Bath Road in 2024, the newest and largest Sikh worship centre, and was warmly welcomed to attend one of the many daily services. I was just asked to remove my shoes and given a scarf to cover my hair. The services are open to all men, women, and children regardless of faith. Volunteers prepare free community meals in the 4 acre centre that includes thriving religious education classes that are also free for the community. The Gudwara received the Queen's Voluntary Service Award in 2020 for the service it provided the community during the COVID-19 crisis. Volunteers kept their kitchen open, continuously serving and delivering free vegetarian community meals. They also offered the site as a large temporary community hospital.

Crime — When I worked in Slough, O2 had offices in a few locations and I used to take a shuttle bus between the offices on the Bath Road and an office by the Slough train station adjacent to the Brunel Car Park and Bus Station. I had been warned by other employees to be very careful about parking at the Brunel Car Park after dark. Unfortunately, I was not careful enough, as I had my

laptop stolen from the boot of my car after working late one evening. The theft was quite brazen as it happened while I was still in the car! The burglars even had the audacity to say 'thank you very much'— polite, if nothing else. Unfortunately, this wasn't the only time my laptop was stolen. My car was again broken into outside a café that I was parked at whilst having lunch — as I clearly didn't learn from the first incident, it is fair to blame my lack of security consciousness as part of the cause.

According to recent national crime statistics (www.crimerate.co.uk), certain aspects of crime in Slough are still very high, such as vehicle related crime and crime related to violence or sexual attacks. The site rated Slough as the most dangerous town in Berkshire in 2023 and one of the most dangerous in the Thames Valley overall. Oxford, Newbury and Windsor are rated as having lower crime levels overall but have a higher number of crime incidents than Slough in certain categories such as in bicycle thefts and shoplifting.

Redevelopment — Since the early 2000s, when *The Office* was aired and I had my experience at the Brunel Bus Station Car Park, a lot of redevelopment has happened in Slough and further work is planned.

- An ultramodern Library and Cultural Centre called 'The Curve' was completed in 2017 as part of the 'Heart of Slough' regeneration project. I visited the centre in 2024 and it does appear to be very well used and popular as a community hub.
- The old Tesco supermarket was replaced with a major new Tesco Extra, one of the largest supermarkets in Europe.
- The Brunel Car Park and Bus Station has been replaced. Even the roundabout itself no longer exists, being replaced with traffic lights. A new bus station, with an ultra-modern design meant to look like an electronic wave, is affectionately referred to by many as 'the slug'. Sadly, the new station caught fire in 2022 and was still out of use as of 2024.

Another landmark that can still be seen when passing through Slough on the train is the old Horlick's malted drink factory. Horlicks was produced on the site from 1908 until the plant's closure in 2017. It is now being developed into 1300 'contemporary, industrial-inspired studios, apartments and duplex penthouses' by upmarket developer Berkeley's Homes in an area now dubbed 'The Horlicks Quarter'.

- Whilst the factory is not officially an Historic England listed building, the Slough Borough Council worked with the developer to ensure that the new development preserves the iconic structure and appearance of the historic factory including the red neon Horlicks sign and original industrial chimney.
- There are only 486 parking spaces planned for the 1300 homes, so the transport plan for the development includes new cycle and footpaths to the town centre and easy access to the nearby train station.
- 325 of the homes will be classified as 'affordable', although others appear to be more high end. As of January 2024, a 3-bedrooom flat is selling for nearly £670,000 with 1 and 2 bedroom apartments going for between £280,000 and £350,000, with some being advertised as only requiring a 5% minimum deposit.

There are at least three other sites targeted for 1000 or more new homes in Slough, including the site of the old Thames Valley University, the site of a former ICI paint factory, and development of Stokes Wharf in a derelict area by the Slough arm of the Grand Union Canal.

Some reports estimate that a total of £3 billion in development is planned in Slough by 2030 in the form of more new housing, a new town centre shopping mall, and two new hotels, including one paying tribute to the *Thunderbirds* TV show heritage. All in all, Slough may be a very different place in the coming years. Even John Betjeman appears to have had second thoughts about his poem. In 2006, on the centenary of his birth, his daughter said her father 'regretted having ever written it', presenting the then Mayor David MacIsaac with a book of his poems in which she had written: 'We love Slough'.

3. Maidenhead, Marlow and Cookham

Marlow is located on the northern side of the Thames in South Buckinghamshire with Maidenhead and Cookham just to the south on the Berkshire side of the river. Maidenhead is the largest town, with a population of around 70,0000 (2021 Census). It is situated off the M4, is close to Heathrow airport and has a quick rail service to London Paddington. Cookham (pop. 5779 – 2021 Census) and Marlow (pop. 14,400 – 2021 Census), are both just upstream, each with their own Thames lock, and both accessible via the small branch train line from Maidenhead, referred to as 'the Marlow Donkey'. Whilst Maidenhead had its heyday in the coaching era and the Edwardian boating period following the establishment of the railway, today Marlow and Cookham are the more sought after, quintessentially Thames Valley villages to live in.

Maidenhead has been host to a number of High Tech firms since the 1970's and '80s, although some have come and gone. It was the UK HQ for Nortel telecoms before it went out of business in 2009, and the base for Three Mobile — before moving to Reading Green Park in 2023. The town is still home to numerous high tech businesses, some from the UK, and some local divisions of international businesses Adobe Systems and Symantec Software, and pharmaceutical companies Johnson & Johnson, Pfizer and Abbott Laboratories. It is home to a recently expanded global headquarters for the up and coming Seqirus, a leader in influenza vaccines. There are a number of private schools popular with residents of this affluent area such as St Piran's, Claire's Court, and Desborough College.

Former Prime Minister Theresa May, the Conservative MP for Maidenhead from 1997 to 2024, lives in nearby Sonning — another beautiful village on the Thames. Like Marlow and Cookham, Sonning is known for its historic homes and well preserved scenery. Local celebrities include actor George Clooney and his wife Amal, an international human rights lawyer. Sonning is also home to the highly regarded Reading Blue Coat private school.

Theresa May had a well-earned reputation for being devoted to her constituency in addition to serving the country as Home Secretary and Prime Minister. She consistently fought for better local services such as new healthcare facilities and improvements to train services to Maidenhead. She can still be seen with her husband Phillip in local coffee shops, attending church services, and at events like the Henley Regatta and Henley Festival, which are technically hosted in her constituency on the river across from Henley.

Quality of life — Marlow and Cookham are indeed special places with beautiful, well-preserved historic buildings, pleasant rural green spaces and scenic walks along the river. Within easy commuting distance to London, most residents earn good incomes and are willing to pay a premium for homes, making the area somewhat exclusive. As I will describe later, residents of both communities have a reputation for doggedly ensuring it remains such a special place.

Amongst the attractions to the area are Michelin starred restaurants and celebrity chefs.
- The Fat Duck in Bray, also just outside Maidenhead, is run by chef Heston Blumenthal. It is known for unusual food combinations such as egg and bacon ice cream and chocolate wine. Most of the recipes are invented in Heston's research lab in Bray. The Fat Duck has had three Michelin stars since 2004 and was even ranked by one list as the World's Best Restaurant in 2005.

Left: Enjoying the good life along the river at Higginson Park in Marlow.
Inset: Phillip and Theresa May at a local coffee shop.

- Also in Bray, the Waterside Inn, was home to the French chefs, the Roux Brothers. It was the first restaurant outside of France to have three Michelin stars for over 25 years. It is now run by Michel's son Alain Roux.
- Tom Kerridge's Hand and Flowers in Marlow is the only pub in the UK with two Michelin Stars. As customers need to book a table six months in advance, Kerridge also runs two further restaurants in Marlow that don't take bookings—the Coach and the Butcher's Block. Kerridge, shown on the right, hosts an annual 'Pub in the Park' foodie festival with cooking demonstrations and big name music acts in Marlow's Higginson Park along the river. The 'Pub in the Park' festival is now an annual touring festival that stops in 10 locations around London and the UK.

In addition to fancy restaurants, Marlow is known for its bustling High Street shopping with plenty of trendy bars and restaurants. Diners are spoilt for choice with local restaurants and coffee shops such as the Vanilla Pod and the Marlow Bar and Grill, as well as a local branches of national chains such as the Ivy, Zizzis and Pizza Express. There are a number of fashion shops and beauty salons for the yummy mummy crowd. The high-end Everyman Cinema offers drinks and food delivered to your seat.

Community spirit — I know from my experience living in the area that both Marlow and Cookham have close knit communities with a mixture of older long-time residents mixing with relatively young, affluent families socialising through various school groups, youth sports teams, fundraising events, and other social activities. When I lived in Cookham, I got to know people through participating in a National Childbirth Trust football league for new dads.

Both towns have long running summer regatta traditions.
- **The Cookham Regatta** dates back to at least 1882. The original regatta, celebrated in some of Stanley Spencer's famous paintings of Cookham life, was a big event involving Thames sculls, punts, Canadian canoes, and a parade of boats with military bands. In 1890, at the height of the Edwardian boating era, a record 10,000 people attended. It was later overtaken by the Henley Regatta, but was revived in the 1980s as a lower key, family-friendly 'fun regatta'. Today's regatta is similar to a village fête that focusses on dragon boat racing and other family activities such as a Dog Show with categories including 'cutest puppy', 'most handsome dog', and 'prettiest bitch'.
- **The Marlow Regatta** originated in 1855 and is still a more serious rowing affair. It moved to the man-made Eton College rowing facilities at Dorney Lake in 2001 and attracts international rowing teams. It is seen as an important qualifying race for Henley. There is also a more fun Town Regatta and Festival in June similar to Cookham's that features dragon boat racing. Marlow resident and Olympic rowing champion, Sir Steve Redgrave, normally gets involved.

The number of Cookham community events designed to get people together seems to be constantly growing:
- **The Cookham Festival** is held every other year in May and features music, arts, lectures, drama, and comedy. The first Cookham Festival was held in 1967 with soprano opera singer Marie Collier acting as president and was partly inspired by the artistic tradition of local artist Sir Stanley Spencer who died in 1959.
- Held on the Cookham Moor by the river, '**Let's Rock the Moor**' started as a musical event as part of the Cookham Festival in 2009, headlined by Nick Heywood of Haircut 100 who lives near Henley. In 2010, Howard Jones, who was based in Maidenhead for a number of years, headlined a follow-on show along with Haircut 100, who specially reunited for the event. Since that time, the audiences have grown from 1200 to a 6500 capacity event on the Moor featuring many of the most well known '80s rock and pop acts each year. Like the 'Pub in the Park', the 'Let's Rock' festivals have now expanded to several different family-friendly festival locations across the UK each year.

A number of community fund-raising events are organised in Cookham Dean by a charity called the Cherry Pickers, historically known as the Kaffirs. The organisation started in the 1800s, when Cookham Dean was known for its cherry trees, and was then just an outback area where 'a rough lot of vagrant workers' were employed to pick them. The Copas family owned the Orchards at Cookham Dean since at least 1901 and have since diversified into other areas including their well known Christmas turkey farm. The Cherry Pickers still meet at the Jolly Farmer Pub that was purchased by members of the community in the 1980s.
- **Boxing Day Games** on the old cricket common in Cookham Dean started in the 1970s. The event consists of a number of silly games such as potato sack races, blindfolded relays, space hopper races and tug-of-war contests that often end up with very muddy participants. There are normally about 150 competitors, and another 200 to 300 supporters and locals turning out to watch. Afterwards, everyone moves on to the Jolly Farmer or Uncle Tom's Cabin pub for a lively traditional Boxing Day drink.

Kim Wilde at Cookham's Rock the Moor, 2022.

Space Hoppers at the Boxing Day games 2022.

Cookham Gravity Grand Prix races outside The Jolly Farmer pub, 2023.

Competitors who have spent Christmas Day with family elsewhere sometimes drive more than 100 miles to Cookham Dean in the morning to take part. Cherry Picker organiser Peter Austen, described it as "exciting and entertaining games fought in their normal highly competitive but not too serious fashion."

- **Gravity Grand Prix** started in 2007 and has gone from strength to strength. It takes place each September in Cookham Dean and attracts people from miles around to see the various carts that have been made by enthusiastic teams.
- **Christmas Carol Singing** — As the Cherry Picker's describe it: "A terrible sound pervades the hostelries of Cookham on the Friday before Christmas as the Kaffirs try to sing and drink their way through the village!"

Maidenhead regeneration — Having been a regular visitor to the area for a number of years, I've seen the Maidenhead town centre go through ups and downs. Despite it being an affluent Berkshire commuter town to London, a lack of investment in the town centre and competition with both on-line shopping and more competitive offerings in Reading and Windsor have led to a decline in the local economy.

Maidenhead's town centre is now going through a £500 million redevelopment approved by Borough councillors in 2021. The centrepiece development is known as the Nicholson Quarter. The main developer is Areli Real Estate, led by Rob Tincknell, who played a key role in the decade long project to redevelop the Battersea Power Station in London. The plan is to demolish the existing 1970s shopping centre and replace it with double the number of shops but half the overall retail space, adding 364 flats and 311 senior living homes. Mr Tincknell believes the future of retailing is 'much more about local, smaller simpler shops and the restoration of what we used to have in towns — the butcher, the baker — specialised stores run by local people who really understand the catchment and their customers. Our approach is to level the whole place, start again and build a proper, original town centre'.

The Royal Borough of Maidenhead and Windsor has embraced Maidenhead town centre regeneration as a 'strategic growth location' for the area in the Local Plan approved for the period of 2013–2033. The Local Plan calls for 2100 new residential units in the town centre and another 2600 units with new schools in the southwest section of the town on the golf course formerly owned by Lord Desborough. As of 2024, a proposal from Cala Homes had been submitted for 1500 new homes on the golf course.

- These two areas of Maidenhead have been allocated the lion's share of growth in the Borough due to the need for rejuvenation of the town centre along with the benefits of having new homes located close to the train station with quick links to London. The long anticipated Elizabeth Line opened in Maidenhead in 2020 providing further convenience for commuting to London.
- Like many Local Plans, it calls for new developments to be 'active travel' friendly with good footpaths and cycle routes tying in public transportation links to reduce traffic and support national climate change targets. Whilst this makes sense and fosters healthy, community-based lifestyles, it can also be a code word for a lack of investment in the required road infrastructure and

Maidenhead town centre redevelopment in 2023.

The Elizabeth Line and active travel in Maidenhead.

adequate parking for new homes. Another reality is that even with sufficient funding, there is little space or appetite for construction of new roads on green open spaces.

- Not everyone is happy with the plans. Some residents think the council just wanted to protect beautiful, affluent places like Cookham, Ascot and Bray, and dump the new housing allocation on the less desirable Maidenhead. Windsor also escaped major development plans as they have less space for growth due to the large areas of royal property, protected Great Windsor Park and the need to support tourism.

Green Belt development — Cookham and Marlow sit within the 'Green Belt' surrounding London which protects these areas from being subsumed by endless urban sprawl from London and towns like Maidenhead. Green Belt national planning policies have been effective in helping to conserve the picturesque nature of these and other towns and villages in the Thames Valley.

National policy states that significant developments on Green Belt land should only be allowed in 'very special circumstances' — and rarely without a fight from local residents. Cookham has long resisted developments that could easily turn the village into an extension of Maidenhead, especially near Widbrook Common that separates the two communities.

- In 1597, Queen Elizabeth I leased Widbrook Common to the village for a term of three lives — meaning they could choose three residents to sign the lease that would stay in effect until the last one died. The village chose a 17 year old bargeman named Thomas Dodson who lived until the age of 86, well into the reign of Charles II. After that, the village simply refused to return grazing rights to the Crown.
- In 1799, Cookham's newly installed vicar gave notice of an Enclosure Act proposal to take over the common land at Widbrook. Despite Enclosure Acts being common by that time, such was the protest by residents of the village that the act was comfortably defeated in Parliament.
- Wary of Cookham's fiercely independent history, the Windsor and Maidenhead Local Plan appears to recognise the need to preserve the separateness and special nature of the village, at least through the 2033 planning period.

Case Study: Marlow Film Studio — Like Cookham, many Marlow residents do not take their special location for granted and have formed a community group called 'Save Marlow's Green Belt' to help keep it that way. The main object of their campaigning has been the proposal to develop a new state of the art Marlow Film Studio on the outskirts of town on Green Belt land. Residents of many towns would be excited and proud for such a development, but this group is running a campaign to stop it at all costs. They point out 'that natural green spaces make an important contribution to our quality of life, protect wildlife and define the character of this area. The Green Belt must be preserved for future generations because once it's gone, it's gone forever'. The Marlow Film Studio planning application was submitted in July 2022. By the end of the year, nearly 1000 objections had been raised on the planning authority's web-site, with many encouraged by Save Marlow's Green Belt web-site that lists 10 detailed reasons people can use to argue against its approval. The Film Studio cited the significant social and economic benefits it would bring the area with support from celebrities such as British director Sam Mendes "as a resident of South Bucks and member of the film community".

In May 2024, plans were refused by the Buckinghamshire Council amidst concerns that this was an inappropriate development for greenbelt land and would have a significant impact on the local road network. It remains to be seen whether the film studio developers will appeal the decision, but as with Cookham, it looks like the forces of conservation are winning in Marlow.

Left: Widbrook Common, with a view to Cliveden in the distance, has been common grazing land since at least 1597, ensuring Cookham village stays separate and distinct from Maidenhead.

4. Henley-on-Thames

Henley is not just a popular tourist destination, synonymous with the famous rowing competition, but also a desirable and a beautiful place to live for those commuting to London or fortunate enough to work locally. It presents a grand image with its impressive market square with outdoor cafés by the Town Hall, its historic five-arched bridge over the Thames and ample walking paths along the river. It is busiest during the summer 'silly season' with the regatta being held the first week in July attracting visitors from all over the world.

Henley Royal Regatta — The Henley Regatta is arguably the most prestigious international rowing event short of the Olympics. There are currently 26 events in total, each with a silver cup prize:
- The 12 open events are open to all amateur rowers including athletes competing at Olympic medal level. These events attract top international crews, with the Men's 8-crew Grand Challenge Cup being the most prestigious event, dating back to the original races in 1839.
- Four events are for members of independent rowing clubs.
- Three student events open to teams from higher educational institutions.
- Three intermediate level events that were previously open only to schools and clubs are now open to all amateur rowers.
- Four junior events that are open to crews aged 18 or under.

Every year Henley is visited by more and more crews from abroad with 172 teams participating from overseas in 2022. Given the limited number of hotels in the area, the Henley community pitches in. Henley 'landladies' have traditionally offered accommodation at their family homes to visiting foreign crews. They typically need to accommodate ten people as a crew of eight plus their coach and cox all prefer to stay together.

Ten of the 26 HRR races are now for women crews, but a separate Henley Women's Regatta has been held along the same course in June each year since 1988. The Women's Regatta offers a much broader range of events, also attracting crews from around the world.

The Henley Town & Visitors Regatta held at the end of July has been going on almost as long as the HRR, but caters to a slightly lower level of competition. The Town Regatta includes crews from Henley's own Henley Rowing Club and Upper Thames Rowing Clubs, crews from many Oxford College teams that are below the Oxford 'Blue' level, and teams from Rowing Clubs in Wallingford, Reading, Marlow, Maidenhead, Eton, Shiplake and many further afield.

The regatta isn't only about the rowing, of course. Many spectators choose to watch up close from private pleasure craft, whilst others have access to the exclusive Stewards Enclosure at the finish line, or perhaps the Phyllis Court Club on the Oxfordshire side.

Opposite Page: Pangbourne College crew prepare for their race at the Henley Regatta with the Royal Barge *Gloriana* in the foreground.
Below: Abingdon School on the verge of defeating a Canadian school team in a heat for The Princess Elizabeth Challenge Cup in the junior event category.

The traditional dress code for the HRR Stewards Enclosure is strictly enforced. Gentlemen are required to wear lounge suits or jackets with flannels, with a tie or cravat. Ladies are required to wear dresses or skirts with a hemline below the knee and will not be admitted wearing divided skirts. Ladies were finally allowed to wear trousers or trouser suits for the first time in 2021. Whilst not a requirement, members and guests are encouraged to wear hats. Use of mobile phones is also prohibited — although this rule is seemingly less enforced in recent years.

The Leander Club, located by the bridge next to the HRR course, is home to the most elite rowers in the UK. Since 1908, its members have won 127 Olympic and Paralympic medals making it the most successful rowing club in the world.

Right: A Leander Club rower prepares for an early morning practice.
Below: A view of the Stewards Enclosure from the river – where everyone appears to be adhering to the dress code.
Opposite top: In 2023, Oxford Brookes rowing teams won a record eight HRR cups, with their supporters showing their joy at one of the wins.
Opposite bottom: Supporters of the Dutch Amsterdam student rowing club Nereus have a tradition of stripping off and swimming up to their team's boat when they win a final, as happened when they won the Temple Challenge Cup at Henley in 2021.

Festival town — Henley's experience with hosting the regatta combined with the attractive town setting along the river makes Henley the logical choice for attracting visitors to countless other festivals throughout the year:

- **The Henley Festival** is a music and arts festival held the week following the regatta on the grounds of the Stewards Enclosure. Like the regatta, the Henley Festival also has a strict dress code of black tie for men and glamorous dresses for women. The main stage floats on the river and the stands from the regatta are used to watch headline acts such as Burt Bacharach, Tom Jones, Lionel Richie, and Madness. Having been a few times myself, I know it can be a lovely summer's evening out, with plenty of bars and fine dining options as well as quirky performance artists, comedians and art exhibitions.
- **The Henley Literary Festival,** founded by local resident and Fleet Street veteran Sue Ryan in 2007, is normally held the first week in October. Now largely run by her daughter Harriet Reed-Ryan, the festival has gone from strength to strength. Full of big name authors speaking at venues across the town, it has firmly established itself as one of the most popular literary festival in the UK. The 2022 festival featured authors Robert Harris and Lucy Worsley, comedian Lenny Henry and Spice Girl Mel C.
- **The Traditional Boat Festival** is the largest gathering of classic river craft in the world, filled with proud boat owners and enthusiasts keen to show off their beautiful craft. The event takes place in mid-July on the Fawley Meadows along the river. You've never seen so many polished wooden boats with costumed crews.
- **Henley Swim** is the name for a growing number of organised swimming races on the river held between June and August with different lengths for different swimmer's abilities. Some, such as the Selkie Henley Classic are on the 1.5 mile course of the regatta early one morning in June before it is busy with rowers.
- **Rewind** is an '80s Music festival held along the river by Temple Island over a weekend in August with dozens of the biggest names from the 1980s such as Boy George, OMD, and Kim Wilde. Established in 2009, it is similar to Cookham's 'Let's Rock the Moor', but bigger, with up to 40,000 suitably aged participants in fancy dress reliving their youth.
- **The Henley Show** is the traditional county agricultural show established in 1891, normally held on the first Saturday in September. It includes everything from cow and horse judging, to vegetable growing and dog training. It takes place on the beautiful setting of Greenland's Farm in Hambleden, part of Culden Faw estate. Other events held at the site include a variety of equestrian events and an annual 'Tough Mudder' extreme sports challenge.
- **The Ploughing Match** is held in October for farmers who take pride in their ploughing, as well as hobbyist 'tractor boys', as we like to call them. According to the rules,: 'Good ploughing always looks good to the eye. Trash must be well buried; the land firm and level, and the start and finish of the work should be neat and not overly high or deep. Furrow entrances and exits should be neat and tidy.'

Below: Judging at the Henley Agricultural Show.
Opposite top: Performers at the Henley Festival.
Opposite bottom: Sir Lenny Henry on his way to his talk at the Henley Literary Festival with BBC presenter Leah Boleto who interviewed him at the event.

Henley glamour — Henley is no stranger to celebrities. There are a number of famous actors, politicians and musicians who have chosen make Henley their home.
- Actors Orlando Bloom, Russell Brand and Rowan Atkinson live in the area, and at the time of writing, James Corden was building a new home for his planned return to the UK.
- Actor Jeremy Irons lives outside Henley in Watlington and often supports local charities such as refurbishment of a vacant home to house Ukrainian refugees. I've run into the actor around Henley on a couple of occasions including one time we were both paddling canoes on the river during the Henley Festival.
- George Harrison was a long time resident and several other rock stars have chosen it as home over the years.
- Politically, Henley has historically been known for being a safe Conservative parliamentary seat at least until the 2024 elections. Previous MPs have included Valentine Fleming during WWI, the father of James Bond author Ian Fleming. There is still a large 'Fleming Estate' near Nettlebed. More recently, Henley's MPs have been former Deputy Prime Minister Michael Heseltine, followed by former Prime Minister Boris Johnson. Since leaving government, Mr Johnson has moved back to the area.

Henley v. Marlow — Henley, has a population of just over 12,000 (2021 Census) so is actually a little smaller than it's neighbour Marlow, a few miles downstream, which has just under 15,000 residents. Henley is clearly the more famous town and it is no secret that there is a bit of a rivalry between the two. Both have attractive river settings with historic, picturesque bridges over the Thames and nearby attractive church towers. Residents of both towns are justifiably proud of where they live and like to compare things such as which town has the most thriving local businesses, which has the better Christmas decorations and which is generally the better place to live. Henley may have the fame and tourists, but some in Marlow pride themselves on its focus towards younger, hipper families, with Henley having a slightly stuffier, more traditional image with a growing number of retirement communities.

A number of residents complained about Henley's Christmas lights in 2022, some citing that they were inferior to those in places like Marlow and Burford. A typical comment seen on the Henley Standard Facebook page was "if the Town Council are looking to attract people to the shops over the festive period, they need to pull out all the stops next year and make Henley the talk of the Thames Valley for decorations". The Henley Town Council duly approved £55,000 spending on new Christmas lights for 2023.

In 2017, there was even talk of a Henley vs. Marlow-style Olympics. A Henley Town Councillor raised the slightly facetious proposal at a council meeting: "It would be a competition between the two towns — we know we're best but we would like the opportunity to prove it. I see the Mayor of Henley and the Mayor of Marlow laying down the gauntlet over the bridge and we can have fun with it. Every age group would be involved. It's potentially 20 sports, with a tug of war across the river could be quite interesting."

In reality, both towns are gems of the Thames Valley offering different things to different people. I know from living in the area that Henley residents are also very friendly and were even voted one of the ten friendliest towns in the UK in 2014 by the *Telegraph* due to the number of charity and fundraising activities held each year.

Left: Marlow Christmas Lights in 2022 — better than Henley's?

5. Reading

Reading may lack some of the glamour and sophistication of Henley, Windsor or Oxford, but it is the primary transport and commercial hub of the Thames Valley making it the largest town in the region and one of the fastest growing towns in the UK. The town's skyline is in a constant state of flux with new high rise offices and flats popping up on a regular basis. It is the economic heart of the Thames Valley, offering a wealth of employment, shopping and entertainment, transport links and diverse neighbourhoods.

- **Employment** — No longer known for 'Biscuits, Bulbs and Beer', Reading is at the heart of the Thames Valley High Tech corridor with several business parks hosting HQs for international companies such as Microsoft, Oracle, Chinese Telecom supplier Huawei, PepsiCo, and Prudential Insurance. It is also the base for UK companies Virgin Media O2 and mobile operator Three UK.
- **Shopping and Entertainment** — As someone who lives near Reading, I see it as a convenient place for shopping or a night out for a movie, dinner, or maybe a comedy or music show at the Hexagon. It has pretty much everything you need between the Oracle shopping mall, the outdoor Broad Street shopping mall, a very large John Lewis, Ikea, and Sainsbury and Tesco superstores. The nightlife tends to be for people who live in town but there is a good choice of bars and restaurants, both national chains and local ethnic food.
- **Transport Hub** — It is accessible via Junctions 10, 11, and 12 of the M4, and boasts a recently modernised rail station to accommodate both the Great Western Railway and the new Queen Elizabeth Line. It is also at the conjunction of the Thames and Kennet rivers, which was more important during the town's history. The rivers are now mostly used for walking and cycling along or for alfresco dining on the Kennet by the Oracle shopping mall.
- **Diverse Neighbourhoods** — Reading may be best known for its city centre shopping district but there are a range of diverse neighbourhoods throughout the town. The leafy suburban neighbourhoods of Caversham include the generous Christ Church Meadows and Caversham Court open spaces along the river. Many choose to live in the more affordable areas of Tilehurst or East Reading that includes the University of Reading Whiteknights campus. I sometimes enjoy exploring the ethnic diversity along Oxford Road that I will talk about shortly.

City status — Reading is considered a town, a borough in the county of Berkshire and a unitary council with the powers of a combined district and county council — but it is not a city. Reading Borough is made up of 16 Wards with a population of 174,000 (2021 Census) an increase of almost 12% since 2011 that is one of the fastest in growth rates in the country. Already larger than many UK cities, the population of the metropolitan area is estimated to be 318,000 if you count Reading's growing suburbs such as Earley, Woodley, Calcot and Shinfield.

In the UK, only the monarch has the authority to bestow city status and normally does so on special occasions such as a Royal Jubilee. Reading has sought the Crown's approval to be called a city four times since 2000, and has

The Oracle shopping mall along the River Kennet.

failed each time. For the Queen's Platinum Jubilee in 2020, Milton Keynes and several other towns much smaller than Reading were bestowed city status. As an American, I sometimes struggle to understand what the big deal is about becoming a city. Different states in America have different rules, but usually settlements can decide for themselves on whether to be called a town or city as long as they meet minimum population thresholds of between 500 and 12,000 residents, depending upon the state. From what I can see, the designation as a city in the UK is purely honorary, conferring no special rights or privileges, beyond the pride its residents may have in the designation and possibly a small boost to tourism — So why is the process for becoming a city so difficult and the criteria so obscure? One of the magical mysteries of England, I guess.

Sir John Madejski — Reading wouldn't be what it is today without businessman and philanthropist Sir John Madejski, best known as owner of the Reading Football club and the stadium that bears his name. Madejski made his fortune after founding the *Thames Valley Auto Trader* magazine in 1977. This turned into *Auto Trader* and he set up a web-site in 1996 giving people to ability to buy and sell cars on-line.

Madejski became chairman of the Reading Royals Football Club in 1990 and largely paid for the modern stadium named after him in 1998. His tenure as Chairman saw the team promoted to the Premier League in 2006 and again in 2012 with great pride for the town. The fact that they were fairly quickly relegated back to the Champions League each time didn't seem to phase local fans, embracing the team and town for what it is despite any shortcomings.

Madejski sold the club in 2012 after more than 20 years as owner. As of 2024 the current owner, Dai Yonge, has mismanaged the 125 year old club resulting in a difficult financial position and the team being further relegated to League One. Fans have not taken this sitting down and have held protests calling for the new owner to go, chanting "Sell before we Dai".

Sir John has long been supportive of local charitable causes. He provided a major contribution for the building of the Falkland Islands Memorial Chapel at Pangbourne College. His name can be seen on a new centre at the Henley Business School, a gallery of the Reading Museum and a lecture hall at the University of Reading.

The diversity of Oxford Road — According to some reports, there are 150 languages being spoken in Reading schools. This diversity is most evident along the Oxford Road on Reading's west side. It can be considered to be a bit of a rough neighbourhood, but walking along the road can feel like a trip to other parts of the world. The shops are nearly all independently and locally owned with a multicultural flair.

- Reading has long had a strong Polish community. Some of it stemming from WWII Polish refugee camps in the area, other from emigration when Britain was part of the European Union. There are several supermarkets and shops specialising in Polish sausages, meats, and other products shipped in from Poland.
- Turkish and Romanian shops also feature heavily, including the Istanbul Food Centre, and car washes run by Romanian crews.
- You will pass a number of women's beauty salons specialising in Afro-Caribbean hairstyles and wigs. There are African-style food shops and restaurants including Betty's Ghana style restaurant. 'Needful Things', is a type of hardware store/pound shop of things that you might need around the house. I recognise the term from work I have done in Africa over the years.
- The imposing Central Jamme Mosque, located half way down the street, is maintained under the management of the Bangladesh Association Greater Reading (BAGR), but is open to Muslims originating from various countries for prayers 6 times a day.
- Food tends to be dominated by kebab restaurants and takeaway shops, specialising in Afghan, Pakistani, and other styles.
- You will also see many signs for butchers with halaal certified meat as required under Muslim tradition and bakeries specialising in vegan eggless cakes, for those practicing Hinduism and Buddhism.
- One of the few coffee shops on Oxford Road, so common elsewhere nowadays, is Workhouse Coffee, a Reading-based independent coffee roastery.
- West Tailoring, one of the few remaining tailors in Reading, is ironically run by tailors originating from the east in Afghanistan. I highly recommend their excellent service with very reasonable prices.
- Things continue to change as, sadly, 'the Shop on the Bridge' electrical supply shop closed in 2017 after nearly 70 years in Reading not long after I took photos of it in 2016. It was an old-fashioned shop in that you could always rely on the staff to find the correct parts you needed for a particular type of bulb, fuse, cable or light fixture. Today these things can probably still be found at B&Q, Screwfix or somewhere on the internet, but it's just doesn't have the same personal touch and Oxford Road is poorer for its loss.

Scenes on Oxford Road clockwise from top left:
- Romanian crew working at Diamond Car Wash.
- A young visitor to the now closed 'Shop on the Bridge' electronics shop gets a surprise from Des Smith and his parrot Tias that he carries on his shoulder.
- West Tailoring is a family run business of tailors originally from Afghanistan.

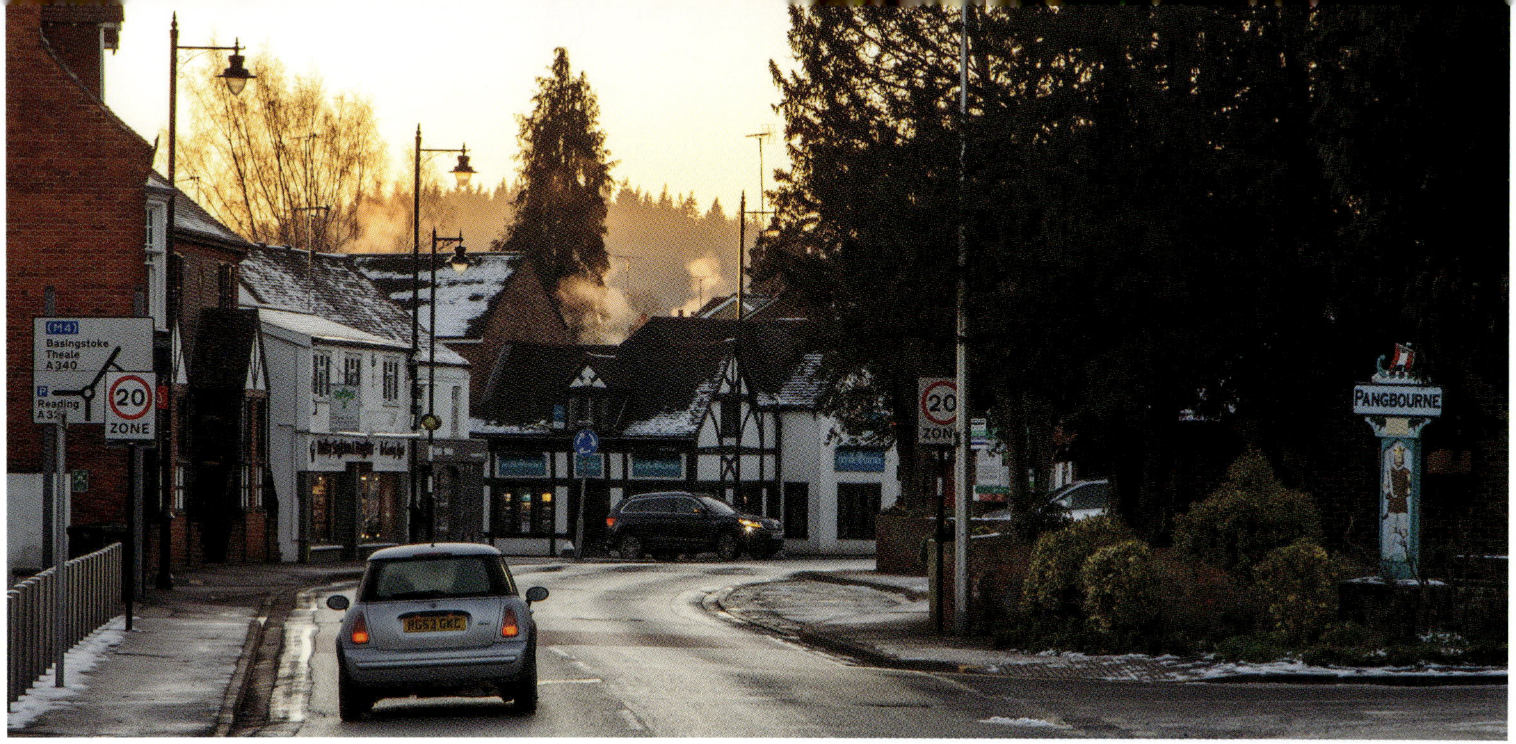
M4
Basingstoke
Theale
A340
Reading
20
ZONE
RG53 GKE
20
PANGBOURNE

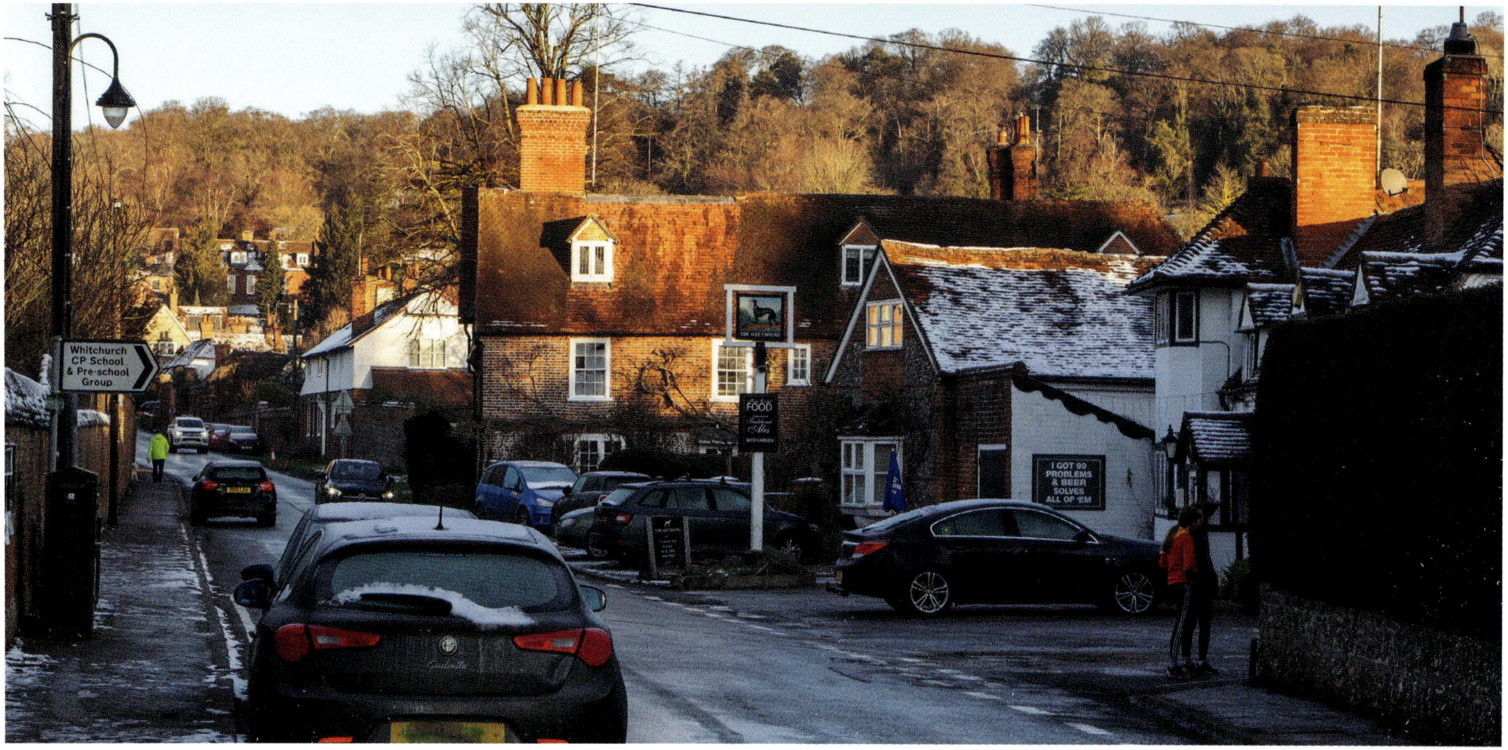
Whitchurch
CP School
& Pre-school
Group
FOOD
I GOT 99
PROBLEMS
& BEER
SOLVES
ALL OF 'EM

6. Pangbourne and Whitchurch-on-Thames

Pangbourne's unpretentious yet vibrant High Street belies the beautiful stretch of the river that it lies on just a couple of blocks behind it by the Pangbourne Meadow. When I say unpretentious, that doesn't take into account the Aston Martin and Lamborghini dealerships, the beautiful setting of the historic Swan Pub along the river, or some of the imposing homes located in the hills above the village. The village has a reputation of being a bit 'posh', or at least an affluent commuter town. This is reflected in house prices, but part of the reason I like living near there is because it actually has an economically diverse population that institutions such as the 130 year-old 'Pangbourne Working Men's Club' hint at.

The High Street is not particularly large but it has all the basic necessities and offers much more than many other rural villages in the area so it acts as a regional centre for shopping in this part of West Berkshire and South Oxfordshire. It has a Co-op supermarket, a petrol station, a few pubs, and a nice selection of restaurants and coffee shops, two Turkish barbers, plus the usual hairdressers and estate agents. Locally-owned independent shops include the Pangbourne Cheese Shop, Birch Bread bakery, Green's award winning organic butcher, Garland's organic grocer and Collins Hardware store.

Thames Twin Towns — If it weren't for the separation of the two villages by the River Thames, Pangbourne and Whitchurch-on-Thames could easily be a single village. Neither village is particularly large. Pangbourne has a population of just under 3000 people (2021 Census), and Whitchurch-on-Thames about 850 (2021 Census). As the retail businesses in Whitchurch are limited to a couple of pubs and an art gallery, residents from both villages make use of Pangbourne High Street shopping. Whitchurch residents can walk or cycle to the shops from home as if they were part of the same community. Pangbourne has a train station to London that commuters from Whitchurch and other nearby villages also make use of.

The River Thames is also the border between the counties of Berkshire and Oxfordshire. Pangbourne is on the West Berkshire side and Whitchurch-on-Thames in South Oxfordshire. Because of this, the villages have separate parish councils, schools, churches, annual fêtes, village magazines and generally separate identities.

The privately owned toll bridge at Whitchurch, which still requires drivers to pay 60p to pass between the villages (47p if you have a pre-paid bridge pass), acts to accentuate the separation of the two villages and perhaps add a little exclusivity and mystique to the Whitchurch side. A bit further out in Oxfordshire are the villages of Whitchurch Hill, Crays Pond and Woodcote, whose residents are also frequent users of Pangbourne services, as long as they are willing to pay the fee to drive over the toll bridge.

There were significant protests in both villages when the private bridge company was allowed to increase the crossing fee from 40p to 60p following the bridge's replacement in 2014. The justification provided by the owners was that the increase was needed to cover unexpected costs due to heavy flooding that delayed construction that winter. A packed public meeting was held at Pangbourne's George Hotel where an independent government inspector heard arguments for and against the fee increase, mostly against. I attended the meeting as the newly elected Vice Chairman of the Whitchurch Parish Council to express our concerns, but in the end, the fee increase was approved as neither West Berkshire Council nor Oxfordshire County Council had any interest in subsidising or purchasing the bridge and were happy to let the private bridge company recoup their costs.

At least now there is no charge for walking or cycling over the bridge as there used to be in the days when *Wind in the Willows* Author Kenneth Grahame lived in Pangbourne.

> *Kenneth used to laugh and say that our sole source of income consisted in not going over Whitchurch Bridge, which we seldom did, though we constantly stood there.*
> Elspeth, wife of Kenneth Grahame

Opposite page: Pangbourne village on top; Whitchurch High Street below. Right: View of St Mary's church from Whitchurch toll bridge with Mr Toad after the 2017 'Yarn Bomb' event that decorated the bridge with figures.

Community spirit —Those who have lived in either village for at least a few years will inevitably run into a number of friends and acquaintances as they walk into town, take a train into Reading or London, or visit a local coffee shop, pub, or restaurant. The villages are large enough to offer a range of opportunities for social interaction, and small enough geographically that walking and cycling is often preferred to driving, very much like the 15 minute neighbourhoods being promoted by some in Oxford. It often feels like everyone is a member of the same social club or even extended family. Everyone has their separate homes, but as soon as you walk outside, you run into members of the close knit community who are all working to support the common good.

As with many other Thames Valley villages, there are a remarkable number of community groups in each village, beyond the traditional school and church communities:

- Both have community gardens run by allotment societies.
- Each village has its own history group.
- Both have active Cricket and Football Clubs as well as a Tennis Club in Pangbourne.
- Both have church bell ringing groups with their respective churches, and also a hand bell group in Whitchurch.
- Both have twinning associations with villages in France and normally alternate visits between the UK and France each year. Pangbourne is twinned with Houdan, near Paris, and Whitchurch and Goring Heath with La Bouille along the Seine in Normandy.
- Pangbourne has an active Choral Society that holds a Christmas Concert each year at the Falkland Island Memorial Chapel at Pangbourne College.
- Pangbourne also has a brass band with a history dating back to 1893 that can normally be seen at the Pangbourne Fête and leading Christmas carols at the annual Christmas High Street event.
- One group that is joint between the villages is the Pangbourne and Whitchurch Sustainability Group (PAWS). This has been working well for over 10 years and includes a very popular Apple Juicing Day that takes place at a small park known as the Maze. There is also a separate Whitchurch-on-Thames Habitat Study group (WOTHabs) that takes on local initiatives to help preserve the natural environment in the village.
- Whitchurch has a Green Team of volunteers to help maintain various aspects of the village open spaces including the recently adopted Polish Church Memorial Gardens in the site of a former WWII camp for Polish refugees.
- There is an Art Café each Saturday morning in Whitchurch that raises money for a different local charity each week. Volunteers serve tea, coffee, and cake and there are many regular visitors who use this as an opportunity to catch up with friends.

Alexa Duckworth-Briggs (right), Sally Woolhouse (centre) and Doreen Gow (left) of the Green Team planning the new Polish Refugee Memorial Garden.

The infamous egg toss at the annual Whitchurch Hill Fête.

The Pangbourne Brass Band leading Christmas carols.

Intrepid early morning swimmers by the toll bridge in the winter.

The Easter dawn service at St James-the-Less church.

A meeting of the Pangbourne Heritage Group at St James-the-Less church.

Pangbourne toilets — There were a number of changes to the Pangbourne High Street between about 2010 and 2020. For the most part, residents adapted to these changes pretty well.
- The local Post Office was not deemed financially viable by the privatised Post Office corporation. It was closed but then moved a few doors down to become part of Collins Hardware store, which seems to suit people pretty well.
- All three High Street bank branch offices closed with the advent of internet and mobile banking. The Co-op installed a free to use cash machine on the High Street which most people now seem happy with.
- There were some protests when West Berkshire Council (WBC) cut back the hours of the Pangbourne Library, but people were at least grateful that it didn't succumb to complete closure of the library which has been the case in so many other communities in recent years .

But when West Berks decided to cut funding for the public toilets with no real alternative available, this was a step too far. As a resident of Whitchurch who was an occasional user of these toilets on forays into Pangbourne, I was one of the outraged voices objecting to this decision. The decision probably impacted visitors to Pangbourne even more than local residents who are normally not too far from home. As with other cutbacks, this was a direct result of the 'Austerity Programme' in the years following the 2010 election of the Conservative-Liberal Democrat Coalition under Prime Minimiser David Cameron. Following an increase in government debt to address the 2008 financial crisis, severe cutbacks were initiated aimed at balancing the budget. Public toilets were apparently not one of the services that local councils were obligated to provide, so whilst not a popular decision, it was one of the things within their powers to cut. I remember attending a Pangbourne Parish Council meeting in 2014 where the West Berks Councillor, stated that they had originally planned to demolish the toilets to make way for a few more revenue-generating parking spaces in the Village Hall car park.

This is where community action took over at an unprecedented level to get the toilets reinstated. Despite objections, West Berks proceeded with closure of the toilets in April 2015. A group of concerned residents of the village formed a Community Trust called Action for Pangbourne Toilets (APT), who eventually got permission to run the toilets on behalf of the parish council and raised the needed £10,000 in contributions from private and public bodies to refurbish it to the point where they could be re-opened in September 2017. APT continues to work as a private organisation to manage operations of the toilets and raise funds for additional improvements. The Whitchurch Parish Council and other organisations continue to contribute each year to APT to help keep the toilets going.

A study by the BBC showed that at least 673 public toilets across the UK have stopped being maintained by local councils since 2010. Pangbourne's actions show how community spirit can be harnessed to devolve powers into the hands of individuals who care about the community.

Left: Grand re-opening of the Pangbourne Toilets in 2017. Local MP Alok Sharma with the button down shirt in the centre and organiser Sir Brian Hoskins with the white beard and sports coat to his right. I am in the back on the right.

Richard Deverrill of Abbootts Shoes on Pangbourne High Street took over from his father-in-law George Abbott in 1982. The shop finally closed in 2023.

Milan, Simon and Peter serving beer at the Pangbourne Fête in 2014 to a thirsty Nick Syfret.

Local tree surgeon Ian Hogg uses a wheelbarrow to transport his rubbish and laundry from his narrow boat *Snapdragon* on the Pangbourne meadow.

Peter McManners, John White, Simon Eely and Caroline Knight help clear the pavements on Horseshoe Road after an increasingly rare snow storm.

Gypsies and Travellers— One of the biggest fears of residents is the thought of Gypsies or Travellers setting up caravans in their village. As Chairman of the Whitchurch Parish Council, I am normally the first person people alert with reports of Travellers in the area. People fear that Gypsies will cause an increase in local crime and leave litter and mess at their camp sites. Parish councils fear the local backlash they would face for allowing this to happen and also the required effort and legal fees to have them moved on. Councils go to great lengths to add security to local parks and open spaces to prevent access by Gypsy caravans. One unfortunate side effect of these concerns has been the seemingly continual increase in the amount of fencing, barricades, ditches and other security measure at both private and public green spaces across the country.

Clearly many of these fears are based on stereotypes of Gypsies that are not always true, but the fears are real nonetheless. Not all Gypsies and Travellers are the same. There are Romany and Welsh Gypsies, Irish Travellers, New Age Travellers, and those travelling for work as showmen. According to a 2018 UK Parliamentary Report, the total number of Traveller caravans in England was 22,662, an increase of 29% since 2008. The majority of caravans were on private sites, 29% were on sites operated by local authorities and registered providers of social housing and 14% were on unauthorised sites.

We have not had Travellers staying in Whitchurch up to this point, but Pangbourne has not been so lucky. There were two recent incidents of Travellers in caravans camping on the Pangbourne Meadows.
- In 2017 a group of Irish Travellers were on the meadows for a period of less than a month without any major incidents. The parish council had to follow a procedure to have them removed by the police that involved thousands of pounds in legal fees and took a few weeks time.
- In 2018, other, more aggressive Travellers came onto the Pangbourne meadows, chain-sawing the fence by the Dolphin Aquatic Centre on the Thames river meadow as they came. There were a number of incidents attributed to the Travellers in the first few days that were considered criminal offences, so the police were able to legally evict them in a matter of days.

The government seems to be walking a tightrope in its polices towards Gypsies and Travellers. On the one hand, the government accepts a responsibility to ensure that there is sufficient access to legal sites to support the rights of Travellers to live a nomadic lifestyle. They also support the need to address the inequalities facing them, including limited access to education for their children. On the over hand, there have also been recent changes to legislation such as the Police, Crime, Sentencing and Courts Act of 2022 that has increased the powers of local authorities to evict Travellers camping on unauthorised sites such as roadside verges. Gypsy and Traveller activist groups are concerned about this act and have had some success in persuading the Supreme Court to provide guidance to limit certain types of enforcement under the act.

Left: Travellers on the river actually come to Pangbourne meadows on a regular basis.

7. Hardwick Estate community

Located on the river at Whitchurch-on-Thames, the Estate forms its own self-contained community with a distinct 'left-leaning, free-spirit, hippy' vibe. It is compromised of approximately 900 acres of woodland, farms, homes, and social enterprises centred around the historic Hardwick House that sits along the Thames. It has been the site of a manor since at least the16th century, and it is still run as an estate with a semi-feudal feel to it, similar to nearby Mapledurham and Englefield Estates.

Hardwick is owned by the Rose family who have a history of supporting progressive ideals. It was purchased by Liberal MP Sir Charles Day Rose in 1909. Sir Julian Rose, who inherited the Estate in 1966, became the 4th Baronet of 'Hardwick House in the Parish of Whitchurch in the County of Oxfordshire'. He is well known for encouraging the availability of unpasteurised milk, and he continues to promote organic farming as well as leading anti-GMO protests.

The Estate is now managed by Julian's daughter Miriam Rose, who works as a human rights activist when not managing the Estate, and chooses to live in a separate off-grid house with her partner and children instead of the main manor house itself. Their house in the Hardwick woods overlooks the River Thames from the edge of the Chiltern Hills. Much of the historic Hardwick House itself is now rented out to provide income that helps cover maintenance costs of the house.

There are 27 houses owned by the Estate and rented out to members of the Hardwick community. The homes on the Estate were originally set up for workers, and most are still used by those working on one of the Hardwick Estate enterprises. Nearly all of the homes are on an 'affordable rent for rural workers'. Miriam says that this rent is well below the standard 80% of market value typically used to define affordable rent. There is no requirement for them to be at this discounted rate, but part of the ethos of the Hardwick community is that local rural workers who work there should able to afford to live there.

Offering the public access on designated rights of way is another part of Hardwick's ethos— something that I have taken advantage of countless times, both on foot and by mountain bike. Riverboat-based Hardwick resident artist and author Nick Hayes is a national advocate for a 'right to roam' across England.

According to Kenneth Grahame's biographer, Peter Green, Mr Toad represented the 'landed rentier squandering his capital on riotous pleasures' that was prevalent in the early 1900s. Green goes on to say that 'this kind of irresponsibility provided the best possible propaganda for radicals who wanted to bring the whole system of inherited wealth and traditional class-values crashing down'. It seems somehow fitting that the descendants of Sir Charles Day Rose, who was a likely model for Mr Toad, are now trying to end this inherited system at Hardwick.

In 2022, Miriam, her father Julian and her brother Lawrence took the decision to turn the Estate into a community-led charitable trust. The change is being made partly for inheritance tax reasons. Present tax laws could mean that a large chunk of the Estate would need to be sold off to cover inheritance tax. By moving it to a charitable trust, the estate can stay preserved largely as it is. A charitable trust would also mean that the 'burden of managing the Estate' can be transferred from the Rose family to trustees with the right skills to manage it. The trustees will probably include

Sir Julian Rose with some of the organic vegetables that can be purchased at the Veg Shed.

Miriam Rose at the Hardwick Estate Office, shortly before giving birth to her second child in 2024.

one or two members of the Rose family, but Miriam and her brother Lawrence would like to largely 'disinherit the Estate' after ensuring that it is preserved for the future in a sustainable manner. They also have no interest in having the baronetcy title transferred to them as they don't believe in the continuation of the landed aristocracy.

Miriam has held community meetings both on the Estate and in the village of Whitchurch to discuss things such as their plans to close the horse stud farm. Closure of the stud farm will enable the nutrient rich horse paddock land to be used for agricultural production going forward in line with their value of promoting food security. The grand Tudor-style horse stables would be converted to retail spaces for selling vegetables, artisan crafts developed locally and tea, coffee and other food for visitors to the Estate. There is also a working group looking at more sustainable energy options for the Estate such as solar and wind power.

Part of Hardwick's ethos is to foster the enterprises that make use of the Estate's land as well as maintaining spaces where members of the community can get together to share skills and enjoy each others' company. The 'beating heart' of the Estate is a number of progressive enterprises:

- **Tolhurst Organic** — has 19 acres of organic farming, having held the organic symbol for 40 years, making it one of the first and longest running organic vegetable farms in England. It has been run by Iain 'Tolly' Tolhurst, MBE since 1987 when Julian Rose invited him to manage the Hardwick organic farm Rose started in the 1970s. All the produce is sold locally via veg box schemes or the recently expanded 'Lin's Veg Shed' that still uses an honesty system for customers to pay for vegetable purchases. It is named after Tolly's former wife who worked to build the new shed before her untimely death. The farm runs annual events open to the wider Thames Valley community, including a Pumpkin and Squash Festival in October and a Strawberry Fayre in June. Tolly was formally recognised with an MBE for his decades of services to agriculture in 2023.
- **Path Hill Farm** — is also managed organically and has been run by tenant farmer James Norman since 1998. James manages several fields of exceptionally biodiverse hay meadows and grassland that traditional Hereford cattle graze on to produce organic beef. He leads annual hay meadow walks to highlight the diversity of the grass and wildflowers on the meadow and sells the hay and seeds for other farmers to establish hay meadows. He also grows organic wheat, oats and beans on about a third of the farm. James was able support growing of hemp again as of 2023 after working with Tolly and Hempen to finally secure a license from the Home Office.
- **Hempen** — was established in 2015 as a non-profit co-operative community made up of like-minded individuals who believe in the immense power of the hemp plant to provide a way of sustainable living.
  - Hemp is a strain of cannabis used for industrial products that was historically used for fibre products such as rope. UK law requires hemp plants grown locally to be less than 0.01% THC, so hemp that is grown at Hardwick is not a strain that could get you 'high'.

Left: Pumpkin and Squash Festival held each October by Tolhurst Organic.

Above: Iain 'Tolly' Tolhurst, MBE on the right, with his partner Tamara in the Veg Shed outside Hardwick gates. Tamara serves as the farm's director of business development. Below: Path Hill farmer James Norman moving cows across a wet field.

- Hempen works to produce products that leverage the ever growing uses for hemp to produce clothing, build houses, provide the healing power of CBD oil, and make food products such as vegetable oil, tea, and pesto sauce.
- The co-operative workers are mostly based at Hardwick on site in a shared house with ancillary caravans or river boats that come and go in a type of communal living.
- Hempen were forced by the Home Office to remove all their hemp plants in 2019 due to difficulty in getting a growing license. During this time, Hempen focussed on processing products from hemp supplied by other farmers. In 2023 they received permission to grow hemp locally again after much difficulty. As a result, they also promote an 'Overgrow the Regime' campaign to train and encourage more small farm holders to push for changes to simplify the licensing laws.

- **Path Hill Outdoors** — is a not for profit company that make use of the woodlands and river to offer outdoor learning opportunities aimed at students who don't necessarily fit within mainstream education. The many activities they offer include learning survival skills, campfire cooking, raft making and canoeing.
- **Green Broom** — is a smaller organic farm in another part of the Estate where a community of nine members live on site in what they call a co-operative of individuals with shared values. Crops are cultivated by hand without the use of fossil fuels, pesticides or artificial fertilisers. All deliveries are made by bicycle. They pride themselves on the model of community they have developed based on the principles of trust, transparency, respect and playfulness. Suz Williams, who practices coppicing and trains basket weaving skills, believes their non-hierachical decision-making and conflict resolution processes are key elements that makes their community so successful.
- **Sadhama Rewild Retreats** — are offered in the warmer weather and feature yoga and meditation practice, wild swimming, ayurvedic food workshops, singing by a campfire, sweat lodge building and tree meditation. Organisers Dmitry Glaskov and his partner Karen live in a house boat on the Thames at Hardwick. They describe the retreats as 'crafted to offer the experience of

Clockwise from top left: Signs for some of the many Hardwick enterprises; Chris Hoadly and Matthew Cottrel Jury working on Tollhurst Organic Farm; Woodsman Tim Sheldon, centre, creating a table from a fallen oak with landowner Alan May and James Norman; Romilly Swann practicing traditional dyeing techniques.

rest, wholesome nourishment and connection to an authentic self. We share the unparalleled beauty and healing nature of Hardwick Estate, tuning into the living wisdom of the ancient oaks and sacred water.'

- **Woodland management and timber** — Ben Manning manages the harvesting and re-growth of trees within the estate. His woodland management strategy includes working to diversify the forest away from historical dependence on ash and beech to provide a more resilient mix of species. Tim Sheldon is the long-time woodsman who manages firewood and timber sales. Tim is shown on the opposite page preparing a large wooden picnic table from a fallen oak tree that is now part of the Whitchurch Maze open space and used for community events such as the annual Apple Juicing Day, organised by the Pangbourne and Whitchurch Sustainability Group.

Right: Cliff Thorne and others from the Pangbourne and Whitchurch Sustainability Group at the annual Apple Juicing Day at the Whitchurch Maze using a table from the fallen oak tree.
Below: Dmitry Glaskov leading yoga practice at a Sadhama Retreat.

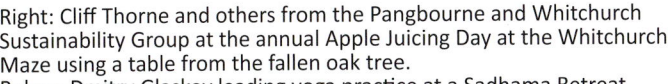

8. Goring-on-Thames and Streatley

Thames twin towns — Five miles upriver from Pangbourne and Whitchurch, the villages of Goring and Streatley are similarly connected by a small, two-lane bridge and have access to a shared GWR station at Goring. In this case, Goring is the larger village in South Oxfordshire with a population of about 3400 (2021 Census) and Streatley has a population of just over 1000 (2021 Census) in West Berkshire. As with Pangbourne and Whitchurch, both villages act as a single community in many ways but are also quite separate and distinct due to the county boundaries at the river.

Goring and Streatley are both very picturesque, affluent villages with historic buildings on well-ordered High Streets set along the river with a number of coffee shops, pubs and restaurants. A dramatic view of the Thames lock and weir combination can be seen at the centre of the two villages as you walk over the bridge. The villages are set in the shadows of the steep surrounding hills that form the Goring Gap, where the river once wore its way through the chalk hills forming a

Goring Town centre, above, and winter view over Streatley and Goring from Berkshire Downs above Streatley, below.

low valley between the Chiltern Hills and Berkshire Downs. Streatley is part of the North Wessex Downs National Landscape to the west and Goring is part of the Chilterns National Landscape on the east side of the river. Good views of the Goring Gap can be seen over Streatley from Lardon Chase National Trust property atop the steep Berkshire Downs, or from the edge of Chiltern Hills just downstream near Gatehampton at Hartslock Nature Reserve. The ancient Ridgeway, now a National Trail, crosses the river via the bridge between the two villages — previously, the Ridgeway may have crossed the river via a nearby ford, such as one upstream between South Stoke at Moulsford or perhaps at the former Goring ferry crossing a little way downstream, by what is now Ferry Lane.

England's planning process — National Landscapes, Conservation Areas and Neighbourhood Plans

The well-preserved beauty of the English countryside does not happen by accident. The UK planning process is a bit complicated and could be considered cumbersome by some, but understanding it is not just for nerds. Countless citizens across the UK are well-versed in these policies and processes and actively take part in them which is a fundamental reason they have been so successful in conserving so many beautiful and historic areas. As a transplanted American enjoying the fruits of this process, I can identify with my compatriot Bill Bryson, who has so often marvelled at the wonders of the British countryside in his books.

I will try to explain some of the many planning processes used in England as simply and concisely as I can using Goring and Streatley as examples. As you read about the work that goes on in these villages in these small parts of Oxfordshire and Berkshire, please try to keep in mind that I am describing activities that are replicated in different ways by hundreds of different communities across the country. I am not making a judgement about whether this amount of planning and scrutiny is too much, too little, or just the right amount, but I think it is safe to say that these processes have significantly contributed to the preservation of the beautiful British countryside, at least in this part of the Thames Valley. What I am describing applies to England, with many aspects of these planning processes varying in Wales, Scotland, and Northern Ireland.

Parish Councils — are the first line of local government that are made up of locally elected councillors. The size, budget and general influence of the council is related to the size of the town or

View over the Goring Weir with the Swan Hotel and Berkshire Downs in the background.

village. The Goring Parish Council has 10 members and Streatley has seven. These are voluntary roles for residents interested in getting involved in their community. Being a councillor can be rewarding at times, but it is often thankless and sometimes stressful when difficult decisions need to be made.

The Goring Parish Council is responsible for things like managing the public parks in the village and community buildings such as the Village Hall and sports pavilions. They manage any common land owned by the village which includes river moorings, cemeteries and war memorials. They tend to be the first port of call for residents complaints about everything from too much dog poo in the village, to bicycle theft, traffic and parking problems, or local sightings of Gypsy and Traveller encampments.

Parish councils are a mandatory reviewer for all planning applications affecting the village. They make recommendations to their respective Local Planning Authority which is responsible for deciding on whether they should be approved or not. For Goring, the Local Planning Authority is South Oxfordshire District Council — for Streatley it is West Berkshire Council.

Local taxes include a precept for the parish council giving them a limited budget to look after the village and make some improvements. In Goring, the annual parish council precept is about £150,000. The parish council typically receives an additional £50,000 to £100,000 in grants and Community Infrastructure Levies (CIL) placed on developers who build new homes in the village. The CIL is meant to help ensure that corresponding local infrastructure is sufficient to support the new homes.

Many council decisions are "no win" where some residents will be unhappy and critical of council decision regardless of the outcome. I attended one meeting of the Goring Parish Council where residents were given the opportunity to provide feedback on a consultant study commissioned by the parish council to provide options to re-organise and improve local parks and open spaces. Feedback at the meeting made it clear that any solution will make some residents unhappy.

- I heard passionate cases from parents wanting to dramatically improve playground facilities for young children, with others supporting skateboard and pump tracks for teenagers that I know were controversial to many other residents.
- Members of the Cricket Club stated that the only realistic place for new cricket practice nets was on sites presently used for bowling and croquet greens.
- Members of the Croquet and Bowling Clubs demanded that their facilities be kept, even though they had previously folded up the clubs due to lack of interest.

The Goring-on-Thames Parish Council making a decision.

Not enough open spaces? Some residents are calling for more space to support Goring youth football leagues.

- The Football Club complained about backlogs of youth having to travel to join football clubs in other villages due to inadequate facilities in the village, whilst others said that the Football Club already had too many pitches.

The Goring Parish Council does have the authority to decide how open spaces and sports facilities are used in the village, however the responsibility for resolving many of the issues raised to parish councils is not fully within their control. Parish councils normally get involved in escalating issues to the local government officials at the county level. In Oxfordshire, there are separate District and County Councils that further confuses things — very few people in the county really understand who is responsible for what:
- Oxfordshire County Council (OCC) is responsible for all roads and transportation related matters, street sewers and drainage, public footpaths, as well as funding of the schools, libraries and health and social care.
- South Oxfordshire District Council's (SODC) primary responsibility is for the planning matters described in this section, but they also manage waste and refuse collections, street cleaning, dog bin collections, and a few other things such as business licenses and public toilets.
- West Berkshire Council, that governs Streatley, acts as a Unitary Council, which means it has combined district and county level responsibly for the western part of Berkshire.

The National Planning Policy Framework (NPPF) — sets out the government's planning policies for England and provides a framework for which locally-prepared plans can provide new housing and other developments requiring land.

Originally approved by the Conservative-Liberal Democrat coalition government in 2012, the 65 page document, along with its 27 pages of technical guidance, consolidated the previous 1300 pages of multiple policy statements and guidance documents into a single, simpler framework. It was meant to cut red tape and speed up the planning process that was seen as making it very difficult to get approval for much needed developments in many parts of the country.

The NPPF calls for local authorities to make a 'presumption in favour of sustainable development—significantly boosting the supply of homes'. Partly as a result, net new housing supply doubled over the next seven years from about 125,000 net additions in 2012 to almost 243,000 by 2019/20.

Local Planning Authorities — Planning applications for new buildings or changes to existing buildings need to be approved by the Local Planning Authority. In Goring, the Local Planning Authority is SODC. All planning applications are made available to the public to comment on for at least three weeks on-line and are usually also posted with notices on the site. Anyone can comment on or object to these applications.

Many SODC planning decisions can be made by one of SODC's full-time planning officers, with more contentious decisions going to the Planning Committee of elected councillors. Depending on the application, SODC will consult with a variety of other specialists either employed by SODC or outside experts:
- Oxfordshire County Highways representatives asses the impacts on local traffic and parking.
- Conservation, Heritage and Archaeology Officers assess the impact on conservation areas or other heritage assets.
- Ecology and Environmental Health Officers check for things like impacts on bat roosts or ponds with great crested newts.
- Landscape Architects and Forestry Officers review plans impacting trees and other flora.
- A Drainage and Flooding Officer reviews changes that could impact flooding of the property or the wider village.
- The Countryside Access Officer reviews impacts on public footpaths or bridleways.

This planning process was demonstrated on the television show *Clarkson's Farm* in West Oxfordshire when Jeremy Clarkson submitted plans for a new restaurant and car park for his Farm Shop in 2022 that was considered controversial amongst residents of Chadlington, where the farm is located. The Chadlington Parish Council ultimately supported the Farm Shop car park plans but the plans were still rejected by the West Oxfordshire District Council Planning Committee. Those voting against it cited things such as it being an inappropriate development within the Cotswolds National Landscape. In 2023, Mr Clarkson appealed the District Council decision to an independent inspectorate appointed by the government's Department of Levelling Up, Communities and Housing. As so often happens, he was later given approval for the car park based on his appeal, however he withdrew his more controversial application for the restaurant.

National Parks and National Landscapes — By the time that National Parks were first set up in the UK in the 1950s, the UK had no truly uninhabited, pristine wild areas remaining, so unlike National Parks in the US, UK National Parks are very much lived in, working communities. National Parks in the UK try to balance objectives for conservation of the parks with making the countryside accessible to the general public. They also have to consider the needs of the residents in the towns and villages within the park, as well as landowners, businesses and farmers based there. UK National Parks are also not owned by the government or some quasi-government agency, but are 98% privately owned.

The Chilterns Hills AONB (now called a National Landscape) stretches about 45 miles from Goring and Whitchurch along the Thames in the southwest to Luton in the northeast.

There are 15 National Parks in the UK, including the Lake District and the Yorkshire Dales, and 46 National Landscape designations in England, Wales, and Northern Ireland. National Landscapes is the new name that the government gave Areas of Outstanding Natural Beauty (AONBs) in 2023. The new name seems to have largely been a branding exercise to emphasize their national importance and to create a term that more easily rolls off the tongue.

Both National Parks and National Landscapes are governed by the same legislation and are subject to the same planning policies that apply to the rest of the country. The main difference is that with National Parks and National Landscapes the policies are more rigorously enforced.
- New development is allowed only if it is are seen to 'conserve or enhance' the National Park or Landscape.
- Major developments in National Parks and Landscapes should be refused except in 'exceptional circumstances.' As Goring sits within the Chilterns National Landscape and Streatley within the North Wessex Downs National Landscape, they should both be relatively immune from the risk of major new developments.
- A key difference between National Parks and National Landscapes is that National Parks have their own planning authorities to provide a coherent development approach

throughout the park. National Landscapes each have several different planning authorities depending on what county borders they cross. So even though Goring sits within the Chilterns National Landscape, the planning authority for Goring is still SODC, one of nine planning authorities for the Chilterns.

- Another difference is that National Parks generally receive more funding for projects to preserve and improve the area — both from central government and from receipts from visitor centres and cars parks.

Green Belt land – As described earlier for Marlow and Cookham, the NPPF has special policies to protect green belts of land around major cities such as London and Oxford to prevent suburban sprawl by keeping some land permanently free from development. More than 60% of the land in South Oxfordshire is covered by either the Green Belt around the city of Oxford or the Chilterns National Landscape where major development should be avoided. This leaves very little unprotected land in the area for significant new housing.

Case Study: Mend the Gap — Network Rail, the organisation that owns the national rail tracks, completed a project to electrify the stretch of GWR from London Paddington to Didcot in about 2015 when trains were converted from diesel to electric. The gantries that were installed to support the electric cables have proven controversial as they are generally seen as ugly. Their appearance negatively impacts the landscape views in the Goring Gap that covers both the Chilterns and Wessex Downs National Landscapes.

A 'Railway Action Group' was formed by concerned citizens in the Goring Gap area to protest the 'devastating visual assault' the gantries made against the National Landscapes in an effort to get them removed or improved. National Rail ultimately accepted that they had not been compliant with all relevant planning policies but determined that there were no other feasible alternatives to the gantries that had been installed. As a settlement, they agreed to provide a fund of £3.75 million to invest in the local area for a 'Mend the Gap' programme to be run by the Chilterns National Landscape organisation. Whilst the ugly gantries won't be removed, the programme funds other projects in the area that would 'enhance' the National Landscapes to compensate for the negative impact of the gantries and 'soften' the impact to the landscape.

One of the *Mend the Gap* projects it funded was an Otter Holt along the river near Goring. As of 2023 I am happy to report that the project was completed and seems to have been successful in attracting at least four otters who live there!

Conservation Areas — In addition to being in National Landscapes, both Goring and Streatley have Conservation Areas within each village, located mostly along the historic High Streets. Conservation Areas are designated by Local Planning Authorities as

Not very attractive — gantries to support electric cables were installed over the GWR line in 2015 that were deemed to have a negative impact on both the Chilterns and North Wessex Downs National Landscapes.

areas that are worth protecting and preserving from a historic or architectural perspective. Key elements are historic buildings, views within the village, and other unique features including trees and vegetation which are deemed to be of special significance.
- Conservation Areas come with further controls on what can and cannot be changed. For example, owners of properties in these areas may need to use special 'heritage approved' types of doors, windows or skylights when making changes to the outside of their building that are typically more expensive. Unlike other properties, they also need to seek permission to cut or remove any but the smallest trees on their property.
- In Streatley, all of the properties along the High Street are covered by the Conservation Area, with many buildings dating from the 17th or 18th century or even the 13th century, in the case of the church. A Conservation Area Appraisal document was created in 2010 that was approved by the West Berkshire Planning Authority that describes why the area is of special interest as a whole and provides the detailed characteristics of specific buildings, views, and architectural elements that should be preserved.

Heritage Assets — An extra layer of protection is afforded to specific buildings that are considered 'listed'. Historic England maintains records of listed buildings, scheduled monuments, World Heritage Sites, and registered parks and gardens. Historic England is the public body given the responsibility for championing the preservation of historic assets and providing expertise when needed to address issues or advise on proposed changes to these assets. The first lists of buildings with 'special architectural and historic interest' were developed after WWII when bombed buildings in England were assessed to determine whether they should be saved despite being damaged. In England and Wales, a listed building can be either:
- Grade II: buildings that are of special interest (over 90% of listed buildings)
- Grade II*: particularly important buildings of more than special interest, or
- Grade I: buildings of exceptional interest

Under the NPPF, any planning applications impacting Heritage Assets should require 'clear and convincing justification' and any proposal to significantly harm a Heritage Asset 'should be refused.'
- The Streatley Conservation Area includes 28 Grade II listed buildings and structures, and one Grade II* building — Streatley House. A further 10 listed buildings sit outside the Conservation Area. Most buildings are now in residential use but the list includes three tombs at the church, a milestone marker along the High Street and a wellhead and pump outside the Bull Inn.
- Goring has a similar number of listed buildings.

Protected **scheduled monuments** in the area include Iron Age earthworks called Grim's Ditch that starts at Mongewell and the site of Bozedown Iron Age Camp on a hill overlooking Whitchurch. Wallingford includes scheduled monuments that protect the sites of Wallingford Castle, Wallingford Bridge, and the Saxon town in the centre now used as the Kinecroft and Bullcroft public parks.

The only **UNESCO World Heritage** site in the Thames Valley area is Blenheim Palace north of Oxford as described in Part 1. The UK has a total of 33 World Heritage sites including nearby Avebury and Stonehenge.

Tree Preservation Orders — known as TPOs, are approved by Local Planning Authorities to protect specific trees, groups of trees or woodlands 'in the interests of amenity', especially if someone suspects that a tree is 'under threat.' Trees with TPOs cannot be removed, damaged or even 'topped or lopped' without permission from the Local Authority. In practice, a tree with amenity value means that their removal would have a 'significant negative impact on the local environment and its enjoyment by the public.' A member of the public can apply for a TPO on anyone's property if they are concerned that a present or future landowner would have the trees removed and this would negatively impact the area. Once approved, the landowner will need to make an application for permission to make any changes including for maintenance to the trees.

Local Plans — are very important. They are the documents prepared by Local Planning Authorities that identify appropriate areas and sites for development of new homes, businesses and community facilities and infrastructure.
- Development and approval of Local Plans can be controversial as they basically decide how many houses should be built in which area. The whole process leading up to approval by elected councillors and government inspectors can take at least 4 or 5 years.
- They start with an assessment of how many and what types of new homes are needed, then look at the available land and develop something called a 'spatial strategy' that basically says where the new homes will go.
- Part of the process is to review proposals by developers to determine which sites are the most appropriate.
- Parish councils, residents and other stakeholders in the affected area are given opportunities to comment on the draft plan at a number of key stages in the process.
- Besides the bottom up housing needs assessment, the overall target for the number of new homes is normally influenced by central government targets, such as 300,000 net new houses a year by the mid-2020s. In the past, the central target has been allocated to each county and planning authority by a special

algorithm designed by central government. Former Prime Minister Liz Truss called it a 'Stalinist' allocation approach and vowed to eliminate specific targets.
- Despite a relative cross-party consensus on the need for more homes, politics demand that each party takes different approaches to achieving this. Policies for making targets will vary depending on which government administration is in power. As of 2024, the government is apparently no longer allocating firm targets.

South Oxfordshire Local Plan —Totalling 354 pages, the South Oxfordshire Local Plan for the period of 2011-2035 is not particularly easy reading. I'll do my best to highlight some of its key elements as an example of a Local Plan in a couple of pages:
- The starting point for the Local Plan is a calculation of how many new houses are required during the 20 year period of the plan. SODC used a standard methodology for calculating the number and types of new homes needed in a planning area called a Strategic Housing Market Assessment. The calculations that are part of this process are complex and involve a degree of judgement and uncertainty, but it is intended to determine the housing needs of the residents and support the ongoing growth of the local economy. The target in the plan was also influenced by a 100,000 new house target during the period from central government set for Oxfordshire overall. The government committed to funding certain infrastructure projects in exchange for the higher target. In the approved Local Plan, the final number SODC arrived at was a target of 18,860 new homes for South Oxfordshire over the twenty year period 2011-2031.
- There was an additional need for 5000 new homes allocated to South Oxfordshire to support the City of Oxford's growth needs that couldn't be met by the city. The city claims it doesn't have enough space due to the Green Belt preventing expansion around the city and due to limited space within the city resulting from its historic developments. Not everyone agrees that the rest of the county should accept this burden.
- The plan approved in 2020 concluded that South Oxfordshire requires 23,550 new homes over the plan period or between 900 and 1100 additional homes per year.
- Getting the plan approved was difficult and somewhat political. It was originally developed by a Conservative-led SODC Council starting in about 2014, but they were unable to get the final plan approved before elections in 2019 changed the SODC leadership to a Lib Dem/Labour/Green alliance. The new alliance then reviewed it and considered throwing it out. The government's Secretary of State for Housing, Communities, and Local Government at the time, Robert Jenrick, gave the council an ultimatum to approve the plan or the government would move South Oxfordshire Planning Authority to another body and decisions would essentially be made from Whitehall. So the plan was finally approved in December 2020. It remains to be seen how much of the targets and vision in the document will be realised. Efforts are underway to develop an updated Local Plan that is more acceptable to the politics of the new coalition, but this new plan appears to be based on most of the same strategic sites and assumptions in the present approved plan.

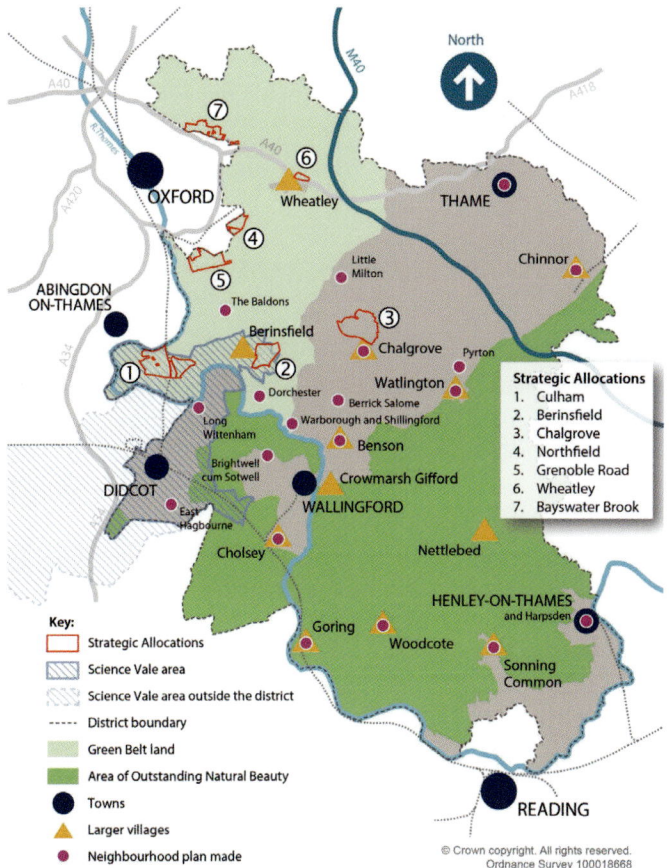

A map of the South Oxfordshire Local Plan showing its spatial strategy, highlighting where the new housing development will go.

The plan's 'spatial strategy' defines where the new homes will go:

Strategic Sites — There are seven strategic sites ear-marked for new large developments that are mostly between 1000 and 3000 new homes each.
- These include major new developments at Didcot (see Chapter 9), new homes adjacent to Culham Science Centre, and some new developments on the outskirts of Oxford City.

- Controversially, six out of the seven strategic sites in the plan require development on the Oxford Green Belt land. As the NPPF policy is to generally not allow this, the plan lists the 'exceptional circumstances' requiring development on the Green Belt:
  - To allow housing to be located adjacent to employers near the City of Oxford, the University Science Centre, and the Culham Science Centre.
  - To support regeneration of communities such as Berinsfield and Blackbird Leys that are adjacent to two of the new developments.

Market towns — Besides Didcot, there are three larger market towns that are given significant housing allocations to be detailed in Neighbourhood Plans developed by each community:
- Henley-on-Thames: at least 1285 homes
- Thame: at least 1518 homes
- Wallingford: at least 1070 homes

Larger villages — There are a further 12 larger villages in South Oxfordshire than have been given a target of increasing housing stock by 15% during the 20 year period, including Goring. Nearly all of these villages have now developed a Neighbourhood Plan to detail where the houses will go. Goring has mitigating circumstances of being within the Chilterns National Landscape and having Flood Zones by the Thames, so this was not considered a firm target for the village. Other villages, such as Woodcote and Sonning Common, have been asked to take on additional quotas for new homes beyond the 15% target.

Smaller villages — There are about 50 other settlements in South Oxfordshire large enough to be considered small villages, such as Whitchurch-on-Thames. The Local Plan asks that these villages consider increasing the number of houses by 5-10%, but does not apply any specific targets.

Business land allocation — No less important than new homes, but slightly less controversial, are the approximately 48 hectares of new 'employment land' for new businesses across the area including new land at Culham Science Centre and other business parks.

Gypsies and Travellers — The council has a responsibility to address the needs of Gypsies, Travellers and Travelling Show People, through the identification of land for caravan pitches. Families are typically allowed to claim the sites if they travel for 6 months or less during a given year. The Local Plan includes land for 10 additional pitches, some as part of future developments in Culham. There are half a dozen other locations in the county managed by the council that are not normally in very attractive locations. The largest site in the county is on the outskirts of Oxford at Redbridge Hollow that has 24 pitches. This site was only expanded in 2012 in an effort to eliminate 'a mountain of waste' on an adjacent space known as a 'superdump for fly tipping'.

Affordable housing — Last and certainly not least, the Local Plan requires that 40% of all new houses in developments greater than 10 homes should be considered 'affordable'. What this really means is a matter of great debate. The ever increasing cost of new housing is one of the UK's biggest issues, so this will be explained in examples with Goring and other communities later.

Neighbourhood Plans — are meant to give local communities a say in where the new homes allocated to them in the Local Plan should go and what they will look like. The process for getting Neighbourhood Plans approved includes having them reviewed by an independent examiner and holding a referendum in the community on whether it should be adopted. I know from experience that the process takes a lot of time and effort to prepare and get approved — but given the importance to the community, many towns and villages a have been successful in completing them in recent years.

Once a Neighbourhood Plan is approved, it becomes a legal part of the Local Plan and is referred to when reviewing new planning applications, especially for significant new housing developments. Unfortunately there are many examples of Neighbourhood Plans

Henley Town Councillor Michelle Thomas, on the left, discusses a draft Local Plan with South Oxfordshire Planning Officer Rosalynn Whiteley.

being ignored or overridden when developments are approved that were not part of the plan agreed by the community. There are also examples of where it seems to be generally working, if not perfect.

Neighbourhood Plans cover more than just homes. They also define where the Community Infrastructure Levy (CIL) funds developers are charged will be spent. CIL funds can be used for things like new schools, sports and community facilities, or road improvements.

Draft versions of SODC's Local Plans identified the need for between 140 and 320 new homes in Goring, depending upon which version you read. But if Goring is part of a National Landscape, shouldn't it be protected against any large new developments? Many residents didn't believe the proposed level of allocations were appropriate for the village and felt it was in their best interests to use the Neighbourhood Plan process to define the level, locations and type of housing they felt were feasible.

It is safe to say that most people in a beautiful spot like Goring would be somewhat resistant to significant new developments threatening the paradise they call home. At the same time, many also understood the need for more homes to keep the village 'vibrant and energetic' and to provide more affordable homes in a place where their children have little chance of being able to afford to live. It took Goring almost four years, from 2015-2019, to develop and get approval for their Neighbourhood Plan. This is a typical time frame and some village Neighbourhood Plans have taken even longer.

- More than 40 volunteers were involved in its development that was led by a Steering Committee of six members working as a sub-committee reporting to the Goring Parish Council.
- The work involved extensive consultation with the community including surveys issued to all households and four open days at the Village Hall that attracted over 300 people each.
- They received grants to hire consultants to produce reports on a Landscape and Visual Impact Assessment, a Flood Risk Assessment, a Biodiversity and Ecology Assessment and a consultant to ensure it complied with relevant European Environment Directives.
- They evaluated five candidate sites for new homes. The team ultimately decided that four sites were suitable for development. The clear preference from the community was for a number of smaller developments that enhanced the existing character of various neighbourhoods, as opposed to one large new development.
- The priorities they identified for the CIL were improved traffic and parking measures in the village, more open space for recreation, rejuvenation the village centre shopping and parking areas, and ensuring the school has sufficient capacity for future demand.

The resulting Goring Neighbourhood Plan recommended development of 94 new homes across the four selected sites. This is less than the 140 to 320 target identified in the SODC Local Plan, but the plan was approved by an independent examiner review and a referendum of residents in the village so the Neighbourhood Plan is now incorporated into SODC's Local Plan. It can be estimated that the development of the 94 new homes could generated CIL funds in excess of £2million. 25% of this, approximately £500,000, would be available for to the parish council to initiate projects, the remainder would be allocated to projects determined by SODC.

How do you define 'affordable'? — Despite the Local Plan calling for 40% of new homes on new developments to be 'affordable', what is considered affordable is relative. As we will see, government schemes for affordable housing are still linked to local market prices and rents.

- The first development to be built under Goring's Neighbourhood Plan was 14 new 2-3 bedroom houses on Ash Hurst Road, which were meant to have 5-6 affordable social rent homes. According to Rightmove.com, the new homes built in 2020 and 2022 were all 2-3-bedroom homes that went for between £470,000 and £725,000. This price range is certainly on the low end of prices for homes in Goring, but they are also well above the national average cost of a home in England, which was £285,000 in November 2023 (UK Government National Statistics).
- Due to the timing of the Neighbourhood Plan approval, only one of the 14 new houses in Ash Hurst Road qualified for an affordable housing scheme. In this case, it was a shared equity scheme that enabled the purchaser to have a reduced deposit, as low as 5%. The shared equity scheme helps get new home buyers onto the property ladder, but they still pay the market rate for the house and also end up having an extra loan to make up the remainder of the deposit.
- A second new development of 20 homes, called Manor Meadow, was under construction as of 2024. As this is a slightly more exclusive neighbourhood near the river, prices for a 3 bedroom house were expected to be on the higher end of the range that Ash Hurst Road homes went for, although they could still be considered relatively affordable for the area. Four bedroom homes in the new development are expected to fetch more than £1million.
- The plans for Manor Road comply with the requirement that eight of the 20 homes (40%) are 'affordable' through a combination of 'affordable rent' and 'shared ownership' two and three bedroom homes.
    - **Affordable and social rent** homes are normally owned by a Housing Association who act as the landlord and can charge up to 80% of local market rents. Still not cheap in Goring.
    - **Shared ownership** is similar to the **shared equity** scheme described earlier to allow deposits as low as 5%. For shared

ownership, purchasers only own a portion of the home, typically between 25% and 75%. The resident then pays a mortgage on the portion of the home they own and pays an additional rent to a landlord for the remainder of the home they don't own. The overall price of the home does not change, but this scheme at least allows new home openers to get on the housing ladder. The new homeowners have the option of increasing their percentage of ownership over time, known as 'staircasing'.

Village Plans — Unlike Neighbourhood Plans, Village Plans do not become legal documents that form part of the Local Plan after approval. Village Plans make sense for smaller villages such as Streatley that are not expecting significant growth in homes but still want to make improvements to certain aspects of the village. Streatley issued a Parish Plan in 2006 that identified a number of issues with agreed actions:

- Addressing traffic safety and congestion especially on the narrow High Street.
- Another priority was to retain the character and charm of the village through development of a village design statement.
- There was also a desire for more community events such as an annual fête and more activities for youth in the village.

Hydro power generation on the Thames at Caversham Lock using Archimedes screws.

Conservation vs. the Environment: Goring Hydro-Power

The need to address climate change is increasingly causing trade-offs between conservation and new environmental initiatives. The case of the Goring Weir Hydro Power project shows that the drive for conservation of historic parts of the countryside still seems to be winning the day in some Thames Valley communities.

- In 2009, Goring was named South Oxfordshire's Village of the Year. The £1000 prize was put towards the village's hydro-electric project to generate electricity from the River Thames using turbines on the Thames Weir. The organisers of the competition were impressed by Goring's hydro-electric plans which was a factor in the award.
- The plans for a hydro-power generation at the weir were completed by the Goring and Streatley Sustainability Group in 2015 after at least 10 years of studies and discussion. The plan was to use three 12 ft-wide fusilli pasta-shaped Archimedes screws powered by water from the Goring weir. The plant was designed to generate an average of 1000 Megawatt hours per year that would provide electricity to the national grid for approximately 300 homes. Whilst innovative, this was not the first such scheme to generate sustainable power from a weir on the Thames. A community-owned hydro-power plant at the weir at Osney Lock in Oxford was opened in 2015, and another one was opened at Caversham Lock in 2021.
- Despite these benefits to environmental sustainability, the Goring Parish Council came out strongly against the project on behalf of residents of the village with a number of objections mainly around the concerns that it would spoil views of the river, generate noise, and cause additional flood risks. The parish council felt strongly enough about this to spend more than £30,000 of tax payer's money on legal fees to try to stop it with an appeal. The appeal went all the way to the High Court which ultimately upheld the decision to approve the plans. The High Court ruling statement of 2016 described 58 residents raising objections to the proposal, but still found the application's approval to be compliant with planning rules, so the approval was upheld.
- Even with this approval, the local sustainability group ultimately gave up on the project. It had been nearly three years since SODC's planning approval so the plans would need to be re-approved. By this time, the government's renewable energy feed-in-tariff scheme was less generous making the project less viable, the elderly chief designer of the hydro-scheme had passed away and the local sustainability group had not had a chance to raise the required funds. It is not clear how many residents supported the project overall, but after three years of fighting the Parish Council and a small but vocal group of residents, they ultimately lost the will to continue. According to one member of the sustainability group 'We got tired of fighting the NIMBYs'.

9. Wallingford to Abingdon

The Wallingford to Abingdon stretch of the river is just upriver from Goring and Streatley and south of Oxford. Both Wallingford and Abingdon are historic market towns that provide many residents with walking distance access to shopping and entertainment in the town centre, encouraging a strong community vibe. Being that much further away from London gives them a more relaxed, rural feel. It also makes living there that much more affordable than other commuter towns in the Thames Valley. The area is also home to a number of other attractive, historic villages such as Dorchester-on-Thames, Brightwell-cum-Sotwell, Clifton Hampden, and Sutton Courtenay.

With a population of 8500 (2021 Census), Wallingford is bit smaller than Henley and Marlow but still one of the largest towns in South Oxfordshire. Abingdon is much larger (population 33,125 - 2021 Census), sitting just outside the Oxford Green Belt, with many commuting from there into Oxford.

One thing that both Wallingford and Abingdon are missing is GWR train stations. Whilst this is less convenient for commuters, it means the towns haven't grown as quickly in recent years and are more affordable. Abingdon is still served by GWR stations at nearby Radley, Culham and Appleford and neither town is too far from Didcot, which has become the central transport hub for South Oxfordshire.

Like other parts of the Thames Valley, the towns and villages in the area have active communities:

- In the warm summer months the river meadow on the Crowmarsh Gifford side of Wallingford Bridge becomes a beach for swimming and paddling about on the Thames. The spot finally achieved a designation of 'Bathing Water Status' in 2024 despite applications being rejected in previous years.
- This quiet stretch of the river at Wallingford is also home to Oxford University's state of the art Boat Club, built in 2006 to train its men's and women's teams for the annual Boat Race with Cambridge in London.
- Dorchester-on-Thames holds a festival for two weeks in May every two years centred around classical music, talks, art, and family events at the Abbey. Highlights include renaissance music from the renowned Tallis Scholars and a 'baroque extravaganza' enthusiastically performed by Red Priest. And of course, you

can't miss the opportunity to abseil down the 100 foot Abbey tower.
- Abingdon is known for the peculiar traditions of 'bun throwing' from the roof of the Town Council building to crowds below to mark significant royal milestones.
- Sandford is home to the world 'pooh sticks' competition each May where contestants drop sticks from the bridge at Sandford Lock to see which ones float downstream the fastest. The competition is a family friendly event inspired by the game played by Winnie the Pooh.
- Brightwell-cum-Sotwell hosts an annual Wassailing event on 12th night in January for their apple trees to ward off ghosts and encourage a good harvest. The event is full of ritual ceremonies, dancing and light-hearted amateur dramatics that some in the village prepare for all year.
- Wallingford hosts the Bunkfest Music, Dance and Beer Festival for three days each September. Visitors are spoilt for choice with dozens of activities across the central part of the town. It is run as a free, family friendly, not-for-profit event to benefit the community. With free music, good beer, food trucks and friendly, welcoming people, it can be a beautiful place to be on a sunny September's afternoon:
    - The festival is named after 'the Bunk' branch line train that used to connect Wallingford to the Great Western line in Cholsey. The Cholsey & Wallingford line closed to passengers in 1959, but it is still being preserved and a vintage train is run for families and tourists on special occasions like Easter, Christmas and for Bunkfest.
    - It is said to be the largest free music festival in the UK. The music is predominantly folk but can feature everything from sea shanties to pub rock bands.
    - The dancing includes a variety of traditional folk dancing demonstrations. For that weekend, Wallingford is probably home to the highest per capita concentration of Morris Dancers anywhere in the world!

Plans for growth – After decades, and even centuries, of relatively slow growth in the area, Wallingford, Didcot and Abingdon find themselves at the centre of Oxfordshire's plans for more and more homes. As housing costs in this area are already at the lower end of the price scale for the Thames Valley, new developments here are more likely to be affordable. Unlike places like Goring an Streatley, the area is not restricted by Green Belt or National Landscape planning policies, making these towns ideal locations for significant growth in South Oxfordshire.

As of 2024, plans for new housing developments are in full swing and seem to be popping up all over the place:
- Wallingford's Neighbourhood plan calls for over 1400 new homes at three strategic locations: west of the town centre at Slade End Farm; in the Winterbrook neighbourhood; at a former Habitat warehouse site; and on a new site just north of the Wallingford bypass.
- Crowmarsh Gifford, directly across from Wallingford Bridge, will be supporting 183 homes at Wallingford Reach, under construction as of 2024; another 91 homes were completed in 2022 on land owned by the disused Carmel College; SODC is now planning to build homes at the site where its former council offices were destroyed in an arson attack in 2015.
- Benson, a couple miles upstream from Wallingford, approved 559 new homes across three major developments in its Neighbourhood Plan, on top of other significant developments already completed outside of the Neighbourhood Planning process.
- Abingdon has been allocated 1000 homes at two sites in the Vale of the White Horse Local Plan. An additional site at Dalton Barracks is now being proposed in a new Local Plan. The developments comes with

A sunny day at Wallingford's Bunkfest.

Wassailing at Brightwell-cum-Sotwell.

approval for an additional access road to the A34 highway that would benefit Abingdon overall.
- Didcot is targeted for the lion's share of the new homes in the Local Plan, contributing over 6000 new homes in South Oxfordshire during the planning period to 2033, and ultimately as many as 15,000, taking into account homes in the neighbouring Vale of the White Horse. Part of the justification for the growth is to provide homes in the growing Science Vale UK:
  - Science Vale is the area around the existing cluster of Harwell Space and Science Campus, Culham Fusion Centre and Didcot's Milton Business Park.
  - The plan includes land earmarked for a new Science Bridge over the Thames at Culham with a bypass highway around the village of Clifton Hampden (known as HIF1) and a number of walking and cycling routes to promote active travel. Local residents have raised concerns about both the noise and visual impact of the bypass, causing SODC to cancel HIF1 in 2023 despite funding being available. This decision is now under review by central government as without it, major developments planned for Culham are unlikely to go ahead.
  - Didcot would become 'Gateway to Science Vale' meaning it is the main route for accessing these campuses and business parks via the A34 highway and Didcot's GWR train station.
  - Didcot is also meant to become a 'Garden City'. Many locals scoff at this name being just a nice marketing ploy, but the Local Plan states that new Garden City homes will be of high quality and good design with plenty of green spaces and community hubs. The infrastructure is meant to encourage green modes of transportation. History will be the judge of whether Didcot becomes a well thought out community or it just has a lot of new houses dumped on it exacerbating traffic and other infrastructure problems.

Affordable housing —Most people are aware that a lack of affordable housing is a national issue. UK house prices have soared since at least the 1980s. Goodmove.co.uk has calculated that the average house that cost £19,273 in 1980 went for £239,927 by 2020 — a 1450% increase overall. This can be a good thing if you own a house and may be able to sell it at some point, but not so good for young people looking to buy their first home. It is also not good for families in expensive areas like Pangbourne and Goring that are looking for a larger home for a growing family or may want to have their children settle in the area.

According to Paul O'Loughlin of Warmingham estate agents in Goring, prices in the Goring to Henley area in 2024 started at about £400,000-600,000 for a 2–3 bedroom home, but there is also no shortage of £1 million-plus 3–5 bedroom houses in the area if you fancy something grander. Even houses that were developed as council-owned homes prior to the 1980s are now in a similar price range.

A view of Abingdon along the Thames.

A major priority for nearly all Local Plans and Neighbourhood Plans in the Thames Valley is to provide more affordable housing. Both Wallingford and Benson's Neighbourhood Plans call for 40% of their 2000 new homes to be 'affordable' as required by the national target. The new developments are expected to come with a selection of smaller one, two and three bedroom properties suitable for a variety of buyers, some of which will be sold at local market value and some on one of the government's affordable housing schemes. For a new house to qualify as part of the 40% affordable quota, it must make use of one of the approved schemes, such as:

- Social rent and affordable rent schemes available to qualifying residents with lower incomes. Social rent is meant to be around 50% of the market rate with affordable rent defined as 80% of market rates. In much of the Thames Valley, these rents can still be relatively expensive.
- Shared ownership schemes are available to reduce down payments to as little at 5%. This still doesn't change the price of the home, but it can help first time buyers with getting on the property ladder. Examples of how this worked in Goring can be seen in Chapter 8.
- There have been various other schemes in recent years, including stamp duty breaks, rent to buy deals, and subsidised prices for first time buyers.

The 300,000 new homes target —One of the underlying causes of rising prices in the UK is clearly the growing demand for homes against a limited supply. This increased demand is due to general population growth that includes ongoing immigration as well as demographic changes in recent decades: people living longer; an increase in the number of people living on their own; and more people being able to afford second holiday homes. The limited supply and high prices has other societal impacts such as children living at home longer with their parents until they can afford to buy their own home.

There seems to a general consensus across political parties that there is a need for at least 300,000 new homes in England per year to meet demand. If this level was reached it would be the highest level of new house building since the 1970s:
- Theresa May's Conservative government set a target in 2015 of building 1 million new homes by 2020, and then to build 300,000 new homes a year by the mid-2020s on an ingoing basis.
- The government was starting to reach this target with a net gain of 243,770 dwellings in 2019-20. The impact of COVID reduced this trend somewhat, with the number of net additional dwellings in 2022 and 2023 was still about 233,000 per year. (National Statistics: Dept. for Levelling Up, Housing and Communities).

Even if the 300,000 new homes targets were met, there will still only be a very limited impact on house prices unless a large percentage of the houses are actually 'affordable.'
- There were 1.15 million households on waiting lists for social housing in March 2020.
- The Housing, Communities and Local Government (HCLG) Select Committee's inquiry into building more social housing received 'compelling evidence that England needs at least 90,000 net additional social rent homes a year.'
- The government now requires that 40% of all new developments are classified as affordable, meaning one of the government-approved affordable housing schemes described earlier.

California Housing Crisis and Granny Flats — England is not alone in having challenges satisfying unmet housing demand. The State of California, with a population of 40 million compared to 56 million for England, estimates that it needs at least 180,000 new homes per year to keep up with housing demand with a recent report estimating that there was a 1.2 million housing backlog. The state is in a self-declared affordable housing and homelessness crisis and has still only managed to build an average of 80,000 new homes per year over the past decade. In a 2022 interview, frustrated by resistance from the state's cities and counties to build more houses, California's Governor Newson declared that "NIMBYism is killing the state".

The state government has tried countless zoning law changes, tax incentives and other schemes, but the one initiative that seems to have been most successful in the past few years has been to allow home owners to convert garages, basements or other small outbuildings in their home as flats for grown children, parents, or any other rent-paying tenants. Commonly known as granny flats in the UK, in California they use the far sexier term, Accessible Dwelling Units (ADUs).

I know this type of development is often frowned upon in both US and UK communities, but in California it has been a way of finally getting around NIMBYs to allow an increase in the number of new residential units and tend to be more affordable as small, 1 bedroom homes. Owners of the flats receive an economic benefit from extra income to pay their mortgages and help with ever rising living costs. There are also social and health benefits for extended families living in close proximity. According to a Harvard study, there were 25,000 ADU permits approved in California in 2022 — a remarkable growth since legislation first allowed them in 2017 in a state where there are only 80,000 new homes are built a year. Other states in America are now considering how ADUs can help them meet their housing targets. Could wider use of granny flats have a future in the UK?

10. Oxford

Known as the 'city of dreaming spires', the final stop on our journey up the Thames is a truly beautiful and historic city that is well worth a visit for the world-class architecture and magical feel about it if nothing else. Spires from the many university college chapels and other historic buildings can been seen from several vantage points including the top of Carfax Tower or even the top terrace of the Westgate Shopping Centre. The view above was taken from South Park on Headington Hill in East Oxford.

A large percentage of Oxford's 162,000 residents (2021 Census) work in the knowledge industry or have some connection to the famous university, but it is a city in its own right separate from the famous university. I'll talk a bit about what its like to live there today from both town and gown perspective. If visiting for the first time, there are many ways to explore the city.

- There is no shortage of popular walking, bus, and cycling tours that provide highlights of the city and university history. Footprint tours operate a range of two-hour tours daily, run by knowledgeable and enthusiastic Oxford students. City Sightseeing bus tours are also popular.
- Tours are available for most of Oxford's 49 colleges, although days and times that tours are available will vary. Any college visit is likely to include tours of their well kept quadrangles with medieval architecture and gargoyles, chapels, and student dining halls. Some of the more popular college tours are Trinity, Merton, and Magdalen College with its Deer Park. Christ Church College is one of the most grand with its chapel doubling as the impressive Church of England Cathedral for the Diocese of Oxford, courtesy of Henry VIII.
- Christ Church Meadows is a lovely place to walk around, where you can watch people punting along the River Cherwell and follow it to the point where it joins the Thames, or the Isis, as the river is known in Oxford. Boat houses for many of the Oxford colleges can be seen along the river here.

A satisfying day out is a walk or cycle ride along the Oxford Canal, perhaps returning via the Thames Path along Port Meadow. Departing from the centre of Oxford, the canal leads up to Godstow Road, and from there you could return back via Wolvercote, perhaps stopping at the famous Trout Inn, with its large decking along the river, site of many *Inspector Morse* and *Lewis* episodes. Book ahead for lunch to avoid disappointment. Then come back to Oxford along the Thames Path on the west side of Port Meadow common land, perhaps stopping at the historic Perch pub on the way. As described earlier, Port Meadow is still common land owned by the City of Oxford since the time of King Alfred. Freemen of Oxford still have the right to graze their livestock there.

Visitors to the city should try to avoid driving into the centre, instead accessing the city via a park and ride bus or train if at all possible — I'll talk more about the traffic challenges a little later.

Statue of Mercury at Christ Church College fountain.

Punting along the River Cherwell near Christ Church Meadows.

Port Meadow commons where Free Men of Oxford have had the right to graze their livestock since the time of King Alfred in the late 9th century.

Oxford neighbourhoods — Beyond the student life at Oxford colleges, the city is blessed with a number of vibrant neighbourhoods, inhabited by residents working at both the university or a variety of other local businesses. The community feel of the neighbourhoods benefit from being in close proximity to local shopping districts that are accessible by foot, bicycle or frequent buses. These are sometimes referred to as '15 minute neighbourhoods', where most of your shopping, work and other community needs are available locally, reducing the need to travel by car. Fewer car journeys is a good thing for many reasons—one being that parking in these neighbourhoods is difficult and can be expensive, unless you live in the area and have a residents parking permit.

Jericho — Located on the north edge of Oxford city centre within easy walking access to the canal and Port Meadow, Jericho has a reputation for being a hip neighbourhood with a strong community spirit. Nightlife includes many trendy wine bars, pubs and restaurants, usually with a bohemian vibe. There is a Phoenix Picture House Cinema that shows first run and art house films, and the Jericho Tavern pub and music venue where local bands Radiohead and Supergrass used to play gigs. Unfortunately the popularity and convenience of the location make Jericho a rather expensive place to live.

Summertown — A little further north, Summertown is known for its smart town houses, private independent children's schools and convenient and thriving neighbourhood shopping along Banbury Road. Like Jericho, it has easy access to Port Meadow. It also offers an easy commute to most Oxford colleges making it a popular location for Oxford academics with families who can afford to live there. All this gives Summertown a rather posh reputation and makes it one of the most expensive places in Oxford to live.

Headington — A little further out and less expensive than Jericho or Summertown, Headington is a large and a growing neighbourhood on the east side of Oxford full of quiet residential areas. It has a large number of pubs, restaurants, and all the services you might need. The city's main hospitals, including John Radcliffe, Churchill and Oxford City are all located here.

Headington is a bit far out for most Oxford University students, partly because it is on a hill that can be a challenge for commuting by bike — but there is no shortage of students in Headington as it is home to the other Oxford university — Oxford Brookes. Founded in 1865, it is still considered quite young for Oxford. Oxford Brookes became a polytechnic in 1970 and formally became a university in 1992 when a number of British universities changed status. It is now highly respected and internationally ranked in a number of disciplines, not the least of which is rowing. As described earlier, Brookes rowers won a record number of trophies in the 2023 Henley Regatta.

Photos on this page: Scenes around Jericho — Oxford is a self-declared "Cycling City" and there are no shortage of cyclists, cycle lanes, and cycle shops in Jericho and other parts of the city.

East Oxford: Cowley Road, Iffley Road, and St Clements are arterial roads leading into the city centre from the southeast that meet at The Plain roundabout just to the east of Oxford centre. Highly diverse from both an ethnic and economic perspective, in previous decades the neighbourhoods in this area were considered by many to be a bit on 'the dark side' and somewhat dangerous. Whilst Cowley Road has a relatively safe feel to it now, it still has the highest crime rate in the city. In 2018, 226 offences were recorded along the long road that included a mix of shoplifting, bike thefts, drugs and sexual offences. Despite this, the area is now an attractive and cost effective place to live for students and other urban dwellers on a budget.

Many pockets have become quite trendy in their own right. I recently took a stroll down Magdalen Road, that runs between Iffley and Cowley Roads, and was struck by the rather woke community feel, with young mothers and fathers chatting over coffee after the school run or a class at the nearby gym and yoga studio.
- I stopped for breakfast at the plant-based Green Routes café where regular customers seemed to be on first name basis. I ordered their version of 'beans on toast' made of butternut beans, with toasted sesame seeds and crispy kale on sourdough toast. Tasty, but with the premium price you would expect.
- Just down the block, the noticeboard in Wild Honey Organic Health shop was full of community activities being offered such as the usual variety of alternative healing services including acupuncture, a self-compassion course and menopause support.

I moved to England 25 years ago from San Francisco, where vegan restaurants and alternative self-help classes were common—participating in some myself. In the time I have lived here, England has gradually become more open to these things—but the extent that Oxford's left leaning culture now seems to have dominated this once gritty urban neighbourhood is striking.

Cowley Road is known for its diverse ethnic restaurants and shops as that are far removed from Oxford University life. Like Reading's Oxford Road and parts of Slough described earlier, it is well represented by many regions of the world, including Turkish restaurants, a Moroccan grocer, and a long standing Hi-Lo Jamaican Eating House.
- Some worry that it is becoming too gentrified in recent years — there is still a selection of ethnic restaurants and cafés, but the area has clearly attracted more students and city dwellers with eclectic tastes who now intermingle with displaced migrants.
- Some shops are clearly targeted at middle-aged urban residents such as Truck Store record shop and café, and live music venues such as the O2 Academy and a growing number of coffee shops and organic cafés. Even Thy Spa, the Thai Massage parlour has an upscale feel to it, with prices for an hour massage starting at £70 and branches in Windsor and San Francisco.
- On recent visits to Cowley, I couldn't help noticing street flyers and advertisements political activism for things such as Palestinian rights, water pollution protests or recruiting residents to join the Just Stop Oil environmental activists—fitting in with Oxford's progressive reputation.

James Attlee paid homage to the Cowley Road neighbourhood in his 2007 book, *Isolarion*, clearly revelling in the diversity of life that he

Above: Cecilia, Manager of the organic grocer Wild Honey, setting up shop on Magdalen Road. Right: Oriental food store on Cowley Road.

183

explored in the book. Whilst I am sure that Attlee would not consider himself as someone who is resistant to change, he clearly wasn't impressed with the 'improvements' planned by the local council. He described his outrage during a council consultation on the future of the road, taking exception to plans to label it with 'gateway signage' at either end of the road, designating it as a type of 'China Town' area of diversity in an effort to attract tourism and business. Attlee argued that Cowley was one of the few areas of Oxford not dominated by the university or tourism, and the scheme would only encourage further homogenisation. In the end, the signage proposal was withdrawn.

A walk down Cowley Road in 2024 still has the feel of a vibrant and diverse neighbourhood, perhaps in a more welcoming way to visitors than it was in years past. Many of the traders Attlee interviewed in 2007 have long since either relocated or gone out of business. This in itself is not unusual, but there clearly have been pressures from increased rents and business rates as the demographic of residents in the neighbourhood becomes more middle class. As described in the next section, Low Traffic Neighbourhoods and other planned restrictions are now making it more difficult for visitors to drive to the area. This has clearly added to the pressure on retail business in the area and has forced at least a few high profile shop closures.

Places such as the somewhat upscale Arbequina tapas restaurant may give an indication of what Cowley Road's future could look like. The restaurant is owned by locally established restaurateurs who employ Spanish tapas chefs producing a well-regarded menu. The restaurant is listed in the *Michelin Guide* allowing it to charge a small premium with a reputation that attracts customers from outside the neighbourhood. Arbequina still seems to fit in with Cowley's urban, ethnic, bohemian chic atmosphere and even pays homage to its history with a store-front that displays the original shop signs of the former dispensing chemist tenants. The watchmaker's sign next door was added as it seemed to fit, but is not based on historic accuracy.

Scenes along Cowley Road: Left- Arbequina tapas restaurant in a former chemist shop. Above left: 'The Damned' performing at O2 Academy Oxford in 2023. Above: Truck Store record store and coffee shop.

Traffic — Congestion, pollution and difficulty parking in Oxford has been a growing problem for a number of years. With many roads originating as part of the medieval city or during the coaching era, there is generally no space or desire to expand existing roads where this may impact the beauty of carefully preserved buildings and parks. Oxford is a cycling friendly city with good public transportation but there is pressure to do more to reduce traffic congestion and pollution even as the population of surrounding Oxfordshire continues to grow. On top of these challenges, some local councillors and activists would like the city to be a world leader in reducing carbon emissions to meet global climate change targets. All this pressure has led the local council to consider difficult choices and has made visitors think carefully before planning trips into the city.

If you can't build more roads and car parks, how do you manage the effects of more and more people wanting to travel into Oxford? This is an issue that Oxfordshire County Council (OCC), which is responsible for the county's road network, has been debating. There are a number of options to address this, but none of them are easy to execute and nearly all of them have negative consequences for at least some community stakeholders. Options include:

- Encouraging visitors to take buses using park and ride car parks on the edge of the city. Four locations north, south, east and west of the city have been in place for a number of years and are working well, with more locations planned.
- Encourage residents and visitors to 'actively travel' by making cycling and walking safe and convenient. Oxford may be cycling friendly but not everyone feels safe cycling in the city as cyclist casualties are still all too common. 16 cyclists have been killed on Oxford roads between 2000 and 2022.
- Provide better public transportation, especially reliable bus and train services. The problem seems to be that buses are often slowed down by traffic and many complain of train services that are all too often delayed or cancelled.
- Place levies on businesses offering employee parking to encourage less driving into the office. This could encourage more working from home, but could also scare away business from the city.
- Congestion charging on cars, as is done in London and is being trialled in Cambridge to encourage use of public transportation. This can be very unpopular as anti-ULEZ (Ultra Low Emissions Zone) votes in London and outraged drivers in Cambridge show.
- Encourage the use of clean electric vehicles and buses to reduce pollution. This seems like a relatively uncontroversial initiative but it wouldn't reduce congestion and can be seen as competing with national initiatives that are already encouraging drivers to transition to electric vehicles across the country.

Busy cycle lanes at the bridge over the Cherwell by Magdalen College, just outside The Plain roundabout.

A ghost bike memorial to Dr Ling Felce, a 35 year-old mum and Oxford University researcher who was killed when she had an accident with a tipper lorry on The Plain roundabout in March 2022. I don't recommend you actually go into the centre of the roundabout to see this up close as you may also be risking your life crossing busy traffic.

Partly due to its academic focus, Oxford has a reputation as a city with progressive left-leaning values and politics. An OCC administration led by a coalition of Green, Liberal Democrat and Labour Councillors that was elected in 2021 has been pushing forward a number of new initiatives to address the problem that some see as rather aggressive 'anti-car' measures. The initiatives may well achieve some of the desired effects of reducing car journeys into the city centre but will also significantly change how many people live and work and may even fragment the identity of Oxford as a city. The changes now being implemented or planned include:

- **Low Traffic Neighbourhoods (LTNs)** — effectively banning anyone from driving in certain neighbourhoods unless they live there. The image below shows planter-style bollards that block cars from entering a road in East Oxford. LTNs are designed to prevent cars using side streets for short cuts, making the neighbourhoods safer for walking and cycling. Residents can still have visitors or deliveries made to them via certain routes. LTNs in a number of East Oxford neighbourhoods were trialled for a little over a year in 2022-23 and whilst there were some benefits, the changes were extremely controversial and there were many negative consequences.

Bollards blocking access to cars and motorcycles in the Bullingdon Road Low Traffic Neighbourhood near Cowley Road.

- The LTNs were successful in making many residential roads quieter with less traffic and pollution and somewhat safer for pedestrians and cyclists, however they have made the made the main arterial roads of Iffley Road, Cowley Road, and St Clements more congested.
- LTNs do seem to encourage more cycling as the roads within the neighbourhoods can feel safer, although cycling on the main arterial roads with more traffic is arguably less safe.
- A study of London LTNs showed that some types of pollution are reduced within LTNs, as you would expect, but levels of pollution that is then displaced to LTN boundary roads and other areas outside the LTN may increase depending upon how the scheme is set up.
- Many local businesses complain of reduced footfall, as it is harder for customers to find parking due to loss of spaces on side streets. An ever growing number of businesses have blamed their recent closure on the LTNs.
- Buses also seem to be getting caught in the congestion, delaying journeys, the opposite of the benefits the LTNs were meant to provide.

- **Zero Emission Zones (ZEZ)** — A ZEZ has been formed in the centre of Oxford, closing off key streets to all but electric private vehicles or taxis and buses. OCC and the City Council are proud that they have introduced the first ZEZ in the world. Some see the ZEZ as discriminatory, as electric cars are still more expensive and only those with sufficient incomes can afford them. This type of scheme would eventually become redundant as more and more drivers purchase electric cars going forward.

- **Bus Filters/Gates** — Probably the most controversial scheme is a series of six bus gates that were due to go into effect in 2024 or 2025. The gates will prevent most private vehicles from entering the centre of the city on current direct routes, effectively dividing the city into sections that make if difficult to travel by car from one part of the city to other parts of the city, unless they return to the Oxford Ring Road and travel back in via another route. As with other initiatives, this aims at encouraging the use of buses and to reduce congestion for buses. It is also hoped that this will encourage residents to focus travel within their immediate "15 minute neighbourhood" instead of travelling to other parts of the city. Like LTNs, those within the segregated neighbourhoods are likely to see some benefits of reduced traffic and pollution, but it also makes it harder for them to get to other parts of the city, potentially fragmenting the city's identity.

- **Business parking levies** – Charge fees on businesses employing staff that need to travel into the city and park. This may be an acceptable cost of doing business for some companies, but it will certainly make them consider whether they should move their businesses outside of Oxford altogether.

The overall result of these changes is to make it harder for people to travel into Oxford with private cars. For those living in the Oxfordshire countryside needing access to services in Oxford, they need to think carefully about whether it is worth it regardless of how far they are from the city. Cycling is clearly the best way to get around within Oxford although it is not for everyone. When researching this book, I tended to park at the Park and Ride with my cycle in my car and then explore the city by bike.

Local retail businesses who depend on trade and tourism from visitors outside the city or even from outside of their 15-minute neighbourhood probably have the most to lose. Some are claiming that business is down 25-50% since the LTNs were introduced.

- Sylvester's Hardware store on Magdalen Road in East Oxford, just across the road form Wild Honey Organic shop mentioned earlier, were forced to shut in 2022 after being a family business since 1910. According to the former owner Stuart Sylvester, "the business has come through two world wars and the pandemic, but LTNs have hit traders the most. They didn't listen to the traders. God knows how people are going to continue to keep running."
- When I spoke to Ben Bateman, the manager of Arbequina tapas restaurant, he said that he understands what the council are trying to achieve but doesn't believe they went about it in the right way. He is concerned that the planned bus gates could be the 'final nail in the coffin' for restaurants such as his.
- Perhaps the most vocal business owner has been Clinton Pugh, owner of Cafe Coco on Cowley Road who resorted to putting up a large billboard stating his complaints. Among his objections were that the County Council claimed to be consulting residents, however, they also made it clear that they were going ahead with the schemes despite the overwhelming negative feedback during the consultation.
- Oxfordshire's largest industrial employer could also be impacted. The Mini automobile plant that sits alongside the south east section of the Ring Road uses manufacturing processes that depend on hundreds of daily just-in-time deliveries from the Swindon plant and dozens of suppliers travelling with components from other parts of the UK and Europe. Whilst it seems unlikely that the UK government would allow this important historic factory to close in the near future, a more congested Ring Road does have a direct impact on plant productivity.

I do have some sympathy for the County Council and the plans they have developed. I'm not saying that I agree with all of it, but I know from experience trying to address traffic and parking in my little village on the Thames that changes to parking and traffic regulations will impact different residents in different ways. A change that helps reduce congestion and improve pedestrian safety for many, may inconvenience other residents and businesses by making parking more difficult.

It is worth noting that the City of Cambridge has similar traffic challenges, but is trying a different approach for reducing traffic through use of a 'sustainable travel zone' that is effectively a £5 congestion charge during peak travel periods to be phased in by 2027-28. The money raised would be used to cap bus fares, increase bus routes and services, and increase footpaths and cycle lanes. Whilst still a long way off from being implemented, it is getting similar outraged responses about shutting down businesses and penalising those who can't afford to live in the city centre.

A call to arms against LTNs and bus gates by Cafe Coco Owner Clinton Pugh.

Wild swimming and Bathing Water status — Wild swimming has become increasingly popular in the Thames in recent years, especially since COVID in 2020-21 and the rediscovery of local open spaces. Despite the desire for more outdoor swimming, studies have shown that Britain's rivers are amongst the dirtiest in Europe. You will often see people swimming in the Thames at Port Meadow or in other parts of the river at their own risk.

Oxford can be proud of a small victory in the battle to clean up the Thames. After more than two years of active protesting, Oxford was awarded a site designated as Bathing Water status in 2022, just north of Port Meadow—only the second river swimming area to be awarded this status in the country.

The bathing area covers Wolvercote Mill Stream, which is an offshoot of the Thames that re-joins the river just by Godstow Lock on the north side of Oxford. Once a site is designated as a Bathing Water site, the Environment Agency has a duty to test the water regularly throughout the bathing season (May to September), and the landowner, in this case Oxford City Council, must display the results of the water quality tests, classified from excellent to poor. After two years of monitoring for E. coli and other bacteria, the Environment Agency still considered the quality of water to be 'poor', meaning that it does not meet the minimum standard for healthy bathing. The hope is that the scrutiny given from the bathing status will lead to improvements in quality going forward.

River pollution protests have been held in a number of communities along the Thames since he start of COVID, including Oxford, Henley, Pangbourne and Wallingford. Henley has also applied for Bathing Water status on the Thames, but has so far been unsuccessful — Wallingford finally received approval for its 'beach' in 2024.

Release of raw sewage into the Thames upstream of Wolvercote is likely to continue for many years to come. Normally, sewage plants only discharge 'treated sewage water' into the river which is considered safe for drinking and swimming in. During periods of heavy rain when sewage treatment facilities are often overwhelmed, Thames Water has permission to pump raw sewage into the river.
- An underlying reason for the sewage discharges is that many sewage pipes in the UK are still shared with rain water drains under roads, similar to the system of Bazalegette's Victorian

Oxford designated Bathing Area at Wolvercote Mill Stream. It is used by many for swimming despite testing showing the water quality to be 'poor'.

sewerage system in London. During periods of heavy rain, the sewers and sewage plants can't cope with all the rainwater, so water companies are allowed to use 'release valves' to temporarily send raw sewage into rivers. If this wasn't allowed, there would be a significant risk of sewage backing up into properties. New housing developments are now required to keep the systems separate.
- There were more than 372,000 raw sewage spills across England in 2021, increasing to 464,000 in 2023. During this period, the number of raw sewage discharges in the Thames Water area increased from 14,700 in 2021 to almost 17,000 in 2023 (Environment Agency, Event Monitoring data). Thames Water blamed the increase on record levels of wet weather and improved monitoring of the spills.
- Thames Water now publishes a map that shows where discharges in the river are happening in real time (https://www.thameswater.co.uk/edm-map). The map also refers to plans for upgrading individual sewage plants to reduce overflows, some of which will not meet government targets before 2050, and even then some less critical raw sewage spills will probably be still be allowed. The closest upstream sewage treatment plant from Wolvercote shown on the discharge map is a plant at Cassington that is scheduled to have an upgrade completed by 2025.

Beside raw sewage discharges, rain run-off from farmland near the rivers can spread chemicals such as phosphorus into the river. This can be especially bad from chicken farming. A report from the House of Commons indicated that, in some areas, pollution from agricultural run-off can be equal to or greater than pollution from sewage plants.

Thames Water is private company that is regulated by Department for the Environment, Food and Rural Affairs (Defra) and Ofwat who put pressure on them to comply with pollution reduction targets under the threat of fines for unauthorised discharges. The government has developed a 'Storm Overflows Discharge Reduction Plan' with targets and plans to resolve the problem by 2050. The work to address the problem across the country is estimated to cost £600 billion that would need to be paid for by the water companies with increases in water bills.

Given the current system in the UK, political pressure on Thames Water may be the only way to address urgent issues in the meantime. MP Robert Courts of Witney helped to secure a £17 million improvement project for a local Thames Water sewage plant that had been causing continued problems on the River Windrush. The upgrades were meant to be completed by the end of 2024.

Many believe that a private company is not properly incentivized to address this costly issue. In the United States, the vast majority of local municipalities manage treatment of drinking and waste water with publicly-owned water companies, although there is a similar ongoing debate about whether privatisation makes sense in certain situations. Some municipalities have chosen private or public-private partnership options.

Countryside vs. climate change – The need to address climate change with more renewable energy is having a direct impact on the nearby Oxfordshire countryside. The proposed Botley West Solar Farms would cover about 3200 acres (about five square miles) of land mostly owned by the Blenheim Estate north of Oxford.

Whilst most people are in favour of solar power in principle, it is understandable that the residents of communities near these massive solar farms would have cause for concern.
- The development would cover vast areas of countryside impacting towns an villages near Blenheim Palace, such as Bladon, home to St Martin's church where Winston Churchill and many Spencer-Churchill family members are buried.
- The village of Church Hanborough would be almost completed enveloped by solar farms, and clearly many residents don't want this massive change to their countryside.
- Residents in the area have formed an actions group called *Stop Botley West* to fight government approval of the development, or at least to ensure that their concerns are sufficiently considered as part of the planning approval process.

Anti-sewage dumping protest in Pangbourne.

But not everyone is against it.
- The developers, Photovolt Development Partners (PVDP) claim that the solar farm would generate enough renewable energy to power more than 330,00 homes, roughly all the homes in Oxfordshire. They have stated that the benefits outweigh the initial downsides and that are only seeking a temporary license of 40 years.
- Dominic Hare, the CEO of the primary landowner, Blenheim Estate, counters accusations that it is just a moneymaking exercise "I think to imagine that the only reason anyone would back a de-carbonising project which generates this amount of clean energy is because it makes money is very sad. There are people and institutions who believe that it is very important that we strain every sinew to arrest and reverse climate change. Blenheim is one of those institutions."
- Another apparently grass roots environment action group called *Botley West NIMBYs* is in support of the proposal and uses environmental rationale stating that the opposition group "is ill-conceived, short-sighted, and fundamentally driven by the petty interests of those running the campaign. They may not consider themselves to be NIMBYs, but NIMBYism is hardwired into every part of their campaign."

As consultations on the proposal proceeds through the planning approval process tensions are rising.
- The Stop Botley West campaigners appear to have numbers on their side with both Labour and Conservative local MPs listening to their constituents and urging central government to reject the proposed plans.
- Meanwhile those in favour of the solar farms, who some might call 'extreme environmentalists' are resorting the name calling and defacing opposition signs with NIMBY, as shown below.
- The Stop Botley West group continues to questions Blenheim Estate's stewardship of the land with some of their protest signs calling Blenheim a 'destroyer'.
- Some have called for more inland wind farms as an alternative as they are more efficient at generating energy. However, given the severe visual impact of windmills on the landscape, this option is unlikely to go down well with those living in the Oxfordshire countryside.

Regardless of which side of the debate you support, it's not clear if climate change has sufficient political weight to overcome the deep currents of conservation in this part of the country. Like the debate over the Goring hydro electricity plant, the local residents seem to be well organised with political support and financial donations to fight any decision in court — but have they met their match with Blenheim Estate?

Inset: Local residents are clearly not happy with Blenheim's plans.
Left: A climate change action group apparently defaced the Stop Botley West group with the NIMBY slur.

Oxford rowing — may be a less controversial way to end this tour of Oxford. Amongst the many sporting activities that Oxford University students can participate in, rowing is clearly king.

The Boat Race — The most famous rowing event is the Oxford – Cambridge Boat Race— a 4.25 mile race held on Thames tidal waters between Putney and Chiswick bridges in London each spring. For this race, a top Oxford 'Blue Boat' and 'Isis' reserve crew, each with 8 rowers and a cox, are formed of the best rowers from each of Oxford's many colleges.

The Oxford University Boat Club (OUBC) uses a dedicated boathouse to train for the Boat Race that was built by the Thames at Wallingford in 2006. The teams also make use of the Redgrave and Pinsent Rowing Lake in Caversham and indoor training facilities at the Iffley Road Sports Centre in Oxford. There is also a Women's Boat Club, and clubs for Lightweight Men and Women Rowing teams that also compete against their Cambridge counterparts.

The competition is fierce to get a slot on the Oxford Blue squad, with top international crew members from America and other countries often participating. The OUBC members elect a student president each year who works with the team coaches to select the crew and make the final decisions about who gets in the boat and what position they sit in. The tension for these much sought after positions was made evident in 1987 when four American elite rowers objected to the president's decision to exclude a key rower and ultimately 'mutinied' — refusing to row. They also questioned the techniques used by the legendary Oxford coach Dan Topolski who had led Oxford to 10 consecutive wins over Cambridge from 1976-1985 — calling them 'outdated'. In the end, the Oxford team found victory without the American mutineers, beating a strong Cambridge team due to their strategy to navigate around unusually choppy waters that Cambridge struggled with.

In 2024, Oxford lost to the Cambridge team where an unusually wet winter and flooding of the river played a factor. Oxford missed a number of practices dues to flooding at the Wallingford site and on the day of the race three members of the men's team complained of illness from e.coli associated with "too much poo in the river" from sewage discharges associated with the flooding.

Inter-collegiate 'Bumps' races – For those not at the level of the highly competitive Boat Race crew, rowing at college-level is open to all university students regardless of their level of experience, making rowing one of the most widely-participated-in sports at Oxford.
- Many colleges have their own boat houses along the Isis near Folly Bridge at 'Boat House Island' where the Cherwell meets the Isis and the 'bumps' races take place.

Wadham College women crew at 2022 Summer 8s Bumps Race.

- This stretch of the Isis is generally too narrow for side-by-side racing so college crews start the race lined up one after the other several metres apart in their positions from the prior day's or year's race. When the starting canon goes off, the boats race up the river from Donnington Bridge near Iffley Lock to just short of Folly Bridge and try to catch up with the boat in front and 'bump' it with theirs (although physical bumping is no longer required).
- Upon successfully bumping, the boats then swap positions on the river on the start line the following day. In May, the 'Summer 8s' also know as 'Eights Week' competition lasts for four days, with the aim being to bump on each of the days, and ultimately reach the top position of 'Head of the River'.
- The winning teams for both men and women are crowned the 'Head of the River' and have the honour of parading through the streets of Oxford carrying their boat— these days a cheaper wooden version of their boat — on their shoulders singing songs along the way. Upon returning to their college quad they have a grand celebratory dinner followed by the burning of the boat in the quad with the winning crew traditionally jumping over the flames.
- The college coat of arms with details of the winning teams and year are proudly painted on the quad walls by winning teams and stay until worn away by years of weathering.

Oriel celebrates their 2022 Head of River win with a parade back to their quad carrying the winning cox on a boat they will later set fire to. The 2022 win gave Oriel College 34 total wins, making them the most successful Summer 8s rowing ream in Oxford history, just ahead of Christ Church. Photo ©Tim Koch.

Left: Oriel team preparing to start a bumps race in first position, with other college teams lined up behind them.
Below: One of many Oriel wins commemorated on the walls of their college quad.

Parting Thoughts

Like the meandering flow of the river in the Thames Valley, this book has been a wide-ranging journey for me in exploring so many aspects of the area — from learning so much about its rich history, meeting people from all walks of life and pondering the issues concerning local residents. I hope that the holistic approach I took to documenting life in this area rings true to those who live here and know the region well.

This book is also clearly also a reflection of who I am:

- A photographer, slightly obsessed with capturing pictures of the beautiful countryside and is always the one at community events taking photos of the activities.
- A resident of an English village who appreciates the community spirit unique to village life in this country.
- Someone who continuously digs to understand the wider historical significance of places in our local stomping grounds.
- A local councillor interested in understanding the causes of community issues with the persistence and patience to find solutions.

Beyond the extensive history described in Part 1 of the book, I hope that the resulting story of the Thames Valley's history gives a sense of the importance of the region, making the case that it deserves a stronger sense of identity. So much of the history of the Thames Valley until now has been centred around local accounts of individual towns and villages or of the river itself. By framing these events and sites within the story of the Thames Valley, I tried to show how many of these events are interrelated, giving an them even greater significance when tied into the history of the region.

None of the local issues described in Part 2 of the book have simple solutions that will be resolved in the near future. Many of the biggest challenges result from expected growth of the area that many other parts of the country can relate to. Based on Local Plans that have been approved or are under review as of 2024, there are plans in place for at least 100,000 new homes in the Thames Valley by the mid 2030s. This number includes some new developments that have recently been completed or are now under construction, but the vast majority of new homes are still to come.

- All these new homes and neighbourhoods won't be a panacea to make housing more affordable, but hopefully they will result in a greater selection of smaller, more affordable homes that are so desperately needed — a mixture of smaller privately owned homes and those with government subsidised social rent.
- There will inevitably be more cars and traffic challenges as many of these developments come with limited new road infrastructure. The need for significant improvements in public transportation and better support for pedestrians and cycling safety will be even greater.
- Provision of infrastructure for things like sewage treatment, health care and schools are likely to struggle to keep up with demand.
- It remains to be seen how successful the largest developments will be in rapidly growing places like Slough, Maidenhead, Reading and in expanded Garden Towns in Didcot and Berinsfield. In recent years we have seen examples of development that could be considered quite successful, however, done the wrong way, large developments could just exacerbate existing challenges.
- The tug of war between forces of conservation vs. demands for more houses will continue. Based on centuries of evidence and the planning controls that have been developed since the Second World War, I am confident that where conservation is a priority, such as in National Landscapes, Green Belts, and Conservations Areas, the forces of conservation will largely prevail.

If nothing else, I hope the photos and stories in the book at least make it clear that the Thames Valley is a beautiful place to live with thriving and diverse communities. The challenges described in the book are not going to go away anytime soon, but the vibrant community spirit shown in many of the case studies is a cause for optimism. One of the most important messages that I hope emerges from these examples is that our future is shaped by the people in our communities — people working together who are passionate about their communities CAN make a difference:

- You can have your voice heard and influence the future of your community through development of Local Plans, Neighbourhood Plans, and countless smaller changes within your town or village.
- Communities can stop the closure of important public services such as libraries and community toilets.
- Community action can prevent your village from being subsumed by developments in neighbouring towns.
- They can stop inappropriate developments from negatively impacting Conservation Areas, National Landscapes and Green Belts.
- Communities can create a new way of communal living and working as they are doing in Hardwick Estate.
- Whilst there is still a long way to go, sustained pressure can make improvements to the quality of river water.

One of the marvellous things about living in England is that you CAN make a difference in the future of your community. The future is up to us.

Acknowledgements

I'd like to thank all of those who I have met, had discussions with and interviewed along the incredible journey of writing this book, some of whom are mentioned as sources below. I'd also like to apologise to family and friends for being such as bore about this book which I admit has been a somewhat of an obsession. A special thanks to those who took the time to reading early drafts of the book to provide invaluable feedback, including local historians Ellie Thorne, Victoria Willcox and Eric Hartley. Reading University Professor Peter Worsley's review of the pre-historic section was extremely helpful. Others who reviewed drafts, including Mark and Alistair Dunstan, my sister Karen Donahue, Paul O'Loughlin of Warmingham Estate Agents and my publisher Steven Pugsley. Thanks to Magdalena Wachnik of Oxford Archaeology for her work on the Thames Valley map graphics.

Sources and Further Reading

The list of sources below this is not exhaustive. The research is also based on:
- Visits to local museums, such as Reading Museum, the Ashmolean and the Natural History Museums in Oxford, and other museums in Dorchester, Henley, Wallingford, and Windsor.
- Interviews and discussions with numerous residents, including local history experts and groups.
- Accounts of community issues in local newspapers such as the *Henley Standard*, *Oxford Times* and the *Maidenhead Advertiser*.
- Countless site visits throughout the region to photograph and understand the context.

Part 1: History

General History of the Area:
- Victoria County History, VCH Berkshire, Volume I, 1936.
- Victoria County History, *A History of Oxfordshire* Volume XX, The South Oxfordshire Chilterns, 2022.
- Jonathan Schneer, *The Thames – England's River,* Abacus, 2005.
- Jean Cook, Trevor Rowley et al, *Dorchester through the Ages*, Oxford Universality Department for external studies, 1985.
- Clive Aslet, *Landmarks of Britain, the Five hundred Places that made our History*, Hodder and Stroughton Ltd, London 2005.

Thames River History:
- The Thames Conservancy & The Thames in Wartime, Where Smooth Waters Glide: 250 years of caring for the River Thames, https://thames250exhibition.com/

Pre-History to the Iron Age:
- Anthony Morigi et al,*Thames Through Time, The Archaeology of the Gravel; Terraces of the Upper and Middle Thames, Early Pre-History to 1500 BC*, Oxford Archaeology, 2011.
- George Lambrick et al,*Thames Through Time, The Archaeology of the Gravel; Terraces of the Upper and Middle Thames, Late Pre-History:1500 BC - AD 50*, Oxford Archaeology, 2009.
- Interview with Peter Worsley, Emeritus Professor of Quarternary Geology at Reading University. March 2024.
- British Archaeology at the Ashmolean museum, https://britisharchaeology.ashmus.ox.ac.uk/index.html
- South Oxfordshire Archaeological Group (SOAG), Bulletin, Issue 42, 1986.

Roman Period:
- J. Malpas, *Roman Roads South and East of Dorchester-on-Thames*, Oxoniesia, 1987.
- Paul Booth, et al, *Thames Through Time, The Archaeology of the Gravel; Terraces of the Upper and Middle Thames, Early Historical Period, AD 1-1000*, Oxford Archaeology, 2007.
- Reading Museum, Silchester Gallery.
- Ashmolean Museum Gallery of Roman findings in Oxfordshire.
- Streatley Village Design Statement – Your Village Your Future, Streatley Parish Council, 2009.

Anglo-Saxon:
- Morris, Mark, *The Anglo-Saxons, A History of the Beginning of England*, Hutchinson, London, 2021. Especially the role of Thegns and accounts of slaves at the time including the quote from Ælfric of Eyshan.
- A lost monastery revealed? Investigating an Anglo-Saxon community at Cookham, The Past, the-past.com, 13 October 2021.
- Dr Paul Kelly, *King Alfred: Man on the Move*, Black Sash publications, 2019.
- Justin Pollard, *Alfred the Great, The man who made England*, John Murray publishing, 2005, p119-22.
- Interveiw with Lord Richard Benyon of Englefield estate, April 2024.
- The Vikings in Reading, Reading Museum, 22 March 2019, https://www.readingmuseum.org.uk/blog/vikings-reading
- Historic England, Scheduled Monument, Anglo-Saxon great hall complex and Roman settlement features at Long Wittenham, Oxfordshire, OX14 4PZ, March 2020.
- Catherine Hanley, *Matilda, Empress. Queen. Warrior.* Yale University Press, New Haven and London, 2020.
- Ruth Buckley, *The Legendary Life of St Frideswide*, Palmcross Publications, 2010.
- Ruth Buckley, *The Edward Burn-Jones, St Frideswide Window Christ Church Cathedral*, Palmcross Publications, 2021.
- *A View from the Hill*, Chapter on Ashdown Battle by Judy Barradell-Smith, editor Peter Cockerell. Published by the Blewbury Village Society, 2017.

- Ashmolean Museum raises £1.35 million reward to acquire hoard of King Alfred the Great. Ashmolean Museum Press Release, 01 February 2017.

Norman England:
- Open-Domesday, www.opendomesday.org
- Morris, Mark, *The Anglo-Saxons, A History of the Beginning of England*, Hutchinson, London, 2021. Including the quote from Ælfric of Eyshan.
- John Burnside, Magna Carta was good for humans – but even better for fish, the *New Statesman*, 28 May 2017.
- Luke Over and Chris Tyrell, *A Millennium in the Royal Borough*, The Royal Borough of Windsor and Maidenhead, 1999.
- The Magna Carta, The British Library - https://www.bl.uk/magna-carta
- Interview with Mr David Barber, Royl Swan Marker, April 2024.
- The Royal Dyer Company, https://www.dyerscompany.co.uk/the-company/
- The Royal Family, Swan Upping, https://www.royal.uk/swans
- The Royal Vintners Company, https://www.vintnershall.co.uk/swans
- A.L. Rowse *Windsor Castle in the History of the Nation*, Book Club Associates, London, 1974.

University of Oxford:
- 'The University of Oxford', in *A History of the County of Oxford*: Volume 3, the University of Oxford, ed. H E Salter and Mary D Lobel (London, 1954), pp. 1-38. British History Online http://www.british-history.ac.uk/vch/oxon/vol3/
- Laurence Brockliss, *University of Oxford, a Brief History*, Bodleian Library, Oxford, 2019.
- Tony Morris, *The Morris Oxford Mini-History of Oxford*, Port Meadow Press, 2021.

Hardwick Estate:
- Emily J. Climenson, from the *Diaries of Mrs. Lybbe Powys*, Hardwick House, 1768. Published 2012, Hanse Publications. – Charles I visit to Hardwick.
- Michael Redley: *The Real Mr Toad: Merchant Venturer and radical in the Gold Age*, 2016.

The Civil War:
- Peter Gaunt, *The English Civil War, a Military History*, Bloomsbury Academic, London, 2014.
- Vicky Wilson, *Walking Oxford*, Metro Publications, 2021.

Blenheim Palace:
- Reports and Financial Statements Blenheim Palace Heritage Foundation, 31 March 2022 and 31 March 2023.

The Coaching Era and new bridges from 1786-1840:
- Charles G. Harper, *The Bath Road, History Fashion, & Frivolity on an old highway*, Chapman & Hall Ltd, London, 1899.
- Report to the Secretary of State for Transport by Mike Moore, an Inspector appointed by the Secretary of State for Transport. WHITCHURCH BRIDGE ACTS 1792 AND 1988 AND THE TRANSPORT CHARGES ACT 1954. 26th June 2015.
- Robin & Valerie Bootle, *The Story of Cookham*, privately published in 1990. - Cookham Bridge building.

Isambard Kingdom Brunel:
- John Pudney, *Brunel and his World*, Thames and Hudson, London, 1974.
- L.T.C. Rolt, Isambard Kingdom Brunel, *The definitive Biography of the Engineer, Visionary and Great Briton*.

WH Smith:
- Stewart Payne, Tycoon pays £38m for idyllic corner of England, the *Telegraph*, 22 June 2007.
- Richard Eden, Abba Singer's Lover Becomes a Viscount, the *Telegraph*, 12 August 2012
- Pangbourne Heritage Group, The Shops, Trades and Businesses of Pangbourne, 2021.

The Great Stink:
- Paul Dobraszczyk, *London's Sewers*, Shire Publications, Oxford, 2014.
- Peter Ackroyd, *Thames – Sacred River*, Chatto & Windus, London, 2007. Pp 272 & 274
- Stephen Halliday, *The Great Stink of London, Sir Joseph Bazalgette and the Cleansing of the Victorian Metropolis*, The History Press, Cheltenham, 2009.

Reading and the 3 Bs:
- Reading Museum, Special Collections, Huntley & Palmer Archive, 2022.
- H&G Simonds Ltd., The Story of the Bridge Street Brewery, Reading, 1785 – 1980, Simonds Family History, www.simondsfamily.me.uk

Pangbourne Manor and Vestry Committees:
- Joan Willcox, *Pangbourne – An Illustrated History*, Berkshire Books, 1992.
- Ellie Thorne, *St James The Less, Pangbourne 1866-2016: Then and Now,* Jim Donahue Images, 2016.

19th and 20th Century Boundary Changes:
- Victoria County History of the Counties of England, A *History of Oxfordshire Volume XX*, 2022.
- Vicky Jordan, Woodcote – *Portrait of a South Chiltern Village*, Windmill Enterprises, 1996.

Whitchurch Manor:
- Interview with Sally Howard and Rodney Cole, March 2024.
- Victoria County History *A History of Oxfordshire Volume XX.*
- A Brief History of Walliscote House by Jackie Moys Verlegh.
- Richard Wingfield, Coombe Park, https://whitchurchonthames.com, June 2019.

Golden Age of Boating:
- Jerome K. Jerome, *Three Men in a Boat*, 1889.

William Grenfell/Lord Desborough:
- William Henry Grenfell, Grenfell Family History, https://grenfellhistory.co.uk/.
- Quote from *Daily Telegraph* from Sandy Nairne and Peter Williams, *Titan of the Thames, The Life of Lord Desborough*, Unbound, London, 2024.

Wind in the Willows:
- Peter Hunt, *The Making of The Wind in the Willows*, the Bodlean Library, Oxford, 2018.

William Morris/Lord Nuffield:
- Oxford Bus Museum, https://www.oxfordbusmuseum.org/william-morris
- Gilliam Bardsley and Stephen Liang, *Making Cars at Cowley – from Morris to Mini*, The History Press, Gloucester, 2013
- Tour of BMW Oxford plant, Cowley.

Sir Stanley Spencer and Dora Carrington:
- Robin & Valerie Bootle, *The Story of Cookham*, privately published in 1990.
- Fiona MacCarthy, *Stanley Spencer, An English Vision*, Yale University Press, 1997.
- Sabine Durrant, Frances Partridge, Bloomsbury Groupie, the *Guardian*, 11 November, 1999.

Grace Kelley and Henley Regatta:
- Daniel J. Boyne, Kelly, *A Father, a Son, and American Quest*, First Lyons Press, 2008.
- Christopher Dodd, Burt Bushnell Obituary, the *Guardian*, 28 February, 2010.

Cliveden and Nancy Astor:
- Alex May, The Cliveden Set, *Oxford Dictionary of National Biography*.
- Cliveden House History, *Cliveden House*, National Trust.

WWII:
- The Thames Conservancy & The Thames in Wartime, Where Smooth Waters Glide: 250 years of caring for the River Thames, https://thames250exhibition.com/
- The GHQ Line, http://dunkirk1940.org.; Chris Kolonko Mapping GHQ Lines in Google Earth -01 December 2015.
- US Army 343rd Corps of Engineers history blog: http://www.6thcorpscombatengineers.com/ArmondeCasagrande.htm - Nettlebed base.
- Nigel Suffield-Jones, *Pangbourne Magazine*, Issue 165, November/December 2021, Lest We Forget, Pangbourne Place-Names, pp 42-43. Bailey Bridge Building in WW2.
- Stephen Billyead, *Pangbourne Magazine*, Issue 166, January/February 2022, Pangbourne in the Second World War, p39.
- Peter Adamson, *A Landmark in Time – The world of the Wittenham Clumps*, P&LA, 2021 - Berinsfield after WW II.
- Mike Cooper, Reading Museum, The Day Reading was Bombed, the People's Pantry 75 years on, 20 January 2018 https://www.readingmuseum.org.uk/blog/day-reading-was-bombed-people%E2%80%99s-pantry-75-years-on
- Robin J. Brook, *Thames Valley Airfields in the Second World War*, Countryside Books, Newbury, Berks, 2002.
- War and State Society, Bombing Britain Dataset, http://www.warstateandsociety.com/Bombing-Britain
- Simon Forty, *D-Day UK, 100 locations in the UK*, Historic England, 2019.
- Whitchurch Camp 1943 to 1960, Transcript of a talk given by Peter Hawley to the History Society in Whitchurch village hall on 20th March 2014.

Rock'n Roll Valley:
- Ian Carroll, *The Reading Festival, Mud, Music and Mayhem, the Official History,* Reynolds & Hearn Ltd, Richmond, 2007.
- Jimmy Page, *Jimmy Page*, Genesis Publications and Jimmy Page, Guildford, Surrey, 2010, 2014.
- Marc Myers, The Making of Whole Lotta Love, *The Wall Street Journal*, 29 May 2014.

Harwell and Culham Campus':
- Dominic O'Connell, Nuclear fusion and the race to save the planet with gas hotter than the sun, *The Times*, 23 November 2021.

COVD-19 vaccine:
- Darcy Jiminez, Covid-19: vaccine pricing varies wildly by country and company, *Pharmaceutical Technology*, 27 Oct 2021.

Film Studio boom:
- Gareth Neame quote from Creative South East A Global Centre of Excellence for Creative Industries, https://www.thamesvalleyberkshire.co.uk

Part 2: Community Life and Future Issues

Windsor and Eton:
- The Crown Estate Integrated Annual Report and Accounts 2022/23, Creating lasting and shared prosperity for the nation, www.thecrownestate.co.uk/
- 'State-school admissions are rising at Oxford and Cambridge', *The Economist*, 11 March 2023.
- www.etoncollege.com/finanical-aid

Slough:
- Hugh Fort, 'Huge housing development will see derelict Horlicks factory revitalised', getreading.co.uk, 10 November 2019.
- Kieran Bell More than £3 billion to be invested in Slough by 2030, *Maidenhead Advertiser*, 28 November 2019.

Maidenhead, Marlow and Cookham:
- Borough Local Plan 2013-2033, adopted 8th February 2022, www.rbwm.gov.uk
- Louisa Clarence-Smith, The small shop blueprint to save town centres, *The Times*, 11 June 2020.
- Adrian Williams, Whacky fun on the field set for Boxing Day in Cookham Dean. The *Maidenhead Advertiser*, 20 December 2022.
- National Planning Policy Framework, 13. Protecting Greenbelt Land, Department for Levelling Up, Housing and Communities, 27 March 2012.

Henley:
- Henley versus Marlow in Olympic-style sports event, The *Henley Standard*, 14 March 2016.

Reading:
- Office of National Statistics, https://www.ons.gov.uk, How the population of Reading changed: Census 2021, 28 June 2022.
- Heidi Blake, The town where schoolchildren speak 150 languages, the *Telegraph*, 08 Feb 2010.

Pangbourne & Whitchurch:
- Peter Hunt, *The Making of The Wind in the Willows*, the Bodlean Library, Oxford, 2018.

Hardwick Estate:
- Interview with Miriam Rose, February 2023.

Goring & Streatley:
- National Planning Policy Framework, https://www.gov.uk/government/publications/national-planning-policy-framework--2
- Goring Neighbourhood Plan, 18 July 2019.
- South Oxfordshire Local Plan 2035. https://www.southoxon.gov.uk/south-oxfordshire-district-council/planning-and-development/local-plan-and-planning-policies/local-plan-2035
- Interview with Felix Bloomfield, former cabinet member for Planning, South Oxfordshire District Council, April 2024.
- Housing statistics: National statistics Housing supply: net additional dwellings, England: 2021 to 2022, 24 November 2022
- Streatley Conservation Area Appraisal, West Berkshire Council Planning and Countryside, August 2010.
- Interview with Paul O'Loughlin of Warmingham Estate Agents March 2024.
- Interview with Mike Stares, Former Chairman of Goring Neighbourhood Planning Committee, March 2024.
- Goring named Village of the Year, 10 July 2009, bbc.news.co.uk.

Wallingford to Abingdon:
- Wendy Wilson, House of Commons Library, Tackling the under-supply of housing, May 2023.
- Affordable home ownership schemes, UK Government, https://www.gov.uk/affordable-home-ownership-schemes
- Conor Dougherty and Soumya Karlamangla, California Fights Its NIMBYs, *The New York Times*, September 1, 2022.
- Accessory Dwelling Units, Lessons from around the country, Harvard University Joint Center for Housing Studies, October 13, 2023.
- Erica Werner, 'Granny flats' play surprising role in easing California's housing woes, *The Washington Post*, May 21, 2023.

Oxford:
- James Attlee, *Isolarion, a different Oxford journey*, And Other Stories Publisher, Sheffield–London–New York, 2020.
- Laurence Sleator, "Gown and Town clash over car fees in Cambridge", *The Times*, Friday December 23, 2022.
- Shosha Adie and Liam Rice, Silvesters Stores to close after East Oxford LTNs 'the last straw', *Oxford Mail*, 08 June 2022.
- Storm Overflows Discharge Reduction Plan, Department for Environment, Food and Rural Affairs, 26 August 2024.
- Environment Agency, Event Duration Monitoring Data Publication, 2021 & 2023.
- House of Commons Environmental Audit Committee, Water quality in rivers, Report of Session 2021–22, 05 January 2022.
- Miranda Norris, Witney MP assured by Thames Water boss on works upgrade, *Oxford Mail*, 26 March, 2024.
- Miranda Norris, Blenheim CEO defends plans for massive solar farm in West Oxfordshire, *Oxford Mail*, 22nd March 2023.
- Stop Botley West Nimbys, https://www.botleywestnimbys.com/behind-the-curtain

Index

A

Abingdon 18, 48, 50, 102, 130, 176, 177
Affordable Housing 173, 178
Alchester 22, 23
Aldbourne 111
Aldworth 35
Allen, Major George 17
Anglian Ice Age 12
Appleford 176
Ascot 91, 120
Ascot Racecourse 72
Ashmolean Museum 31
Aston Tirrold 33, 35, 46
Astor, Nancy 10, 105
Avebury 17

B

Bailey Bridge Building 113
Bampton 27
Band of Brothers 111
Basildon House 110
Bathing Water Status 176, 188
Battle of Britain 108
Bazalgette, Joseph 10, 86
Benson 18, 31, 46, 113
Benyon, Richard 63
Berinsfield 115, 173
Berkshire 123, 129, 132, 168
Berkshire Downs 12, 13, 75, 166
Betjeman, John 54
Bicester 22
Big Rings 17, 18
Bisney 27
Bix 23
Blackbird Leys 24, 173
Black Horse Pub 115
Blenheim Palace 64, 73, 114, 171
Blewburton Iron Age Hillfort 33

Bodleian Library 53
Boulters Lock 91
Bourne End 84
Bozedown Camp 20
Bracknell 3, 121
Bray 46, 125
Brightwell Barrow 19, 21
Brightwell-cum-Sotwell 19, 177
Bristol 81
British Museum 23, 29
Bronze Age 19
Brunel, Isambard Kingdom 10, 81
Bunkfest 177
Burcot 7

C

Caesar, Julius 4, 9, 22
California 179
Cambridge University 52
Cameron, David 53, 133
Carrington, Dora 104
Carroll, Lewis 54
Castle Hill 21
Caversham 46, 98, 175
Caversham Park 61
Chalgrove 113
Charles I 10, 61, 69
Charles II 58, 63
Checkendon 46, 115
Chiltern Hills 12, 13, 75, 98, 166
Chilterns National Landscape 166
Chiltern Strip Villages 97
Cholsey 46, 81, 177
Christ Church Cathedral 27
Churchill, Winston 74
Cirencester 23
Civil War 9, 52, 61, 69
Clifton Hampden 176
Coaching 77

Conservation Area 170
Cookham 12, 30, 37, 39, 46, 79, 84, 98, 100, 103, 109, 116, 117, 128, 138
Cook, Hugh of Faringdon 10, 60, 93
Coronavirus 123
COVID-19 Vaccine 123
Cowley 45, 101
Cricklade 5, 37
Cromwell, Oliver 69
Crop marks 17, 26
Crowmarsh Gifford 46, 176
Crown Estate 130
Culden Faw Estate 64, 85
Culham 173, 176
Culham Centre for Fusion Energy 122
Cursus 17

D

Danesfield House 109
D-Day invasion 110
Deacon's Garage 18
Desborough, Lord 10, 29, 89
Devizes 81
Didcot 84, 173, 176, 178
Dillon, Anna 35
Domesday Book 45
Dorchester Abbey 47, 60
Dorchester Museum 60
Dorchester-on-Thames 17, 21, 22, 23, 26, 29, 37, 45, 46, 115, 116, 176
Dorney 132
Duchy of Cornwall 131
Duchy of Lancaster 131
Dyke Hills 21

E

Earley 16
Edward III 56, 57

Eisenhower 110, 112, 114
Elizabeth I 142
Elizabeth Line 83, 126
Emmer Green 109
Empress Matilda 10, 48
Enclosure Acts 97
Englefield 33
Englefield Estate 63
Environment Agency 8
Eton 46, 83, 117, 129, 132
Eton College 10, 59, 81, 132
Eton Wick 129, 132
Evenlode River 24

F

Flash locks 7
Flooding 117
Folly Bridge 79
Frilsham 27
Fusion Energy 122

G

Gatehampton 13, 23, 29, 166
George III 58
George IV 58
Gervais, Ricky 10, 135
Gewisse 26
Goring 12, 46, 79, 84, 98, 108, 109, 113, 120, 123, 165, 174
Goring Gap 12, 23, 81, 170
Goring Heath 98, 109
Grahame, Kenneth 10, 62, 100
Great Western Railway 8, 9, 23, 81
Green Belt 142, 170, 172
Greenham Common 110, 114
Greenham Common Women's Peace Camp 10, 114
Grenfell, William 89

Grim's Ditch 97
Gypsies and Travellers 159, 173

H

Hambleden 46, 85, 95
Hampstead Norries 113
Hand axes 15
Hardwick Estate 61, 64, 100, 128, 160
Hardwick House 62, 100
Harwell Campus 122
Headington 45, 182
Heathrow Airport 116
Henley 7, 23, 50, 51, 79, 85, 97, 113, 120, 144
Henley Royal Regatta 5, 75, 144
Henry I 10, 43, 47, 48, 56, 129
Henry II 48, 55, 56
Henry III 56
Henry VI 10, 59
Henry VIII 10, 52, 58, 180
Heritage Assets 171
High Wycombe 84, 109
Hillforts 17, 19, 20
Holyport 125
Holywell 45
Home Park 131
Hounslow 77
Hungerford 81, 84, 110
Huntercombe Golf Course 101
Hurley 46

I

Iffley 8, 45
Iffley Road 183
Ipsden 16, 46
Iron Age 20, 21, 29
Isis 5

J

Jericho 182
Johnson, Boris 53, 133, 149

K

Kelly, Grace 104
Kemble 5
Kennet and Avon Canal 81, 108
Kerridge, Tom 138
Kidmore End 98
King Æthelred the Unready 39
King Alfred 9, 30
King Alfred's Way 126
King Alfred the Great 32
King Charles III 129
King John 10, 55, 56

L

Leander Club 145
Lechlade 5
Led Zeppelin 10, 119
Lewis, C.S. 54, 107
Littlecote House 110
Local Plans 171
London 7, 50, 86, 126
London Paddington 81, 84
Long Wittenham 26
Lowbury Hill 23, 33, 36
Low Traffic Neighbourhoods 186
Lullebrook Manor 100
Lyd Well 6

M

Madejski, Sir John 10, 151
Magna Carta 10, 53, 55, 69
Maidenhead 8, 12, 29, 46, 77, 81, 83, 84, 90, 91, 98, 109, 117, 121, 126, 129, 138

Mapledurham 8, 64, 67
Mapledurham House 100
Marlborough 81
Marlow 8, 12, 46, 47, 79, 84, 109, 116, 125, 138, 149
May, Theresa 10, 138
Mercia 30, 31, 32, 37
Mongewell 97
Morris, William 10, 101
Moulsford 33, 35, 84
Mount Farm Airfield 115

N

National Landscapes 169
National Planning Policy Framework 168
Neighbourhood Plans 173
Nettlebed 23, 114
Newbury 3, 77, 84, 109, 110, 121
NIMBYs 128, 175, 190
Norman Conquest 9
North Stoke 18, 97
North Wessex Downs National Landscape 166
Nuffield 97
Nuffield, Lord 10, 101
Nunham Courtenay 46

O

Ofwat 189
Old Windsor 117, 120
Order of the Garter 57
Oxford 7, 37, 39, 42, 45, 46, 51, 69, 79, 81, 91, 100, 101, 109, 113, 128, 173, 180
Oxford Brookes 182
Oxford Castle 44, 48
Oxford Green Belt 176
Oxfordshire 98, 123
Oxfordshire County Council 168, 185
Oxford University 9, 37, 47, 52

P

Page, Jimmy 10, 119
Palmer, George 10, 95

Pangbourne 23, 30, 45, 46, 65, 84, 85, 91, 93, 98, 100, 113, 119, 123
Pangbourne Working Men's Club 113, 154
Parish Councils 166
Phyllis Court Club 23, 144
Polish Refugee Camps 115
Port Meadow 27, 98, 180
Pound Locks 7
Prince and Princess of Wales 10, 131
Profumo Affair 105
Purley 98

Q

Queen Anne 72, 77
Queen Charlotte 58
Queen Elizabeth II 129
Queen Victoria 58, 83

R

Radley 176
RAF Aldermaston 111, 114
RAF Benson 109, 115
RAF Greenham Common 112
RAF Harwell 122
RAF Heston 109
RAF Medmenham 109
RAF Membury 112
RAF Ramsbury 112
RAF Welford 111
RAF Woodcote 115
Reading 3, 8, 16, 33, 35, 46, 47, 62, 77, 81, 84, 93, 95, 108, 109, 113, 121, 126, 128, 150
Reading Abbey 10, 47, 60
Reading Festival 119
Reading Museum 23, 42
Redgrave, Sir Steve 10, 75, 139
Ricardo, Colonel 100
Ridgeway 13, 33, 97, 126, 166
River Kennet 47
River Thame 4, 21
River Thames 4, 17, 21, 86, 91, 100

Rock and Roll 120
Roman Britain 22
Roman Road 22, 23
Rose, Sir Charles Day 10, 61, 62, 100
Royal Borough of Windsor and Maidenhead 129
Runnymede 55

S

Sandford 5, 177
Sashes Island 37
Science Vale UK 178
Sewage 8, 86, 188
Shinfield 125
Shiplake 51, 84, 98
Silchester 22, 23
Slough 3, 77, 83, 84, 121, 123, 126, 128, 129, 135
Sonning 78
Sonning Common 98, 173
South Oxfordshire District Council 168
South Stoke 46, 97, 98
Spencer, Sir Stanley 10, 103
Stagecoaches 77, 81
St Albans 12, 22, 23
St Birinus 9, 26, 115
Steventon 84
St Frideswide 9, 27
Stoke Row 98
Stone, Robert 93
Streatley 13, 23, 33, 46, 79, 109, 116, 120, 165
Sunbury 8, 50
Sutton Courtenay 48, 176
Swan Upping 49

T

Tæppa's Mound 29
Taplow 29, 46, 92, 109, 126
Taplow Court 20, 29, 89
Teddington 5
Thame 109
Thames 108

Thames Conservancy 89
Thames Estuary 4
Thames Path 108
Thames River Basin 3
Thames Water 8, 88, 189
Theale 77, 113, 120
The Boat Race 191
The Compleat Angler 49
The Great Stink 86
The Thames Conservancy 8
The Thames Path 126
The Tideway 5
The Tuddingway 59
The Upper Thames Patrol 108
Thorne, Hedley 35
Tidmarsh 93, 104
Tilehurst 16
Tolkien, J.R.R. 10, 54, 107
Tree Preservation Orders 171
Twyford 84, 126

U

University of Oxford 53
Upper Bucklebury 132

V

Vale of the White Horse 81, 178
Vikings 9, 31, 33, 39, 63, 126
Village Plans 175
Vodafone 121

W

Wallingford 37, 42, 46, 84, 101, 176, 188
Wallingford Castle 43, 48, 58, 69
Walton 45
Wantage 32
Watlington 31
Weirs 5
Wessex 30, 31, 32, 33, 39
West Berkshire Council 168
West Saxons 26
Whitchurch 16, 45, 79, 98, 115

Whitchurch Hill 20, 98
Whitchurch-on-Thames 16, 39, 46, 65, 98, 109, 113, 173
White Waltham 113
WH Smith 85, 87
Widbrook Common 98
Wild Swimming 188
William the Conqueror 9, 42, 43, 131
Wind in the Willows 100
Windsor 3, 42, 46, 55, 83, 84, 117, 121, 125, 128, 129
Windsor Castle 9, 43, 56, 86, 129, 130
Windsor Great Park 131
Winnersh 125
Winter Hill 12
Wittenham Clumps 17, 19, 20, 21
Wolsey, Cardinal Thomas 27, 52
Wolvercote 180, 188
Woodcote 98, 113, 154, 173
Woodley 113
Woolhampton 77
Woolly Mammoths 17
World War II 108
Wraysbury 117

Y

Yattendon 16, 27